EDITED BY KIRSTY BENNETT, IMOGEN MIDDLETON, MICHAEL PAGE AND JULIET WARREN

IN THE SHADOW OF
THE GREAT
WAR SURREY 1914–1922

The History Press

First published 2019

The History Press
97 St George's Place, Cheltenham,
Gloucestershire, GL50 3QB
www.thehistorypress.co.uk

British Library Cataloguing in Publication Data.
A catalogue record for this book is available from the British Library.

ISBN 978 0 7509 9306 7

Typesetting and origination by The History Press
Printed and bound in Great Britain by TJ International Ltd.

CONTENTS

FOREWORD

Between 2014 and 2018, communities, boroughs and indeed the country came together to remember the ultimate sacrifice paid by so many of our young men during World War I. There were few families who were not affected by the loss of a loved one. I am sure I am not alone when I say that I have learnt a great deal about my family's experience in the Great War. I participated in two moving battlefield tours and retraced the steps of my grandfather, who survived the conflict. I am fortunate enough to remember every activity I did with him. Like all brave men, he was incredibly modest and, of course, never talked about his experiences.

My great-uncle also served in the Queen's (Royal West Surrey) Regiment, as a captain. He received the DSO for crawling to within 25 yards of a German stronghold, bombing it and then returning with a sergeant and a private to take forty uninjured German soldiers prisoner. He sadly died in action and is buried in Heninel Communal Cemetery, France.

Like so many others in the county, I attended a great number of events to mark the centenary of the end of the Great War: from the small, such as the anniversary presentation of a Victoria Cross to a Coldstream Guardsman in Brookwood Cemetery, on a day with the sunshine pouring through the trees, to the large, such as the event at the Peace Garden, Woking, organised by the Shah Jahan Mosque, Woking Borough Council and the Princess of Wales' Royal Regiment, to remember the 400,000 Muslims who fought for our king and country during World War I. On this occasion it poured with rain, but somehow it was appropriate to the conditions that were experienced in the trenches. Finally, there was the weekend of remembrance at Guildford Cathedral, with its climax of Armistice Day. Many organisations played key roles in these events, including Surrey County Council, Surrey's Borough and District Councils, the armed forces, the cadets, the Royal

British Legion and faith groups, to name but a few. In addition, almost every parish used imagination and invention to make us all reflect and remember.

I feel honoured to have been asked to write a short foreword to this excellent book, which reveals the vital importance of the part played in the Great War by those on Surrey's Home Front. Surrey was mobilised as never before, both men and women, whether for the production of food, the manufacture of armaments (including some of the most iconic aircraft of the war), the raising of funds, the tending of the wounded or the defence of the county. As the book makes clear, almost no aspect of daily life was left unaltered by the war and the legacy of the conflict changed the face of Surrey in so many ways.

After the war, my grandfather returned to Loseley Park with several of his men, including his machine-gun officer, who became the head carter; his batman, who helped in the house; and two others who worked on the farm. Comrades-in-arms remained comrades in peace. The memory of World War I, and indeed of World War II, and the contribution that was made by so many, must never be forgotten. It is imperative that educating the young continues, so that in 100 years' time the poignancy of Remembrance Sunday will be just as vivid as it was in 2018.

Michael More-Molyneux
Lord Lieutenant of Surrey
April 2019

INTRODUCTION

The four-year centenary commemoration of World War I sparked an extraordinary worldwide outpouring of activity and creativity, inspired by a desire to reflect the significance of the conflict that marked a turning point in Britain's social, economic and political structures, and has so gripped our nation's consciousness. From individuals searching for information on a grandfather who fought, to organised projects such as Surrey Heritage's *Surrey in the Great War: A County Remembers* (*SGW*), which has sought to investigate the war's impact on a wider scale, it has been a time of great historical exploration and discovery.

World War I caused unprecedented upheaval in Britain. Six million men were mobilised, with, for the first time, civilians called up to join the professional armed forces. Women not only had to keep the family together during the absence of male relatives, but also to fill the gaps in the workforce, whether on the land, in factories or in voluntary roles. They took on jobs previously perceived as the preserve of men, earning a wage and enjoying new social freedoms. It is no coincidence that the campaign for women's suffrage gained momentum during the war, with some women aged 30 and over winning in 1918 the right to vote.

Wartime loss was suffered indiscriminately: from the brother of a factory worker to the sons of Lord and Lady Ashcombe (respectively Lord Lieutenant of Surrey and President of the Surrey Branch of the British Red Cross), everyone lost a loved one or knew someone who had. It was a time of enormous change, too. War demanded each side strive to gain a technological advantage; this stimulated (often deadly) innovation, such as radio, the tank, poison gas, aerial bombardment, submarine warfare and the wristwatch (personal timepieces had previously taken the form of a pocket watch, which was too cumbersome and impractical for trench warfare). New weapons and tactics wounded soldiers in fresh, horrific ways, driving medical advances including prosthetic limbs, X-rays and blood transfusions.

Surrey Heritage (part of Surrey County Council) is responsible for the archive and local studies library for Surrey, collecting and preserving the records of the county's past and present. Its base is the purpose-built Surrey History Centre (SHC) in Woking. Its ambitious project *Surrey in the Great War*, made possible by a generous grant from the Heritage Lottery Fund (now the National Lottery Heritage Fund), was inspired by a desire to both galvanise and bring together in an enduring form the responses of the county's communities and individuals on the centenary of this terrible conflict. As well as exploring the stories behind the names on war memorials, the project sought to understand the impact of the war on the Home Front and reveal the extraordinary contributions made by the county's people throughout the conflict and beyond, as demobilised servicemen returned home, and Surrey slowly recovered. This book is just one of its achievements.

Fundamental to the ethos of *SGW* was the involvement of individuals, families and groups from across Surrey and beyond and, indeed, the project has enjoyed a global reach. Research and family stories from all over the world have been shared with us. The project was fortunate to draw together a team of marvellous volunteers, incorporating over its lifetime more than 100 people of various ages, interests and backgrounds. They have supported *SGW* in manifold ways, including indexing war-related articles in Surrey's contemporary newspapers, photographing memorials, helping with school workshops and delving into SHC's archives to uncover the information to be found in school logbooks, anti-invasion plans and soldiers' letters home to name but a few. Their work has fed directly into the narrative of this book.

We are indebted to the six authors of this book's chapters, who have sought out material on a variety of themes to tell the many facets of Surrey's wartime story. They have uncovered tales of individual heroism and tragedy, of the war's impact on town and village life, and of the experiences of communities and religious groups. Surrey played a key role in the mobilisation and training of British and overseas troops and experienced acutely the international dimension of the war from the start.

This book also looks at the war's impact on Surrey's women, conscription and objection, how the county fed its residents in the face of severe shortages, British Red Cross activity and the care of the wounded, Surrey's wartime industry, and how Surrey's communities chose to commemorate their war dead. This focus on the Home Front reflects the aim of the *SGW* project as a whole – to bring to light the civilian experience of 'total war', in which the impact of the conflict was not restricted to those fighting, but directly affected life at home: ever decreasing food supplies were prioritised for servicemen, German Zeppelins carried out air raids over the south and civilians found themselves working in industries that had been adapted to support the war effort. The Surrey discussed in this book is the administrative county as it was at the time of the war, including, therefore, the present-day London boroughs of Croydon, Kingston, Merton, Richmond, Sutton and Wimbledon. It includes also the part of the former county of Middlesex that now forms the modern-day Surrey borough of Spelthorne. Please visit the 'Places' page of the *SGW* website (www.surreyinthegreatwar.org.uk) to view the full geographical area covered.

This book forms an important part of *SGW*'s legacy and will provide an engaging and thought-provoking read beyond the end of the project's active life in 2019. However, there is more to explore. The project's website holds over 1,000 articles published by project volunteers and staff and members of the public, ranging across a huge diversity of topics. The website also contains research guides, images, contemporary film footage and our indexes to war-related content in contemporary Surrey newspapers that, at the time of going to press, extend to over 80,000 entries. All of this acts as a reference point to encourage and aid further research. Much of it has been incorporated into bespoke learning resources, aimed at Key Stages 2 and 4 pupils, whether in formal or informal educational environments. Closely focused on Surrey, these resources include digital copies of primary sources from SHC's archives, activities and advice for educators and are freely available to download from the site. Finally, the *SGW* website allows users to listen to the voices of people who grew up in Surrey in the aftermath of the Great War, thanks to project volunteers who have recorded oral testimonies that bear witness to the conflict's long reach.

We hope that you find this book an informative and absorbing tribute to Surrey's courageous people: Flora Sandes of Thornton Heath, the only British woman recognised to have served as a soldier during the 1914–18 conflict, the thousands of men and women who volunteered in medical roles, the foreign soldiers (so far from home) brought to the county for training, those who were stigmatised for their conscientious objection and, of course, the Surrey men who joined the armed forces, many losing their lives in this terrible conflict. Surrey's Great War story is, above all, a human one, focused on the men, women and children who lived through the period. We hope that this book does justice to their courage, service and sacrifice.

Kirsty Bennett, Imogen Middleton, Michael Page and Juliet Warren
Surrey History Centre, Woking, Surrey
April 2019

AUTHOR BIOGRAPHIES

Marion Edwards

Marion Edwards has been a volunteer for Surrey Heritage since 2005, having been employed at The National Archives from 1972 to 2007. She has catalogued a range of archives, including letters relating to Sir Barnes Wallis and the World War I correspondence of the Lushington family of Cobham. Her involvement with the present volume arose from her various contributions to the *Surrey in the Great War* project website.

Keith Grieves

Professor Keith Grieves has a research interest in English rural society during, and after, World War I and teaches at Kingston University, London. In 2017 he organised and led a workshop on war memorials for the *Surrey in the Great War* project.

Sue Hawkins

Dr Sue Hawkins has a PhD in nursing in the nineteenth century. Her research interests have since expanded to explore women's roles in the world, medicine and nursing. Sue has published on nursing in the nineteenth century, on the Voluntary Aid Detachment in the Great War and on the history of the Hospital for Sick Children (Great Ormond Street), among others. Her research interests came together in the *Surrey in the Great War* project, for which she has investigated the role of Surrey women in the Great War and the complex infrastructure for the treatment of casualties, which arose out of almost nothing.

Nicholas Howgill

Nick Howgill is a leading member of the Royal Borough of Kingston upon Thames War Memorial Association (www.local-hero.org.uk). His research interest is in the military and naval contribution to World War I of Kingston's boys, the subject of his MA thesis at Kingston University, London. Nick is also interested in the involvement in the conflict of international groups such as the Chinese Labour Corps. He is a member of the Western Front Association, gives talks across the county and sits on the *Surrey in the Great War* steering group.

Michael Page

Michael Page studied history at St John's College, Oxford, and in 1985 received a diploma in Archive Administration from University College London. Now County Archivist at Surrey History Centre (SHC), he has worked with Surrey's historic records for thirty years, including those of the East Surrey and Queen's (Royal West Surrey) Regiments. He has also compiled an online guide to SHC's World War I collections.

Martin Stilwell

Martin Stilwell explored London County Council's social housing for his Master's dissertation at Kingston University London, his research specialism being the earliest London County Council housing and the council's creation of an effective housing regime between the wars (see www.socialhousinghistory.uk). He is a volunteer researcher for *Surrey in the Great War*, and contributor to its website. His research into Surrey's agriculture and into Brooklands during World War I for the project has been expanded for this book.

ACKNOWLEDGEMENTS

The genesis of this book lies in Surrey Heritage's World War I centenary commemoration project *Surrey in the Great War: A County Remembers* (*SGW*). That project, like so many nationwide, was enabled by a heritage grant from the National Lottery Heritage Fund (formerly the Heritage Lottery Fund), whose support we would like to acknowledge. The Fund's backing for commemoration activities across the country has been magnificent.

Surrey's Great War story is here told thanks to the dedication of six authors, who have sifted through countless contemporary newspapers, archival sources (many located in the strongrooms of Surrey History Centre) and scholarly works in order to research and shape their chapters. We are very grateful to them for weaving their research into compelling narratives that cover an impressive amount of ground. The many stalwart volunteers for the *SGW* project have created collectively an enormous bank of stories, newspaper indices, war memorial data and information on which our authors have been able to draw. The heart-wrenching, quirky and previously untold stories that our volunteers unearth never cease to fascinate and inform. We would like to thank all of our volunteers for their inquisitiveness, enthusiasm and camaraderie over the years. *SGW* would not have been possible without their commitment and dedication.

Surrey Heritage staff have also played an integral role in bringing this book to fruition. The current and former members of the *SGW* project team and others of our colleagues at Surrey History Centre have contributed expertise in managing data uploads and our website, digitising images, newspaper indexing, research and data inputting. We are grateful to them for their enthusiasm and support. We would like to record our thanks to Surrey Heritage's digitisation team, led by Teresa Gray, and to Phil Cooper, for expert help in preparing the book's images for publication. Thank you also to our colleagues in the Surrey County Archaeological Unit for sharing with us their research on Witley Camp and to Dr Simon Maslin, Finds Liaison Officer for Surrey County Council working on behalf of the Portable Antiquities Scheme, for helping to research the Strachey badge. We would also like to express our appreciation to Surrey History Trust for its steadfast support for both the project and Surrey Heritage.

This book includes some wonderful, evocative images that aid our authors in telling Surrey's wartime story. We are grateful to the following organisations for permission to reproduce images in their care: Bramley History Society, British Red Cross Museum and Archives, Brooklands Museum, Caterham and District Local History Centre, Chertsey Museum, Museum of Croydon, Dorking Museum, Guildford Borough Council Heritage Services, Hocken Collections at the University of Ontago (New Zealand), Horley Local History Society, the Imperial War Museum, Kingston Heritage Service, the National Portrait Gallery, London, Screen Archive South East, Sue James and Sutton High School for Girls (Girls' Day School Trust – GDST), The National Archives of the UK and Wairarapa Archive (New Zealand).

Several individuals have kindly supplied information or allowed us to use digital images from their private collections. For this we would like to thank Vivienne Bennett, Jeremy Gordon-Smith, David Hassard (www.kingstonaviation.org), Sheila Lumley, the descendants of the MacDonald family, Councillor M.I. Raja, Philippa Scarlett (indigenoushistories.com) and Martin Starnes (www.thebignote.com).

We are grateful to The History Press, in particular our commissioning editor Nicola Guy and our project editor Ele Craker, for accepting our book as one of its publications marking the centenary of the Great War, and for its support during the writing, production and publishing processes.

The editors would like to extend a personal note of thanks to their families for their patience and understanding while this book has been put together, for (un)willingly listening to all the Great War stories that have been shared with us, for proofreading and for supplying hundreds of cups of tea!

Kirsty Bennett, Imogen Middleton, Michael Page and Juliet Warren
Surrey History Centre, Woking, Surrey
April 2019

ABBREVIATIONS

AA	Anti-Aircraft
AC	Agricultural Company
ANZAC	Australian and New Zealand Army Corps
BEF	British Expeditionary Force
BOA	Board of Agriculture
BRC	British Red Cross
CGHS	Croydon Girls' High School
CO	Conscientious objector
CWGC	Commonwealth War Graves Commission
DORA	Defence of the Realm Act (1914)
ESR	East Surrey Regiment
FAU	Friends' Ambulance Unit
GC	Golf club
GDST	Girls' Day School Trust
GRU	Graves Registration Unit
HAOF	Housing Association for Officers' Families
IWGC	Imperial War Graves Commission
IWM	Imperial War Museums
KC	King's Counsel
MOM	Ministry of Munitions
MP	Member of Parliament
NAF1	National Aircraft Factory 1
NUWSS	National Union for Women's Suffrage Societies
OTC	Officer Training Corps
POW	Prisoner of war
QAIMNS	Queen Alexandra's Imperial Military Nursing Service

QRWS	Queen's (Royal West Surrey) Regiment
RAF	Royal Air Force
RC	Red Cross
RFC	Royal Flying Corps
RNAS	Royal Naval Air Service
RNVR	Royal Naval Volunteer Reserve
SCC	Surrey County Council
SCWFL	Surrey Committee for Women's Farm Labour (later renamed the SWAC)
SHC	Surrey History Centre, Woking
SPAD	Société Pour L'Aviation et ses Dérivés
SWAC	Surrey Women's Agricultural Committee (formerly the SCWFL)
TNA	The National Archives of the UK, Kew
VAD	Voluntary Aid Detachment (of the British Red Cross)
VTC	Volunteer Training Corps
WAAC	Women's Army Auxiliary Corps (later the Queen Mary's Army Auxiliary Corps)
WAC	War Agricultural Committee
WLA	Women's Land Army
WRAF	Women's Royal Air Force
WRNS	Women's Royal Naval Service
YMCA	Young Men's Christian Association
YWCA	Young Women's Christian Association

Imperial currency and measurements used in the text:

Shillings	*s*
Pence	*d*
Pounds	lb
Ounce	oz

A PRELUDE TO WAR

BRITAIN'S WAR WITH GERMANY.
MOBILISATION OF TROOPS: SCENES IN WOKING.
EFFECT ON FOOD PRICES: TRADERS' COMMENDABLE ACTION.
RAILWAY GUARDED BY TROOPS. – TRAIN SERVICE DISLOCATED. – PROSPECTS
OF UNEMPLOYMENT.
GREAT BRITAIN DECLARED WAR UPON GERMANY AT 7 O'CLOCK [sic] ON TUESDAY
EVENING

This momentous decision, which the people of this country feared was inevitable, though hoping till the last that it might be averted, put an end to the period of suspense caused by the high-handed action of the German Emperor.

The quarrel between Austria and Servia [sic], arising over the dastardly assassination of the Archduke Ferdinand Frederick [sic] and his wife, has embroiled the whole of Europe. Russia, in defence of her own interests in the Balkan peninsula, took up Servia's [sic] case, whereupon Germany, Austria's ally, immediately declared war upon Russia, and sent an ultimatum to France demanding to be informed of her attitude, she being an ally of Russia. France's reply was regarded by Germany as unsatisfactory, and war was declared upon her. Germany lost no time in moving her troops, and to avoid the strongly fortified frontier of France, sought to enter French territory by way of Belgium. In this she violated the law of nations, and when Belgium insisted on her neutrality being respected, she was met with the reply that the Germans would resort to force if necessary for the passage of her troops through Belgian territory.

The independence of Belgium is a vital matter to Great Britain, as if Germany became possessed of that country she would be a constant menace to the shores of England. Great Britain accordingly asked for assurances that the neutrality of Belgium would be respected, but this request was summarily rejected by Germany, and Great Britain on Tuesday night declared war on Germany.

The mobilisation of our naval and military forces has proceeded with the utmost expedition, the men in the reserve responding cheerfully and with alacrity to the call to re-join the Colours, whilst the Territorials, who have been embodied for home defence, have shown an equally patriotic spirit.

There have been several stirring scenes and incidents in the Woking district which will be found recorded below. The horrors of war have not yet been realised, but prudent people are taking steps to economise as much as possible so as to eke out their slender resources, as employment at such times is very precarious. The Woking traders, to their credit, have taken steps to prevent the undue depletion of their stocks by refusing to supply well-to-do people with large orders, the effect of which would be to raise prices of foodstuffs to panic figures, thereby increasing the hardships of the poor. It has been stated by the Government that, so far as corn and provisions are concerned, there is an ample supply, and the importation from America and our Colonies will continue. There is, therefore, no reason to apprehend any permanent great increase in prices, although some increase is unavoidable.

For the benefit of the wives and families of the Surrey men who are serving with their colours, efforts will be made, as in the Boer War, to raise a special fund to supplement the allowances of the War Office, and the press of the county will co-operate in the appeal.

Excerpt from the *Woking News and Mail*, 7 August 1914, p. 5.

1

SURREY GOES TO WAR

NICHOLAS HOWGILL

*(with contributions by Imogen Middleton,
Kirsty Bennett and Michael Page)*

Mobilisation

In the last days of July and the first days of August 1914, that Europe teetered on the brink of war mattered little to Surrey. The *Dorking and Leatherhead Advertiser* of 1 August 1914 might refer to the 'dread, enthralling word – war', but considered the most likely source of conflict to be the crisis over Irish Home Rule.[1] Preparations for receiving refugees were reported, but they would be from Ulster, not Belgium.[2] Reports on military movements were all about the mobilisation of the Home Counties Territorial Division (which included the Territorial battalions of both the East Surrey Regiment and the Queen's (Royal West Surrey) Regiment) for its annual camp.[3] On 4 August 1914, the day the British Government issued its declaration of war on Germany, more column inches of the *Surrey Mirror* were devoted to local government proceedings than to the prospect of war.[4] However, the following Friday's edition (7 August) referred to 'The Great War' and the 'European War'.[5] The enthusiastic reporting of local military preparations still displayed an innocence oddly at variance with the imposition of press censorship by the government's invocation on 8 August of the Defence of the Realm Act (DORA).[6]

In 1914 the British military had a considerable presence in Surrey. The heathland in the county's north, due to its open nature, unsuitability for agriculture and proximity to key military establishments like Aldershot and Sandhurst, was ideal for the

Mobilisation of the 4th Battalion, the Queen's (Royal West Surrey) Regiment, Croydon, August 1914 (SHC QRWS/5/7/1)

development of firing ranges and training areas, and had become the home of military camps such as Pirbright and Deepcut, while Camberley housed the recently developed Staff College, responsible for training selected officers in the management and control of large bodies of troops.[7] Surrey's two infantry regiments were the East Surrey Regiment (ESR), its depot at Kingston Barracks, and the Queen's (Royal West Surrey) Regiment (QRWS), its depot at Guildford. Each had two regular battalions, one on Imperial service and the other stationed at home, plus a 'Special Reserve' battalion (the ESR actually had two) that were embodied on the outbreak of war to train new recruits for the regular units. Each regiment also had two Territorial Force battalions, consisting of part-time volunteers.[8] The four Surrey Territorial battalions belonged to the Home Counties Territorial Division that, when war broke out, was actually assembled and on its way to Salisbury Plain for its annual training camp.[9] Surrey also had a mounted Territorial regiment, the Surrey Yeomanry (Queen Mary's Regiment).[10]

The mobilisation of the British Expeditionary Force (BEF) for service in France was ordered on 3 August 1914. To bring units up to full strength required calling up army reservists – men who had completed full-time service in the army under terms that required them for a set number of years thereafter to return to the colours if needed.[11] Mobilisation telegrams went out on 4 August; consequently, the depots at Guildford and Kingston saw reservists arriving in droves, being kitted out and then despatched to their units. QRWS reservists had a short journey to Bordon, Hampshire, where its 1st Battalion was stationed; ESR reservists had a much longer journey to Dublin to join their 1st Battalion. An infantry battalion's

The 1st Battalion, the Queen's (Royal West Surrey) Regiment in August 1914, Bordon Camp, Hampshire (SHC QRWS/30/HENR/3)

established strength was 1,000 men and the number of reservists involved shows their importance: the war diary of the 1st Battalion QRWS records 450 reservists arriving at about 11.30 p.m. on 5 August and a further 130 at 4 p.m. on 6 August, with mobilisation complete by 5 p.m. on 7 August.[12] The war diary of 1st Battalion ESR records the arrival of 402 reservists at 4 p.m. on 6 August, a further 242 at 6 a.m. on 7 August, and a final fifty at 10 a.m. on 8 August, the later schedule no doubt due to the longer journey.[13]

The arrival and departure of the reservists at both Guildford and Kingston depots attracted considerable numbers of onlookers, who also accompanied the drafts to the local railway stations.[14] Surrey's newspapers recorded when local police officers departed to fulfil reservist commitments and commented on how reservists' obligations might affect local businesses.[15]

The government mobilised the Royal Navy on 1 August 1914. While the major warships in the Grand Fleet were fully manned, the crews of older ships brought out of reserve were augmented by naval reservists, called up on 2 August. There were nowhere near as many naval reservists in Surrey as there were army reservists, but local newspapers reported the departure for army and naval service on 3 August of several Kingston police officers and employees of the Metropolitan Water Board at Long Ditton.[16] The same paper also noted the departure of the chief instructor of the training brig *Steadfast*, moored in Kingston, Chief Petty Officer J.T. Goodyear.[17] Sadly, some older ships became early casualties of the war. The *Surrey Advertiser* reported on 26 September 1914 that a stoker from Kingston, Frederick Hammond, was among the missing from the cruiser HMS *Aboukir*, sunk by German U-boat U-9 off the Dutch coast on 22 September. Hammond had been a policeman in Kingston and his departure for service had been recorded by that newspaper just weeks earlier.[18]

One element of mobilisation came through impressment rather than volunteering. In August 1914, the army's peacetime establishment of horses was 25,000, but the BEF about to be sent to France required 165,000.[19] Following a review after the South African War (1899–1902) of problems with the supply of horses, the Army Remount Department had conducted a national census to identify suitable horses for army needs; on the outbreak of World War I, selected animals were called to centres such as Guildford and inspected, and those approved were purchased at market price for military service.[20] Horses used to pull carts and delivery vans were prime targets, as the vast majority of army horses hauled supply wagons and artillery pieces, rather than being cavalry horses. The supply of horses in Britain proved to be greater than anticipated, and so it was only from 1915 that greater numbers were provided from overseas.[21] Surrey's newspapers reported on potential problems caused by the perceived lack of horses, such as difficulty preparing the land for future crops, and some traders (such as Gray's Garage, Guildford) sought to take advantage of the shortage to push the sale of motor vehicles. Nonetheless, the army got its horses.[22]

Surrey's Territorial Force units, which had been on their way to summer camp when war was declared, returned to their various homes on 4 August. The following day, the Territorial battalions were embodied, marched to local railway stations and proceeded to the war station of the Home Counties Division in Kent.[23] It quickly became clear that not only did Britain's existing units in France require reinforcement, but additional units needed to be formed, and those could only come from the Territorial Force. However, members of the Force had signed up for home defence and had no obligation to serve overseas. Furthermore, like regular units, Territorial units were not up to strength: for example, the 5th Battalion QRWS comprised some 590 officers and men from an actual strength of 750 and a war establishment of over 1,000.[24] Steps were taken immediately to persuade as many men as possible to accept the 'Imperial Service Obligation' and so undertake service overseas. On 15 August, such men were formed into first-line ('foreign service') units, while the remainder became second-line ('home service') units.[25]

Major St Barbe Russell Sladen, an officer of the 5th Battalion QRWS, was responsible for gathering the horses (over fifty) that the battalion required before it moved off, initially to Strood, then to Maidstone (setting up its HQ in the Girls' Grammar School) and then to Canterbury. Sladen had to reject two water carts provided by Lord Lovelace as they had previously been used to carry liquid manure. It was decided that the two Territorial battalions of the QRWS (the 4th and 5th) should exchange personnel, the 4th taking all those who had volunteered for foreign service and the 5th becoming a home service unit. However, on 8 September, after the exchange had taken place, it was decided that the men of 5th Battalion should be asked if they would, in fact, volunteer for foreign service ('the only honourable course', thought Sladen). Despite the commanding officer giving a speech the following day 'that ought to damp the ardour even of thrusters', a majority volunteered and the men who had transferred to the 4th Battalion returned.[26] The Home Counties Division embarked for India on 30 October 1914 to replace the regular army units that had been recalled from there to France. It was renumbered 44th (Home Counties) Division, while the Surrey Brigade became 131 (Surrey) Brigade.[27]

Surrey as an Army Camp

The new Secretary of State for War, Lord Kitchener, immediately realised that the tiny (by European standards) BEF and Territorial Force would be entirely insufficient to wage a modern, industrialised land war in Europe. On 7 August 1914 he issued his first appeal for volunteers who could be forged into New Armies. The response was overwhelming, at least initially. Surrey's resident aristocracy, Members of Parliament, clergy and wealthy elite led the recruiting drive, addressing rallies and organising marches. Around Dorking, Henry Lee-Steere of Jayes Park, Cuthbert Heath of Anstie Grange, Reginald Bray of Shere and Henry Cubitt of Birtley Court, Lord Lieutenant of Surrey (later 2nd Lord Ashcombe), were at the forefront of efforts.

Recruitment meeting in Epsom (SHC PH/58/207)

Some employers offered incentives to their workers to join up. Leopold Salomons of Norbury Park offered all his unmarried estate workers half pay and those who were married full pay for the duration of their service.[28] Surrey County Council encouraged its staff to volunteer, provided cover could be arranged, and continued to pay them their customary wages, less the service pay they received from the army. In addition, the Council guaranteed to reinstate the men at the end of the war and organised an insurance scheme that would provide up to £100 for the family of any who died in service.[29] Half of the 126 council workers who were serving with the colours by October 1914 were elementary school teachers, causing something of a staffing crisis in schools that endured for the rest of the war.[30] Major Gordon Watney of the South Lodge Motor Works, Weybridge, was still more proactive: with the approval of the War Office, he raised a Mechanical Transport Supply Column within the Army Service Corps from local Weybridge men – 'Watney's Boys'.[31]

Others looked to glorify the patriotic spirit of those who had enlisted (and shame those who had not). Edgar Horne of Hall Place, Shackleford, MP for the Guildford Parliamentary Division, booked a full page in the *Surrey Advertiser* of 5 September on which he listed the names of all those in the division who had volunteered; a further list published on 19 September contained 4,200 names.[32]

Across Surrey's downs and commons, camps sprang up to house and train raw recruits. The miners of the 11th Battalion Sherwood Foresters (Nottinghamshire and Derbyshire Regiment) found the countryside around Frensham 'an unmixed delight' and a tonic: 'almost immediately an improvement came over the appearance of the men, the exercise in the fresh air did wonders for them in the physical sense'. The number of men who required accommodation placed an enormous strain on existing facilities: the 7th Battalion Somerset Light Infantry, in Inkerman Barracks, Woking, endured 'a pretty rough time … there have been very few beds and a great lack of blankets, most of the men having to sleep on the floor. Also the rooms are overcrowded, a room for 22 is made to hold 60 and over.'[33]

As autumn turned to winter and the weather deteriorated, tents had to be abandoned in favour of billets in local towns and villages. In Dorking, troopers of the Surrey Yeomanry first had to be found billets, then in January 1915 the 179th Brigade of 60th (2/2nd London) Division, including men of the London Scottish Regiment, Civil Service Rifles and Queen's Westminster Rifles of the London Regiment, came to town.[34] In December 1914, Guildford had to accommodate 1,500 men of the 46th and 47th Brigades Royal Field Artillery, householders receiving 2s 6d per man housed per day. In November 1916, around 6,000 men were compulsorily quartered in the borough for weeks in homes, public buildings and empty houses.[35]

Some celebrated volunteer units briefly found a home in Surrey: the 17th Battalion Middlesex Regiment, raised from the ranks of professional footballers, spent a few months in 1915 at Holmbury St Mary encamped around the country residence of William Johnson-Hicks, MP for Brentford, who had appealed for players to volunteer. Among them was Walter Tull, the celebrated black footballer, who before the war had defied prejudice and hostility to play for Tottenham Hotspur and Northampton Town.[36]

The closest Surrey approximation to the famous Pals Battalions (specially constituted battalions of the British Army comprising men who had enlisted together in local recruiting drives, with the promise that they would be able to serve alongside their mates) were the 12th (Bermondsey) and 13th (Wandsworth) Battalions of the ESR. In early 1915, Lord Kitchener appealed to London boroughs to raise their own units and John Hart, Mayor of Bermondsey, and Lieutenant Colonel Sir Archibald Dawnay, Mayor of Wandsworth, took up the challenge. The Bermondsey battalion chiefly comprised dock and tannery workers who were fed and paid by the borough until the War Office assumed responsibility.[37]

In January 1915, in atrocious conditions, several of the new divisions were inspected by Lord Kitchener and Alexandre Millerand, the French Minister of War, on Epsom Downs. Thousands of freezing men, standing in snow, had to wait several hours for the dignitaries, enclosed in a car, to arrive. Second Lieutenant Melhuish of the 7th Somerset Light Infantry recalled that the 'only recreation and amusement we had was to count the people who fainted and had to be carried out. The engineers won with thirty-two, our company had eight only.' With only one

Snowball fight at Woldingham Camp, January 1915 (courtesy of Caterham and District Local History Centre)

Barrack huts, Farm Camp, Woodcote Park, Epsom (SHC 6529/4)

Witley Camp in 1916 (SHC 8511/159)

ambulance on hand, many of those who collapsed 'had to lie in the slush, some almost covered, until help arrived. Of course some suffered from exposure, fortunately only two died.' A plan to hold a major exercise in August 1915 for 24th Division on Chobham Common, which was covered in trenches for the purpose, was similarly thwarted by the weather and had to be abandoned. Within a few weeks, the inexperienced division was thrown into action at Loos and suffered appalling casualties.[38]

Makeshift canvas camps gradually became more elaborate and comfortable. In 1914, existing military camps in Britain could house some 174,800 soldiers, but accommodation for some 800,000 men was needed, as were, since the purpose of Lord Kitchener's call for volunteers was to create new divisions of 18,000 men, camps large enough to accommodate and train that number.[39] The privations of the newly enlisted showed that tents and billets were not enough, particularly as autumn approached.[40] Proper hutted camps were necessary. In one respect the War Office met the challenge admirably, soon having the design for a standard hut ready.[41] Suitable locations, with access to railways, good water and drainage, could be identified, but it required time and labour to establish camps properly. Surrey saw several major sites established during the war's early months.

The camp at Woodcote Park, Epsom, came about in a way reflective of the combination of private initiative and military hard work that so characterised this early period. It was built by the War Office on land belonging to the Royal Automobile Club (RAC).[42] Work commenced in November 1914, much of it done by members of the unit that was to inhabit it.[43] Due in part to the bad weather over the winter of 1914–15, the camp was not ready for occupation until February 1915.[44]

The camp was occupied by the Universities and Public Schools' Force (UPS), also known as the Public Schools' Brigade. This originated from a call for public school and university-educated men to form a special unit. Recruiting was nationwide; the resulting brigade-strength force arrived in Epsom for training from 18 September.[45] As Arthur Stanley, the RAC Chairman, had also become chairman of the UPS organising committee, Woodcote Park camp became the force's home.[46] Until the camp's completion, the force was billeted in Epsom, Ashtead and Leatherhead and commenced training on the open areas nearby, including Epsom Downs.[47] Once the UPS had left Woodcote in May 1915, the camp became a convalescence centre, initially for Australian and New Zealander troops and latterly for Canadians, some of whom remained until 1919.[48]

A larger camp was constructed on Witley Common, near Godalming, from October 1914.[49] This was a divisional-size camp with, eventually, space for 10,000-plus infantry soldiers, with additional camps nearby, particularly at Milford, for artillery units.[50] The camp had its own electricity supply, piped water and sewage

A New Heaven

Perhaps the most famous soldier to pass through Witley camp was Wilfred Owen, the renowned poet. He was stationed there with the Manchester Regiment in 1916, during which time he wrote 'A New Heaven', which he later reworked to form his famous 'Anthem for Doomed Youth'.[1] Owen's letters to his mother describe life in camp. Upon arriving at Witley, he wrote:

> Got a car from Milford to the Camp two or three miles off: a vast affair on the top of the hill with Pines interspersed amongst the huts. The Officers' huts form a big settlement apart ... The site is delightful for a camp; but we are all confined to it.[2]

He also describes training across the Surrey countryside: 'I often have a Platoon completely to myself on the Moors [the Surrey Downs].'[3] Owen enjoyed exploring the locality. On 20 June 1916, he wrote to his mother:

> This afternoon I borrowed a (very groggy) bicycle and rode through Godalming to Guildford, in perfect weather ... Guildford is an old town of great charm, with suggestions of Shrewsbury. I had tea in an old casement overlooking the High Street ... I remained there an hour longer so pleasant was the place ....

Two weeks later: 'I made my usual sally into Guildford and had a happy enough ramble around Thorpe's Bookshelves and the Town and the little River.'[4]

Owen was killed in action on 4 November 1918, one week before the Armistice.

Wilfred Owen (image in public domain)

treatment works.[51] Given its rural location and large number of inhabitants, appeals were made to local people to help run institutes and provide entertainment there.[52] In February 1915, the *Surrey Advertiser* noted the excellent response to this call, in particular language classes in French and German. Conditions at Witley were challenging: the same report observed that its inhabitants 'impressed' with their 'wonderful cheerfulness' despite 'the mud and floods'.[53]

Across Surrey, communities rallied to provide facilities and entertainments such as concerts and afternoon teas for the troops. In Guildford, church halls were turned into rest and reading rooms and a Young Men's Christian Association (YMCA) hut with a canteen opened in the town in January 1917. In 1916, a Kitchener Club was established at Bishop's Croft, Mount Pleasant, as a regulated venue where soldiers could meet young women. Men in uniform paid 1*d* per visit and could bring up to two women at 2*d* each. A few young women were also admitted as members for 2*d* a week, provided they could produce a reference from a clergyman, headteacher or employer. The club held reading, French and dancing classes 'and a good moral tone was maintained throughout'.[54] Across the county women patrols also endeavoured to maintain decent behaviour, but for troops seeking a less elevated tone, army camps attracted many prostitutes, as evidenced by the upsurge in convictions for brothel-keeping and prostitution (see Chapters 2 and 5).

Specialist camps provided for the training needs of the Kitchener's New Armies. In Bisley, the firing ranges of the National Rifle Association were turned over to the War Office in 1914 and members of the association were recruited as expert instructors to train officers and non-commissioned officers in the art of rifle shooting. Students who passed the exams were sent back to their units to instruct the men who had volunteered for the New Armies. In the 1915 report of the school it was estimated that it had, indirectly, trained around 1.5 million men to shoot straight. Machine-gun classes were also provided.[55] Similarly, in the east of the county, the Godstone School of Bombing on the Marden Park estate provided training in the use of grenades.

Conscription

As the realities of war hit home, the number of men volunteering to join the armed forces declined significantly. The government had to act to boost numbers. The National Registration Act of July 1915 having established that several million British men of military age were yet to volunteer, the Group Scheme (known popularly as the 'Derby Scheme' after its originator, the Earl of Derby) was introduced in October. Under the scheme, which ultimately ran until mid December,

The 'Willing Badge'

In September 1914, John St Loe Strachey (1860–1927), Surrey's High Sheriff and editor of *The Spectator*, published a description of his scheme to issue a 'Willing Badge' to those who had attempted to enlist for military service but had been rejected on medical grounds or for failing to reach the recruitment grade. He wanted to offer 'proof of service proffered to the state' and to prevent such men being stigmatised on the assumption they had refused to serve. A letter from Strachey to accompany the badge stated that it 'must be considered as a pledge of honour that the recipient will again offer himself should the standard be lowered, or if for any other reason he believes that he would now be accepted', and urged that 'you must not part with the Badge … it is most important that Badges should not fall into any hands but those of men who have tried to join the King's forces.'[1]

Strachey's badge is inscribed 'Surrey 1914' and 'when the people willingly offered themselves' (a paraphrased Biblical quote on service and sacrifice). Around 4,500 were issued between autumn 1914 and December 1915, when the government's announcement of the introduction of its similarly purposed Silver War Badge led Strachey to cease to issue it. Only three surviving specimens are currently known: rare examples of an object that tells of the patriotic fervour and intense social pressures of the home front early in World War I.[2]

'Willing Badge'
commissioned by John St Loe
Strachey (SHC SGW/18)

men could either continue to enlist voluntarily, or could attest but then return to civilian life until they were required by the forces. The scheme met with some, but insufficient, success: a more radical solution was required.[56]

On 27 January 1916, following much deliberation, Parliament passed the Military Service Act, which introduced conscription (compulsory enlistment into the armed forces) for the first time in British history. The Act decreed that all single men aged between 18 and 41 were deemed to have enlisted on 2 March 1916; this was extended in May 1916 to married men and in 1918 to men aged below 51. The Act specified four grounds on which exemption from conscription could be requested: working in a reserved occupation in the national interest; that enlistment would cause exceptional hardship to family, finances or business; being medically unfit or ill; and conscientious objection to combatant service.[57]

Whether a man's request for exemption was granted was determined by local tribunals, set up in each urban or rural district in Surrey and staffed mainly by volunteers. Those who wished to appeal against the decisions of local tribunals could take their case to the Surrey and Croydon Appeal Tribunal, which divided its work among three area tribunals. Few records and no individual case files of any of Surrey's local or area tribunals have survived, although those for the Middlesex Appeal Tribunal (which covered the modern-day Surrey borough of Spelthorne) do survive and have been published online thanks to The National Archives.

Most applications for exemption were on employment, hardship or medical grounds. Employers often appealed for exemption on behalf of workers whose loss to military service they felt would be detrimental to their business. The employer of Thomas Caley of Staines, a foreman in the linoleum industry, requested Caley's exemption on the grounds that his 'principal and usual' work was included in the government's list of exempted occupations. Exemption was refused.[58] George Wheatley of Shepperton, a master butcher, was granted temporary exemption because 'it is expedient in the national interest that the man should, instead of being employed in military service, be engaged in other work in which he is habitually engaged' and 'serious hardship would ensue … owing to his exceptional financial or business obligations or domestic position'.[59] Francis Mills, Wrecclesham's only baker, was granted conditional exemption because baking bread was, at a time of food shortages, deemed to be of national importance.[60] In 1916, Captain M.L. Sant, Chief Constable of Surrey Constabulary, appealed for the exemption of one of his overworked constables, George Edwin Bruce Bord. Perhaps surprisingly, his request was refused.[61] The many police officers lost to military service left Surrey's forces short staffed. The increasing presence of women in the workforce caused some employers to try and cling on to 'valued' male employees, who were deemed more capable and suited to managerial roles. An application by the owners of

Kingston's Bentall's department store is instructive: Leonard Bentall stated that his staff comprised 483 women of a total 500, most male staff having been lost to the services, and that there was only one man managing each 100 women. Bentall's requested that its last three male managers be allowed to remain in order to manage the female staff.[62] Some employers' appeals seem slightly dubious: on 17 November 1917 the Honourable Mrs Greville of Polesden Lacey sought exemption for one of her gardeners, stating that it was in the national interest for him to maintain his current employment.[63]

		2 O'CLOCK.		
Appellant.	Man's Name & if attested Group.	Grounds of Appeal.	Local Tribunal & Decision thereof.	Decision of Appeal Tribunal.
17. Henry Leopold Bennett, Market Gardener & Pig Breeder, Pirbright.	No.	Certified Occupation & domestic reasons.	Guildford R.D.C. 7-3-16 Dissented from. Brother granted exemption till 7-9-16.	
18. Ernest Seymour Osborn, Timber Hauler, Shere.	No.	Indispensable.	Guildford R.D.C. 7-3-16 Dissented from. Conditional exemption to brother while in present occupation.	
19. Royal Horticultural Society, Wisley.	John William Blakey Yes - 22		Guildford R.D.C. 10-3-16 Application refused.	
20. Frank Lloyd Parton, Student for Bar, Chertsey.	No.	Conscientious objection.	Chertsey U.D.C. 28-2-16. Exempted from combatant service only.	
21. J.B. Chandler, Nurseryman & Florist (Employer).	John Norman Chandler Yes - 9	Indispensable.	Farnham U.D.C. 22-2-16 Application refused.	
22. S. Hide & Sons Ltd, (Employers), Farmers, Market Gardeners & Nurserymen, Farnham.	Arthur Hide, Yes - 33		Farnham U.D.C. 22-2-16 Application refused, work could be done by a man not of military age.	38. 12
23. T. Lampert & Son, (Employers), Contractors, Farnham.	William Wilkinson Yes - 10		Farnham U.D.C. 22-2-16 Work could be done by a man not of military age.	26.
24. Mark Goddard, Carpenter & Joiner, Farnham.	No.	Domestic reasons.	Farnham U.D.C. 29-2-16 Application refused, No serious hardship.	12..6 13.6
25. Albert Arthur Brake, Chief Cashier, Farnham.	Yes - 15.	Domestic reasons & indispensable.	Farnham U.D.C. 6-3-16 Application refused. No serious hardship & work could be done by man over military age.	
26. James Corfe, Butcher, Farnham.	Yes - 11	Business reasons.	Farnham U.D.C. 6-3-16 Temporary exemption for 1 month.	
27. Capt. M.L. Sant, Chief Constable of Surrey.	No. George Edwin Bridger Ford.	Police Constable.	Windlesham 2-3-16. Application refused.	
28. Recruiting Officer, Weybridge.	Thomas Clarke Bagshot Yes - 4	Attested man & not yet a Minister.	Windlesham 2-3-16. Exempted from combatant service only.	
29. Edmund Audley Downes, (Employer), St. Johns School, Leatherhead. Appeal out of time.	Charles Dabby Linnell Yes -	Indispensable.	Leatherhead 25-2-16. Postponed for 2 months.	
30. Bernard Clement Stenning, Solicitor, Leatherhead.		time to settle up business affairs.	Leatherhead 3-3-16. Application refused.	
31. Recruiting Officer, Epsom.	Charles Birts Wholesale Bookbinder Ashstead	Need of men ... provision of Bibles.	Epsom Rural. 25-2-16. Exempted conditionally so long as man unable to get efficient substitute.	
32. Philip Edward Blackmore (Employer), Horse Trainer & Dealer, Ashtead.	Henry Walter Broughton, Yes - 13	Reserved Trade & Indispensable.	Epsom Rural 18-2-16. Not indispensable or serving national interest.	
33. do	Harry Watson Yes - 11	do	Epsom Rural 18-2-16. Not indispensable or serving National Interest.	
34. Samuel Dean, Baker & Confectioner, Haslemere.	Horace Isidore Percival Dean Yes -	Indispensable.	Haslemere 3-3-16.	

Captain M.L. Sant seeks exemption for one of his police constables at the Guildford Military Service Appeal Tribunal, March 1916 (SHC CC28/303B)

Roll Up!

Following the introduction of conscription, Surrey's newspapers regularly carried notices listing the names, last known whereabouts and descriptions of men who, under the Military Service Act, ought to have, but had not, enlisted. In August 1916, a notice in the *Surrey Advertiser* listed no fewer than seven employees of Lord John Sanger, circus proprietor, based at Burstow Lodge, Horley.[1] The world-famous Sanger's Circus continued to perform during the early part of the war, but in response to a governmental speech on national service, Lord Sanger announced in February 1917 his decision to close the circus for the duration, an 'unprecedented occurrence, our doors having remained open since the year 1842'.[2] Shows continued, however, as in June 1917 Sanger applied for exemption for two of his employees: Herbert Sanger, also known as 'The Inimitable Pimpo, England's foremost Equestrian Comedian', and circus artiste James Freeman. Stating that his other performers had been 'captured' that summer, that these two had accepted an engagement in Blackpool and that he had no one to tend his elephants, Sanger appealed for help through this difficulty. Temporary exemption (until 30 September) was granted to the men.[3] Might the fact that his elephants had assisted, in the absence of horses, with agricultural work in Horley in 1917 have influenced this decision?[4]

Lord John Sanger's elephants at Burstow (courtesy of Horley Local History Society)

As the war continued and the army sought desperately to fill its depleted ranks, many of the men brought before tribunals were of dubious medical fitness. A.E. Maisey of Wodeland Road, Guildford, had already been rejected from the army on the grounds of ill health (heart strain and epilepsy) five times when he was called before a tribunal.[64] Similarly, a gardener was summoned to the Croydon tribunal despite being blind in his right eye and producing a medical certificate showing that he had 'old-standing ulcers on both legs'. Fortunately for him, the tribunal unanimously agreed that he should continue his work in food production and would be of no use to the armed forces.[65]

Contrary to popular myth, appeals on grounds of conscience formed only a small proportion of cases. The Surrey and Croydon Appeal Tribunal heard in total 7,077 appeals against the decisions of local tribunals. Only 117 of these appeals (a mere 1.65%) were made on grounds of conscience: sixty-five of the 117 appellants were granted conditional (time-limited) exemption if they undertook work of national importance and fifty-two joined the Non-Combatant Corps; no one was granted an absolute exemption.[66] Dorking Local Military Tribunal received few applications for exemption on the grounds of conscience, but Mr E.W. Turner of Holmwood was one of those who managed to secure exemption for that reason, provided he carried out work of national importance: an offer of work by a local umbrella handle and walking stick manufacturer was deemed unacceptable by the tribunal and he was sent to a flour mill at Ewell.[67]

Not all conscientious objectors received such sympathy. A young man in Epsom appeared before his local tribunal to explain the difficulty of getting the work that he had been ordered to do. He had gained employment at the Epsom Council sewage farm, but his colleagues had objected to his presence, forcing him to leave. Another opportunity at a local building firm brought the same trouble.[68] The opprobrium and social ostracism faced by conscientious objectors could be severe. Cobham businessman and diarist Frederick Robinson sneered at the creation of the Non-Combatant Corps for those willing to join the army but not participate in combat, rejecting their views as 'extravagant'. He repeated approvingly the view of the *Financial News* that 'the bulk of this class consists of the most despicable type of man – the degenerate and effeminate worshipper of brute force and indescribable depravity' who should lose the right to vote and hold public office after the war and should be forced to wear a brassard 'which should enable decent people to avoid social or physical contact with them'.[69]

One avenue of war work for conscientious objectors was to carry out medical duties with the British Red Cross (BRC), or the Quaker-run Friends' Ambulance Unit (FAU), which served at the Front. Surrey BRC volunteers included the novelist E.M. Forster, a pacifist who was deemed unfit for military service and

Frank Lloyd Parton

Frank Lloyd Parton of Chertsey worked from 1915 as an ambulance driver for the Friends' Ambulance Unit (FAU) in France. Believing that this helped the armed forces too much, he returned to England on 8 February 1916 and was discharged from the FAU two weeks later.

Receiving his enlistment papers shortly thereafter, Frank sought conscientious exemption before the Chertsey Local Tribunal and the Appeal Tribunal at Guildford; both granted him exemption only from combatant service. He then applied to the Central Tribunal, the final arbiter, which decreed that should he undertake twenty-one days' ambulance service, he would be exempted also from non-combatant service.

Frank approached the King's Bench, asserting his right to argue his case in person. It was heard on 18 April 1916, to public ridicule, and dismissed, the judges ruling that they could not set a precedent of personal hearings. Frank was ordered to serve in a non-combatant role. He refused, was arrested that July, fined and handed to the military authorities. Frank was court-martialled (stating at his trial that his objection to service arose from his Christian values) and sentenced to six months' imprisonment with hard labour. After his release he worked as a forester in Chertsey. Frank committed suicide by taking cyanide of potassium in August 1918. His inquest found that 'death was due to taking poison while of unsound mind'.[1]

Frank Lloyd Parton, one of many pacifists who volunteered with the Friends' Ambulance Unit (© Religious Society of Friends (Quakers) in Britain)

volunteered in Alexandria, Egypt, from October 1915.[70] The FAU assisted the BRC; it boasted over 1,000 members, both Quaker and non-Quaker, and promoted itself as providing alternative war work for those who refused to fight.[71] Women could also serve with the FAU and Woking's Dora Champion was one, motivated by her desire to 'do her bit': her three younger brothers were of military age and the youngest was killed in action in 1917.

Overseas Troops in Surrey

Many thousands of overseas troops passed through Surrey over the course of the war, mainly for training or treatment. Witley Camp was used increasingly by battalions of the Canadian Expeditionary Force and was entirely taken over by Canadian troops in December 1916. Soldiers of the South African Infantry were based for training at the Inkerman Barracks in Woking. The soldiers played football against local teams and even helped to relieve the pressure of the 1917 Christmas rush at Woking's post office.[72] Inkerman also housed a military hospital. In addition to being treated at Woodcote Park (alongside Canadians and Australians), wounded New Zealanders were cared for at Mount Felix (Walton-on-Thames) and Oatlands (Weybridge) hospitals.[73]

Surrey's newspapers record romances between local women and the wounded of Mount Felix. In March 1918, for example, Edith Knapman of Hersham, a long-serving Voluntary Aid Detachment nurse at Mount Felix, married 2nd Lieutenant Randall Browne, of Wellington, New Zealand. The groom had been wounded at Gallipoli and nursed at Mount Felix for eighteen weeks by his future wife.[74]

ANZAC soldiers at Mount Felix Hospital (courtesy of Wairarapa Archive, New Zealand, 16-97/1-24)

When at the end of February 1916 the temporary military hospital established in the grandstand of Epsom Racecourse closed, it had over its fifteen-month lifespan treated 672 servicemen, including seventeen New Zealanders, nineteen Australians, thirty Belgians, six Canadians, and one Frenchman.[75] Many overseas soldiers still lie buried in Surrey cemeteries.

A Canadian unit of a special kind found a first home in Surrey. Trench warfare placed a high value on the supply of timber, needed as duckboards, supports for trenches, sleepers for railway lines and pit-props for mines. Yet pre-war sources of timber (Scandinavia and Russia) had been rendered inaccessible, and from February 1915 importing by ship from North America ran the risk of supplies being lost to attack by German U-boats. Exploiting sources of timber in Britain (and later in France) would therefore not only supply the quantities needed, but also free up shipping space for other essential items.[76] Consequently, on 15 February 1916 the British Government formally requested that the Canadian Government supply a 'Battalion of Lumbermen' for 'the exploitation of forests of this country'. Within six weeks, 1,600 men had been recruited into the 224th Canadian Forestry Battalion. Its first personnel arrived in Britain on 12 April 1916; the unit produced its first sawn lumber on 13 May 1916.[77]

The first timber was harvested around Virginia Water. By June, some 124 men were at work there, with an additional party of forty-nine working at Ripley Lake, near Bagshot.[78] Britain was quick to notice the new arrivals, the *Surrey Advertiser* noting a visit on 3 July 1916 by the king and queen to see the Canadians at work in 'Clock Case Woods, near the Wheatsheaf Hotel'.[79] A less favourable report appeared in the same paper on 24 June 1916: Private Adrian Lederoute of the Forestry Battalion had been arrested in Egham for being drunk and disorderly and assaulting Police Inspector Knight, one of his arresting officers. Lederoute was sentenced to three months' hard labour.[80]

Overall control of the forestry units was vested in the Canadian Forestry Corps, established on 6 January 1917.[81] The corps was administered by district and each district controlled lumber companies located in its area. The headquarters of No. 53 District, which controlled London, the south-east and East Anglia, was established in London in November 1916, but moved to Runnymede House, Egham, on 6 November 1917. Egham also provided the corps with yard space with railway sidings, acquired from the London and South-Western Railway, and all railway equipment it used was sent there.[82] No. 56 District, formed on 16 August 1918, was headquartered at East Sheen. The companies it controlled worked with the Royal Air Force on airfield construction.[83] No. 101 Company operated at Virginia Water throughout the war and generated over 2 million cubic feet of timber, the largest quantity produced by any lumber company in Britain.[84] From 1917, the company farmed 55 acres of land at its camp at Virginia Water, producing potatoes, cabbage, carrots and grain. There was also a very successful piggery. The produce fed the camp and was sold on to forestry companies that did not have farms.[85]

As the corps expanded, it took on other than Canadians, including ex-seamen (described generally as Finns), Portuguese, and German prisoners of war. Some Portuguese served at Virginia Water.[86] At the end of the war, the corps had on strength in Britain 12,533 men.[87] Its success can be measured by Sir Douglas Haig's report in December 1917 that the corps had ensured that the British Expeditionary Force had 'become practically self-supporting as far as regards timber'.[88] Britain's timber imports fell from 11.6 million tons in 1913 to just over 2 million tons in 1918, which released shipping space to carry food for 15 million people.[89] The cost was the devastation of the woodlands of Surrey and Britain, and when in 1919 the Forestry Commission was created, part of its role was to revive British woodlands from the depredations of war.[90]

The presence of Indian troops with the British Expeditionary Force on the Western Front from October 1914 necessitated the provision in Britain of treatment facilities for those wounded, and religiously appropriate funeral arrangements for any who died in the country. The most famous such site was the hospital established within Brighton's Royal Pavilion. The cremation of deceased Hindu and Sikh soldiers took place at a site on the downs at Patcham, above Brighton, while deceased Muslim soldiers were brought to Woking because of the presence there of the Shah Jahan, Britain's first purpose-built mosque.[91]

The mosque was crucial to the proper burial of Muslim soldiers, thereby countering German propaganda about Britain's lack of respect towards them.[92] The first burial was that of Ahmad Khan of the 3rd Sappers and Miners, on 17 November 1914, in the Muslim section of Brookwood Cemetery.[93] A dedicated burial site was desired, however, and Maulana Sadr-ud-Din from the Shah Jahan and British officers agreed to establish a burial ground on Horsell Common, just outside Woking. Once the site had been prepared, burials were moved there from Brookwood.[94] The Royal Pavilion Hospital's Assistant Quartermaster, D.R. Thapar, was responsible for the disposal of the bodies of those who had died there and became the chief mourner at Horsell, despite not being Muslim.[95] Horsell continued to receive bodies for the rest of the war.

In 1916, Miss Constance Faithfull, of Walton-on-Thames, offered 4 acres of land there for use as a Muslim burial ground, but the War Office declined: in December 1915, the Indian Infantry Divisions had left France for the Middle East and it was felt that Horsell would be sufficient to meet future burial needs.[96] Wounded Muslim soldiers came to Woking on 13 August 1915 to meet some 400 other Muslim guests and attend the festival of Eid-ul-Fitr, marking the end of Ramadan, in the grounds of the Shah Jahan Mosque.[97] (See Chapter 8 for further discussion of the Muslim Burial Ground.)

Major (retired) Raja Alaf
Khan in full dress uniform,
wearing First World War
medal, *c.* 1916 (SHC
Z/45 4/4/8, courtesy of
Councillor M.I. Raja)

Any perception that World War I was a 'white man's war' disguises the ethnic diversity of the conflict. Some countries with an ethnically varied population initially sought to recruit predominately white forces only, but the desire of other sections of the population to serve their country gradually overcame early misgivings. The *Surrey Advertiser* of 27 May 1916 records the marriage at Walton Church of Private Peter Poi Poi, a New Zealand Maori, to Miss Winifred Maud Alderton, of Walton-on-Thames. The groom was a patient at Mount Felix Military Hospital, where he met his wife.[98]

Canada was another country whose ethnic minorities overcame their authorities' early 'white only' recruitment policy (at the time, First Nation Canadians were not actually citizens). Corporal Francis Pegahmagabow, a First Nation Canadian from Parry Island, Ontario, serving with the Canadian Expeditionary Force, was stationed briefly at Witley Camp in 1918.[99] He was one of the most decorated First Nation Canadians of the Great War, thrice winning the Military Medal. He was also probably the deadliest sniper of the conflict and an accomplished scout.[100] A Canadian with a varied background was John Baboo, who spent time at the Epsom Military Convalescent Hospital in 1917, suffering from severe leg wounds that eventually saw him invalided out of the army. He was a Sikh, born in India in

the Punjab, and had served for four years in the Indian 28th Madras Cavalry before
moving to Canada. His name was apparently only 'Baboo' – 'John' was given on
enlistment to conform to Anglo-Saxon naming patterns.[101]

African-Canadians were also present within the Canadian forces in Surrey,
and references to them reveal something of the tensions inherent in this diversity. On 27 May 1918 a mixed-heritage member of the Forestry Corps, Private
John Monroe, was charged with the manslaughter of a fellow soldier. The charge
arose from an incident outside the Castle Inn, Egham, in which the deceased
had racially insulted and hit another mixed-heritage soldier. Monroe had
taken exception to the deceased's actions and hit him, with fatal consequences.
Monroe was remanded and later committed for trial. The deceased was buried at
Englefield Green with full military honours.[102] By contrast, on 9 January 1919,
Canadians from Witley Camp (there is no indication of their ethnicity) stormed
a police station in Godalming, angered by the mistreatment by Military Police of
a black boxer and war hero.[103]

That was not the end of the troubles at Witley. The Canadians had been welcomed by the locals, who also enjoyed the boost the camp provided to the local
economy. In 1916, a female volunteer, perhaps rather naively, described the men as
'Nature's Own Gentlemen', both religious and considerate, and in 1917, between
1,500 and 1,600 Canadian servicemen from Witley were entertained in Guildford
on Christmas Day, arriving there in two special trains.[104] To mark their sojourn in
Witley, memorial panelling was installed in the church in which the 123rd and
85th Canadian Infantry Battalions had deposited their regimental colours while in
the field. However, in June 1919, mounting frustrations caused by the slow demobilisation and repatriation of the Canadian troops prompted the soldiers to run riot
over two nights, destroying the local shops serving the camp, known as 'Tin Town',
and setting fire to the Garrison Theatre. (Once the last troops had finally left, the
military and government were reluctant, despite earlier promises, to restore Witley
Common to its pre-war state, but following local protest, the camp's structures
were dismantled and auctioned off: the camps were rebuilt in World War II for
use by Canadian troops and the local Home Guard.)[105] In the same month, 400
Canadian soldiers from Woodcote Park Convalescent Camp laid siege to Epsom
Police Station in an attempt to rescue two of their fellows who were in custody
for brawling. Surrey Police Sergeant Thomas Green was killed and other Surrey
policemen injured.[106] It was a sorry postscript to an extraordinary chapter in the
county's history, when thousands from across Britain and the world had found a
home in Surrey's towns and downs.

2

KEEPING SURREY SAFE

MARION EDWARDS

When Britain declared war on Germany on 4 August 1914, both government and people sprang into action to defend the country against possible German invasion. Surrey was no exception and this chapter outlines local reactions to the wide-ranging measures put into force.

The Defence of the Realm Act

The Defence of the Realm Act (DORA) was passed in Britain, without debate, on 8 August 1914, four days after the onset of war. It was amended and extended six times over the course of the war, and gave the government far-reaching powers during the conflict, such as those to requisition property, or to make regulations creating new criminal offences. DORA facilitated the introduction of a variety of authoritarian social control methods, principally censorship of journalism and letters home from the Front. The press was subject to controls on reporting troop movements and numbers or any other operational information. Seemingly trivial peacetime activities such as flying kites or starting bonfires (either of which could attract or signal to Zeppelins), buying binoculars (possible spying equipment) or feeding bread to wild animals (waste) were all banned under the powers bestowed by DORA, as was discussing military matters (spies were thought to be lurking everywhere). Alcoholic drinks were increasingly watered down and the opening times of public houses restricted, so that drunkenness did not impact on munitions production.

Captain M.L. Sant, Chief Constable of Surrey Constabulary (SHC 9017/4/3)

All of the new measures introduced under DORA had to be enforced locally, and the major burden of so doing fell on the police forces, aided by Special Constables. The Chief Constable of Surrey, Captain Mowbray Lees Sant, was quickly overwhelmed by the flood of directives from central government, as detailed in the reports (usually quarterly) he submitted to the Standing Joint Committee that oversaw the Surrey Constabulary. These reports outline the extra duties and demands placed by the war on the overburdened and under-strength force and the blizzard of orders and requests for information arriving by post, telephone and telegram from London. It was no wonder that early in August 1914, the harassed chief constable 'drew out the full scheme for enrolment of Special Constables', anticipating by a week the Home Office instructions to do so.[1]

The deluge of demands began as early as July 1914, when the Home Office sent instructions for the Surrey Police to 'co-operate with the Military Authorities in any matter in which they might require … assistance'. Thereafter, remote communications were joined by personal visits from representatives of the armed forces, with further injunctions regarding action against 'individuals suspected of spying' (later resulting in 'spy mania' among the general public); guarding railway bridges and 'vulnerable points on railway lines'; pasting up mobilisation posters; 'keep[ing] an eye' on private wireless stations; collecting horses for army purchasing officers; monitoring 'aliens' travelling by night by car 'for the purpose of committing outrages', seizing cars belonging to those aliens and warning garages not to hire cars to the same; enforcing the Alien Restriction Order (although no copy of the order itself or the 'necessary books' had yet arrived); protecting telephones and telegraph poles; the local billeting of army personnel (on 8 September, Sant stated proudly: 'Found billets for 9,000 troops at 24 hours' notice'); tackling civil disturbances; the enforcement of DORA itself; accommodating prisoners of war; enforcing regulations against the keeping of carrier or 'homing' pigeons or sketching; recording the number of 'Alien Reservists' registered (including Germans, Austrians and Hungarians) and arresting German reservists. To add to the burden there were civilian requests for police 'attention' relating to the protection of post offices and 'waterworks' (the latter were deemed to be the responsibility of the owners), and

PHOTOGRAPHY

AND

SKETCHING.

Defence of the Realm Regulations.

IN EXERCISE of the power conferred on me by Regulation 19 of the above-mentioned Regulations, I, General Sir Archibald Hunter, G.C.B., G.C.V.O., D.S.O., A.D.C.Gen., Commanding-in-Chief, Aldershot Command, a Competent Military Authority for the purposes of the said Regulations, with the approval of the Army Council, **DO HEREBY ORDER** that no person shall, without my permission, make any photograph, sketch, plan, model, or other representation of any place or thing within the area specified in the Schedule hereto.

AND I GIVE NOTICE that by virtue of the said Regulation no person in such area shall, without lawful authority or excuse, have in his possession any photographic or other apparatus or other material or thing suitable for use in making any such representation.

PROVIDED that nothing in this Order shall be construed as prohibiting (where otherwise legal) the making of a photograph, sketch, plan, model, or other representation within any photographic or other studio or a private dwelling-house or the garden or other premises attached thereto of any person or things therein, or as prohibiting (where otherwise legal) the possession of photographic or other apparatus, materials, or things intended solely for use within such studio, dwelling-house, or other premises.

The Schedule.

In the County of Surrey:—The Rural Districts of Chertsey, Guildford, Farnham and Hambledon; the Urban Districts of Egham, Chertsey, Woking, Frimley, Farnham, Windlesham and Haslemere; and the Municipal Boroughs of Guildford and Godalming.

Commencement of Order.

This Order shall come into force at noon on the first day of October, 1917.

Given under my hand this 22nd day of September, 1917.

ARCHIBALD HUNTER, General,

Competent Military Authority.

PRINTED AT THE HEADQUARTERS PRINTING OFFICE, ALDERSHOT COMMAND.

Poster forbidding photography and sketching under the Defence of the Realm Act, 1917 (SHC CC98/23/2)

reports of poor discipline among newly enlisted army recruits. Inhabitants of the county made matters worse by sending in 'all sorts of unnecessary and trivial correspondence' and demanding to see the chief constable personally, without waiting for the issue of instructions or 'making enquiry of the nearest Police Officer'.[2]

The pressures put on Surrey Constabulary by DORA, along with other defence and counter-invasion measures, did not abate for the entire war. It was with obvious relief that Sant authorised the ringing of church bells and the use of fireworks and bonfires upon the 'welcome information that an armistice has been signed by Germany'. It was not until well after 11 November that he was able to cancel all DORA regulations.[3]

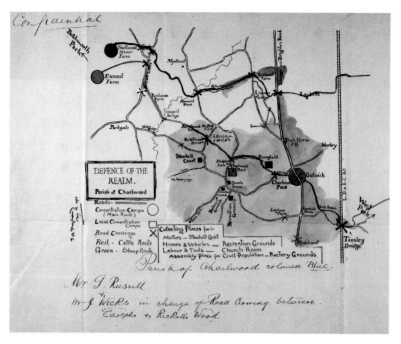

Plan of counter-invasion measures drawn up by the Charlwood Local Emergency Committee, 1916 (SHC 734/1)

London Defence Scheme

In 1859, it had been believed that London was practically indefensible against invasion, and a scheme for a line of simple earthworks for infantry and movable armaments, intended to be dug and manned in an emergency by a Volunteer Force, was proposed. This line was to be supported by permanent defence works, the London Mobilisation Centres, at 5-mile intervals. These would act as stores and ammunition dumps. This 'London Defence Scheme' was announced in Parliament in March 1889. Stretching across the North Downs, from Guildford to the valley of the River Darent in Kent, and across the Thames into Essex, the 70-mile line contained thirteen sites for mobilisation centres. In Surrey, these were Pewley Hill, Denbies (near Dorking), Box Hill, Betchworth, Reigate, East Merstham, Fosterdown and Woldingham. Trenches to link the sites could be excavated rapidly on the outbreak of war.

During World War I, part of this scheme was resurrected to form a 'stop line' of trenches in the event of invasion. As early as 3 October 1914, a circular from the War Office to local councils required all the men they could supply to dig trenches, clear ground of trees, brushwood, etc., and carry out 'rough timber work'. It was expected these men would only be needed for three days, with each authority being responsible for its own foremen, gangers and timekeepers. Dorking Urban and Dorking Rural District Councils supplied two labour gangs, numbered 80 and 81. There were about 800 men in labour gang No. 80, but by 9 February 1917 both gangs had fallen to 150 men, who were to assemble at the council offices in Church Street, Dorking, each morning. The men were to be paid by their employers during the time they were working on the defences. Their company would then send an invoice to the War Office.[4] A 1915 map of the defences held at The National Archives, Kew, shows an almost continuous loop of fortifications from the Thames at Dartford to the Hog's Back, west of Guildford.[5]

Defence Against Attack from the Air

In fact, the greater threat to Surrey came from the air. World War I was the first in which aeroplanes played an important role. While the central role of the air forces was reconnaissance to assist the artillery, the use of aircraft offensively, through tactical and strategic bombing, ground support and strafing enemy forces, developed rapidly. Shooting down enemy aircraft (or at least frightening them off) naturally followed as an important aspect of defence.

No army organisation for anti-aircraft purposes existed prior to August 1914, although the Admiralty had established a programme for the design of high-angle quick-firing guns for the Royal Navy. On the outbreak of war, the Admiralty assumed responsibility for the anti-aircraft defence of London and established an Anti-Aircraft (AA) Corps of the Royal Naval Volunteer Reserve (RNVR). The War Office was made responsible for the defence of important locations, such as munitions factories, and set up a small staff organisation to consider how to proceed.

The RNVR units set up guns atop key buildings in Whitehall and at the Thames docks, as well as near facilities at Woolwich (Arsenal), Waltham (Ordnance Factory) and Chattenden on the Medway. Acetylene-lit searchlights provided night illumination against the threatened Zeppelin raiders. Ordnance stores were combed for any other useful guns, and various older types were installed to cover naval installations at Dover, Harwich, Liverpool and the Tyne and Humber, among others. To protect west London, there were nineteen gun stations, thirty-six searchlights and thirty-eight observation posts in place between 1917 and 1918. In Surrey, searchlights were placed at Englefield Green, Chertsey, Esher, Chessington, Banstead, Croydon, Morden, Addington and Purley and guns at Norbiton, Morden and Croydon. Observation posts were sited near Chertsey, Kingston and Croydon. All were connected by telephone lines.[6]

Zeppelin caught in searchlights, from an album of the Royal Fusiliers' Camp at
Woodcote Park, Epsom (SHC 6529/4)

Locally, further measures could be put in train against the aerial threat. In 1915,
Chief Constable Sant mentioned 'Anti-Aircraft motor cars'[7] – presumably for
spotting approaching Zeppelins and taking the warning to an appropriate recipient, such as local anti-aircraft emplacements, one of which was on the site of the
Chilworth Gunpowder Works.[8] Vigilance against aerial attack was another of the

many duties carried out by Surrey's Special Constables and protective arrangements were put in place. The authorities in Dorking, 'whilst not anticipating air
raids in this district', had looked to establish a satisfactory shelter as a precaution
and 'recommended the Council to approach the Swan Brewery Company with the
view of obtaining their permission to utilize, if necessary, the large caves at the "Old
Rock Brewery" in High-street for the purpose'.[9]

Only two Zeppelin raids took place over Surrey during the war, at Croydon
and Guildford, although the raids on London were clearly audible and visible from parts of the county. Both local raids occurred on the night of 13–14
October 1915. Zeppelin L15, one of five, heading inland for London and seeing
the railway lines and roads of Croydon, perhaps thought it had reached its target
and began to drop its bombs shortly after 11 p.m. Damage was extensive and
nine people were killed, with fifteen seriously injured.[10] Zeppelin L13 seems
to have attempted to locate and bomb the Chilworth Gunpowder Works, but
although it circled the site several times, wartime 'lights out' precautions worked
and the airship continued west towards Guildford, where it dropped twelve
bombs, ten around St Catherine's and two on Shalford Park. A witness recalled:
'I heard plainly enough the tremendous strumming of an airship, sounding like a
bluebottle's buzz magnified a thousand or two times.' Although a number of
buildings were damaged and windows shattered, the only casualties were a swan
on the river and seventeen chickens.[11]

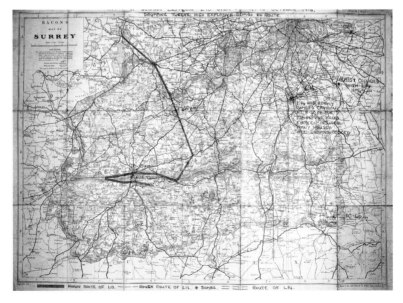

Bacon's Cycling Map of Surrey, the heavy black line indicating the route taken by a
German Zeppelin on 13 October 1915 (SHC 4414/4/1)

There was an ongoing debate over how to warn the populace of a possible imminent air raid. An experiment in Dorking in 1915 to sound the hooter at the electricity works was abandoned after it was mistaken for a fire alarm. In Guildford, by October, it was reported that 'expert opinion is against warning by blowing of sirens or ringing of bells in case of air raid' because it brought people out into the streets, and it was decided to 'discontinue such warnings in Guildford in future'. Popular concerns continued, however, despite the *Surrey Advertiser* advising people not to get into 'a state of funk' about air raids.[12]

With the advent of raids on London by Gotha bombers, it was evident that more was needed. In the parts of Surrey nearest to the capital it was decided to use 'the same sound signals in case of air raids, as are used within the ten mile limit from Charing Cross', that is, two rockets with a fifteen-second interval. 'Take Cover' and 'All Clear' notices were to be circulated by the police. Confusion was never far away. At Whyteleafe Grammar School, the girls sheltered in a ground-floor corridor during raids and did needlework to occupy themselves. Once they mistook the 'Raiders Passed' siren for the 'Take Cover' siren and sat in the corridor for ages needlessly.[13]

In 1916, the shooting down of Zeppelins, as witnessed by Surrey residents and 'Specials', was reported in local newspapers.[14] Special Constable Percy Webb, in his brief memoir 'The Diversions of a Special Constable', describes vividly the night destruction of three Zeppelins (although he admits to having missed actually witnessing the first, having gone off duty); the third, the 'Cuffley [Hertfordshire] Zeppelin', he saw 'glowing like a great elongated sun … till it collapsed and streamed downwards to the earth'.[15]

Local Emergency Committees

To counter the threat of invasion, a network of Local Emergency Committees, based on the Petty Sessional Divisions of the county, was formed. Within each parish, a committee oversaw local anti-invasion measures, principally the safeguarding of property of potential use to an enemy invader. In November 1914 county worthies gathered at Redhill to determine how 'to secure the civil populations and to assist the military in case of hostile invasion'. It was reported:

> … in the event of the landing of a hostile force on the south or south-east coast that military authority would issue orders to denude Kent, Sussex and Surrey (possibly not the north portion) of all cattle, sheep, horses, vehicles (both horse and motor), consumable stock suitable for man or beast and all commodities

which may be considered of use to an invading force and at the same time they would call upon civilian labour to prepare earthworks etc.

A man was to be chosen to tour each parish daily to inspect the cattle and any found to be unfit to travel were to be destroyed. However, in the event of an enemy landing, on no account were bridges, railways, electricity supplies and telephone lines to be destroyed unless permission had been received from the military authorities.

The minutes and papers of the Local Emergency Committee appointed in Horley provide a very detailed account of its work during the early years of the war. This included enforcing directives for the removal of 'intoxicating liquor' from any area to be cleared (as 'many of the atrocities in Belgium were perpetrated by German soldiers when drunk'); the compilation of a list of all those who owned cars and bicycles (109 people owned 536 vehicles, ranging from motor cars to horse and carts, and there were 779 bicycles in Horley); and a census of all livestock within the parish. To enforce regulations there were twenty-five Special Constables divided into five parties under a committee member, plus an additional twenty-four Special Constables, some of whom were assigned responsibility for a specific geographic area. In the event of an invasion, the Special Constables were to divide livestock into herds of not more than 150 head of cattle and lead them to the designated rendezvous, where another Special Constable would take charge of them. The Dorking committee planned, in the immediate aftermath of a hostile landing, to commandeer civilian motor vehicles to evacuate vulnerable people such as the young, aged or infirm to either Royal Holloway College in Egham or the Chertsey Union Workhouse. Cattle were to be moved to Windsor Great Park, Burwood Park and other similar areas to the north. All motor vehicles left behind were to be disabled through the removal of wheels, magneto and carburettor.

On 21 August 1916, the Chairman of the Surrey Emergency Committee, based at Caxton House, London, wrote to parish committees informing them, 'In view of the changed [local] military situation … [it] was no longer necessary that supplies of food and fodder should be destroyed, that live stock should be destroyed or removed or that the civil population should be required to leave their homes.' However, it remained the responsibility of Local Emergency Committees to arrange the removal of horses, motors and other vehicles, control the movements of the civilian population, and supply a fit workforce, equipped with spades, pickaxes and other tools to do any work required. After 3 October 1916, the Horley Committee did not sit again until 8 January 1919, when it was disbanded. At its last meeting, a letter from the Home Secretary and Lord Lieutenant thanking it for all its hard work was read.[16]

Surrey's Police Forces

At the outbreak of war, as discussed earlier, the four police forces within Surrey (the Metropolitan Police, which operated within those parts of Surrey within 15 miles of Charing Cross, the Surrey Constabulary and the Guildford and Reigate Borough forces) found their responsibilities greatly increased by the introduction of such war-time measures as the control of aliens, blackouts, air-raid warning arrangements and enforcement of restrictive licensing laws. At the same time, the number of police fell as officers enlisted and recruitment became more difficult (see Chapter 1 for details of Sant's efforts to prevent his officers being conscripted). In December 1914, the strength of the Surrey County Constabulary was 351; by November 1918 it had fallen to 236.[17]

The head constables of the two borough forces, like Surrey's Chief Constable Captain Sant, had to submit annual reports to their Watch Committees. The Reigate Borough reports, though mostly statistical, give some insight into the war's effect on the local constabulary. The declaration of war 'imposed much onerous and anxious work on the Police. A great number of Home Office and War Office Orders and Communications has been issued, necessitating constant and diligent attention by the Police for efficiently carrying out the same.'

Camberley Special Constables, 1918 (SHC 9152/2/2/4/1B)

Herbert Brockman of Eaton Cottage, Thames Ditton, in his Special Constable's uniform, as drawn by his daughter Nancy, 1916 (SHC 9497/1)

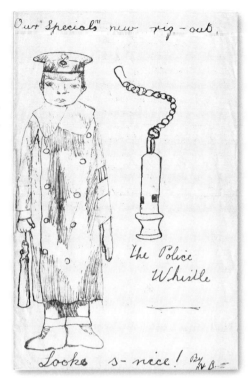

Our "Specials" new rig-out,

the Police Whistle

Looks s-nice! By N.B.

The Reigate force was small. In 1914, it had forty officers: the head constable, two inspectors, seven sergeants and thirty constables. By 1918, although the strength of the force was officially still forty, the Reigate Constabulary had been reduced to twenty. Fourteen men had enlisted and there were six vacancies. Although three members of the Guildford force were killed on active service, it seems that none of those who enlisted from the Reigate Constabulary died.[18]

The increased workload and dwindling numbers of officers placed an intolerable burden on the police. This was partially alleviated by the appointment of Special Constables to assist the police with the implementation of DORA. Their duties covered emergencies arising from air raids and counter-invasion preparations, as well as more prosaic activities such as enforcing blackout conditions, overseeing rationing arrangements and general law enforcement. Numerous collections at Surrey History Centre provide lists of Surrey's Special Constables and detailed correspondence concerning their enrolment and management.[19] By the end of August 1914, over 150 Specials had been sworn in, and numbers continued to rise. In January 1919, Surrey's total was reported to be 1,612.[20] In February 1916, newspapers carried an appeal from the Guildford Borough Emergency Committee for women to join the ranks of the Special Constables, in order to 'deal with the population in times of national emergency'.[21] (For a discussion of the role of women in policing wartime Surrey, see Chapter 5.)

Relations with Chief Constable Sant of the Surrey Constabulary could be strained, especially regarding what equipment should be supplied to the Specials. Sant is referred to in one letter as 'that arch rotter'. The authority of the volunteer constables did not always go unchallenged – a Special Constable lamented that a gardener, when asked to make himself scarce, responded, 'I won't move on for you or any other bugger of a special policeman.' The memoir of Percy Webb, Clerk to Walton-on-Thames Urban District Council and a Special Constable, paints a vivid picture of life as a Special, though he admits that he 'would rather have worn the more honourable uniform' of a soldier. He describes the discomforts of night duties, especially wet ones, and the long periods of tedium interspersed with occasional drama. While attempting to enforce the blackout, Webb admired the stoical reaction of a 'cheerful hawker' – 'Are you frightened Mr Webb? I'm not: what I says is, if they 'its me they 'its me, and if they doesn't, they doesn't'. Webb himself was slightly less blasé about nocturnal terrors. On one occasion he was alarmed to hear a 'ghostly footstep' preceding him along the road, only to find that the sound was an echo of his own 'wet and heavy coat' against his leg. Early morning patrols had their compensations: 'I was sorry when the 3 to 6 patrol was given up. In peaceful times one rarely sees the night grow grey and darkness give place to form and colour, till the rim of the sun appears above the horizon, and living nature awakes.'[22]

The Volunteer Training Corps

When war was declared in August 1914, many men over military age, or with business or family commitments that made it difficult for them to volunteer for the armed forces, looked to join the informal civilian local defence groups that began to spring up. The High Sheriff of Surrey (and editor of *The Spectator*) John St Loe Strachey, of Newlands Corner, urged rifle clubs to form local guard units. One such was the 'Useful Service Brigade', founded by Mrs Janson of Newdigate Place, deemed 'a fine body of men' by the parish magazine.[23] The first elements of central organisation were established by the formation of the London Volunteer Defence Force. Proposals as to the nature and role of the movement ranged from simply drilling volunteers in preparation for their enlistment into the regular or home armies, through augmenting the home army's defence of vulnerable points, to providing a force that would actively oppose invasion using guerrilla tactics. Concerned that such a body would undermine recruitment into the regular army and hinder more than help home defence, the War Office banned the movement.

Despite official antipathy, indeed hostility, civilians continued to organise themselves and, realising that the government could do little to prevent them, the Undersecretary of State for War decided in September 1914 to allow the Central Committee of the London Volunteer Defence Force to continue. Until the War Office itself had the time and resources to devote to the movement, the Central Committee, adopting the name 'Central Association of Volunteer Training Corps', became the body to which individual corps could affiliate. In November 1914, the association was officially recognised as the administrative body of the Volunteer

Training Corps (VTC) and formally subjected to conditions that prevented inter-ference with recruitment into the regular army, barred members from holding military rank and denied state funding.

In October 1914, Major MacLaughlin held a meeting in Woking to raise a vol-unteer force for Surrey and by June 1916 there were twelve local VTC battalions in the county (organised, since July 1915, into a county regiment), with a combined strength of 5,304 men, the largest being the Sutton Battalion. Members were issued with red armlets inscribed with a 'GR', which had to be worn while the men were on duty. Each battalion had to supply its own arms and ammunition. Although not compulsory initially, where uniforms were worn they were to be the same colour throughout the county and were usually grey-green rather than khaki. In 1914, to help clothe the 130 men of the 7th Battalion, Major MacLaughlin made a public appeal that raised £286 9s 6d, but along with the men's own contribution the bat-talion was still short by £93 3s 9d.

In December 1916, the Army Council instructed that all officers were to wear service dress uniforms as worn by the regular army, and non-commissioned offic-ers had to wear 'a special pattern of cloth, which will be known as Serge Volunteer Force'. Rifles (which had to be of a non-service pattern) were in short supply and dummy rifles sometimes had to be used: Guildford Borough Council furnished its corps with old South African War rifles and a number of Russian rifles.[24]

However, drills were intensive, rising to fourteen a month by December 1916 (although down to twenty-four a quarter by 1918). Eventually, as the War Office grudgingly came to accept the Volunteers, members were allowed to wear

Richmond Volunteer Training Corps (SHC ESR/25/MARSD/1)

khaki uniforms and equipment began to be supplied officially. In July 1918, the War Office integrated the VTC battalions into the county infantry regiment system. The twelve Surrey battalions were amalgamated into six, each styled a Volunteer Battalion of the East Surrey or Queen's (Royal West Surrey) Regiment.[25]

Members of Surrey's VTC participated in digging the trenches of the London Defence Scheme and on the 1915 August bank holiday 4,000 Volunteers converged on Ranmore Common for a field day. Crowds flocked to watch as they staged a mock defence of London, followed by tea for the officers at Denbies and a wander around the gardens for the 'other ranks'.[26]

Spies, Internees and Prisoners of War

The threat (both real and perceived) of spies and enemy agents occupied all minds. Instructions under DORA regarding action against 'individuals suspected of spying' resulted in an outburst of 'spy mania' among the public, who were assiduous in their zeal to catch anyone they suspected. Frederick Robinson of Cobham recorded, a fortnight into the war, the false rumour that two spies had been shot for attempting to pollute the water supply at Aldershot with bottles containing typhoid germs, news that had been 'kept out of the papers'. Robinson was also half persuaded of the veracity of stories that a 'hidden hand' was at work, subverting government: as the *Financial News* put it, 'That there is some unseen influence incessantly at work in high places on behalf of Germany is so palpable a fact that it would be ludicrous to deny it.' E.F. Kernick, owner of the King's Arms Hotel, Godalming, shared this view, writing in 1917 to journalist Arnold White 'There are hardly any British hotels … four-fifths of the hotels of all sizes are Germany's hotels. Their managers – Foreign pro-Germans – all know one another … All of them are Spies.'[27]

Dangers could sometimes be misinterpreted. Reports of a possible spy firing a gun close to the railway in Gomshall turned out to be a local farmer shooting rabbits.[28] After the reported escape of prisoners of war in 1916, Special Constable R.D. Hutchings stopped a speeding car at Horsell Bridge, only to find that the irate driver was Francis P. Neville, chauffeur to Mr L. Waddington of Easdale, Horsell Common.[29]

The public mood was febrile. After the sinking of the *Lusitania* in May 1915, a naturalised German watchmaker was attacked in Hersham and Special Constable Percy Webb was called to the scene. Tempers ran high, windows were broken and a policeman knocked unconscious. In Percy's opinion 'the women were the worst and most bitter', although he sympathised with one, who said: 'Why should I go away, they've killed my husband.' When, in October 1915, a Zeppelin passed over Walton on its way to bombing Guildford, it was thought that it was being signalled to by a flare from the garden of a house 'then in the occupation of foreigners' (who turned out to be blameless Belgians).[30] After the Guildford raid there were rumours of lights on the hills or cars signalling to the invaders and for a period cars were stopped and checked near the town.[31] Chief Constable Sant reported that the severing of telephone wires near Blackheath in April 1917 by persons unknown caused much excitement, but enquiries suggested that 'some malicious or mischievous person', rather than a spy, was responsible.[32]

Anti-German sentiment and popular fears of spies led to the internment of German and Austro-Hungarian male civilians in Britain between 1914 and 1919. The main waves of internment, in October 1914 and May 1915, coincided with outbreaks of violence across the country, during which German-owned property was destroyed or looted. After the *Lusitania* riots, the government moved towards wholesale internment of male enemy aliens aged 17–55. Although women, children and older men were not interned, some were repatriated or found their daily lives controlled under the Aliens Restriction Act of 5 August 1914 and subsequent orders in council. They had to register their names with the police, obey local curfews, refrain from entering prohibited areas (which by November 1914 included the east and most of the south coast), and could not own cars, motorcycles, cameras, military maps or homing pigeons.

There were a number of sites in Surrey for interned civilians or prisoners of war (POWs), notably at Frith Hill, Deepcut. From August 1914, firstly German civilian internees and then German military prisoners taken in France were held there.[33] The camp became a local spectacle, with several references to crowds of onlookers.[34]

German prisoners of war marching to Frith Hill Camp, *c.* 1917 (SHC PC/68/23/1)

Edward Unmack

The case of Edward Unmack, the 'German' Rector of West Horsley, generated much correspondence between Chief Constable Sant and the War Office from 1916 almost until the end of the war.[1] Unmack, whose middle name was Carl, was reported to the authorities by a parishioner of West Horsley because he spoke fluent German, was 'thoroughly German in his ideas and speech' and 'spends all his holidays in Germany and preaches in German'. Further to his discredit, he asked another parishioner, whose husband was in the Royal Navy, for news of the whereabouts of her husband's ship, and asked 'to have his correspondence to preach a sermon on'. It was also reported in the *Surrey Advertiser* that Unmack had been fined for ringing the church bells at 6.20 p.m. and failing to black out the church windows (both contrary to DORA, as things that might assist Zeppelins).[2] He was suspected of having 'pro-German sympathies', despite assurances of his loyalty to Great Britain. In fact, it was discovered, he had been born in Australia and was a naturalised Briton. By July 1918, the War Office conceded that Unmack 'must be accepted as a British subject' and merely requested to be informed of evidence of disloyalty should it arise.

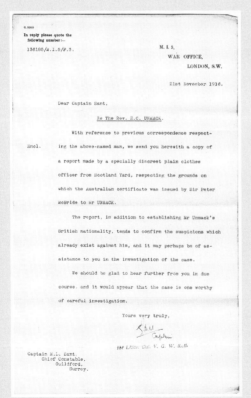

Letter from the security service M.I.5 to Chief Constable Sant enclosing a report on the Reverend E. Unmack, November 1916 (SHC CC98/14/8)

Inmates were initially housed in tents. Probably due to the weather, the camp was closed in November 1914 and reopened in 1915; this pattern was repeated in subsequent years. Concerns were raised locally about the disposal of effluent from the camp.[35] An interesting record of Frith Hill was created by George Kenner (1888–1971), a German-born artist, interned there between May and September 1915, who painted a series of watercolours depicting the camp's daily life.[36]

By 1918, all civilian internees had been moved and the camp had two compounds for military prisoners: one for Germans and one for Austrian and other nationalities, who were mostly at work nearby.[37] Keeping the prisoners secure was another matter: on Monday, 25 September 1916, five German prisoners from Frith Hill, named and described in a local newspaper, eluded their guards while working on the railway near Deepcut.[38] The Surrey Constabulary, anticipating such a possibility, had obtained its first dogs, three bloodhounds kennelled at Camberley.[39] One was used to track the escapees' movements, but failed to locate them because they had crossed a railway line. All five were, however, recaptured by 28 September.[40]

Other Surrey prison camps were set up in Belmont Hospital, Sutton, and Woking Detention Barracks. POWs were employed later in the war to provide labour for agriculture, forestry and industry. Felday Camp in Holmbury St Mary opened in 1917 to house such prisoners.

In September 1917, Chief Constable Sant detailed the case of Hugo Greef, a registered enemy alien who had bought Durfold Farm, Dunsfold (close to the signalling station at One Tree Hill and the prohibited area of Sussex), and whose son had brought twenty-two homing pigeons from Leicester with a permit from the Leicester Police. In his December report, Sant noted (with great satisfaction) that Greef had been ordered to return to 'the place from whence he came, viz, Carshalton' and his 'unwelcome presence' removed. Greef's 'British-born' son enlisted.[41]

In 1918, Sant reported the case of Andre von Drumreicher, who had served in the German cavalry and subsequently in the Egyptian Civil Service and had now come to England. Sant noted that he had been, 'for some inexplicable reason', released by the Home Office from internment and was now residing in Farnham.[42]

At the end of the war, the British Nationality and Status of Aliens Act of August 1918 gave the Home Secretary sweeping new powers to repeal the naturalisation certificates of alien subjects.

Wartime Crime in Surrey

The removal of thousands of young men into the forces during the war reduced the criminal population countrywide. However, offences linked to the presence of servicemen and large army camps, such as prostitution and brothel-keeping, increased. Some soldiers did not endear themselves to the civilian population, often because of their behaviour towards local women. One letter to the *Woking News and Mail* complained that women were often followed by drunken soldiers (although in subsequent editions of the newspaper, many residents, including women, wrote in support of soldiers).[43] Canadian soldiers based in the county found themselves in all sorts of trouble, from assaulting local women and committing bigamy to being arrested for drunken behaviour and theft.

Incidents continued after the war had ended, as soldiers let out their frustration over the slowness of demobilisation. In February 1919, for example, Henry Drummond White, a Canadian at Woodcote Park Camp, was charged with being drunk and disorderly, using obscene language, assault and damage to property.[44] Around 400 Canadian soldiers later rioted in Epsom on 17 June 1919, damaging the police station and killing Sergeant Thomas Green.[45] (See Chapter 1 for further discussion of Canadian troops and the demobilisation riots in Surrey.)

The war saw the creation of many new criminal offences, including displaying lights on houses and vehicles, evasion of the Military Service Act, possession of literature likely to prejudice recruitment and discipline, offences against food and fuel control orders and selling intoxicating liquor during prohibited hours. Blackout conditions and food shortages probably tempted some to commit crimes such as poaching, while others took advantage of situations of panic and disturbance to loot.

Surrey County Council's published Annual Reports include crime statistics.[46] The number of serious, indictable offences committed, and persons charged with those offences, fell during the war as conscription removed many of those most likely to commit such violations. However, the number of certain minor, non-indictable offences committed saw a sharp rise. Convictions under the intoxicating liquor laws plunged from 351 in 1914 to forty-nine in 1918; there were two convictions for brothel-keeping in 1915 and four in both 1916 and 1917, but none recorded for any other year, while convictions for prostitution reached a high (forty-three convictions) in 1916. In the category of 'other offences', which must have embraced many of the new crimes created under DORA, the number of convictions rose from ten in 1914 to a high of 1,213 in 1916.

Animal stealing peaked in the 'hungry' years of 1917 and 1918, and food shortages could prompt desperate measures. On 7 June 1918, burglars broke into Chertsey Golf Course's clubhouse, their main target the store of margarine, butter and lard – strictly rationed products.[47] Soldiers and civilian workers alike were responsible for break-ins at army camp kitchens to steal food. Civilian crime in wartime Surrey was significantly shaped by new restrictions imposed by the government.

3

FORGING THE
WEAPONS OF WAR

MARTIN STILWELL

World War I turned Surrey into a county with a lasting reputation for engineering and technology. The demands of the conflict, particularly from 1917, transformed local industries into major contributors to the war effort. Some Surrey companies that undertook war work continued to be significant to the economy of the county – and, indeed, to that of the country – for decades afterwards.

In 1914, Britain moved onto a war footing. There could be, however, no long-term plans until military needs had been ascertained. Early orders for goods and equipment required for the campaign, such as munitions, were for existing designs from a limited number of established suppliers.[1] There was no central control over the distribution of such goods and the War Office (the army) competed with the Admiralty (the navy) for supplies. By the end of 1914, it was clear that the war was not going to be short and industrial supply was at breaking point.[2] Modern warfare demanded huge quantities of high-explosive shells, but also other ordnance and equipment such as mortars, grenades, ammunition, barbed wire and steel helmets. As a result, production expanded from, predominantly, the foundries and steel works of the West Midlands and the north to wider industrial communities such as London and the Home Counties.

Significant changes to the military machine came in 1915, particularly after a political crisis caused by the dire shortage of high-explosive shells forced the recognition that industry needed to be controlled and supported to enable it to expand sufficiently to facilitate a long-term military campaign. The first important change came in March, when women were allowed to sign up at Labour Exchanges for vacancies in trades from which they had been excluded previously (to inevitable objections from trades unions).[3] What to sign on for had not yet been established, but it was the start of a major, and vital, change in the workforce: while the armed forces needed men to fight, industry needed workers. Reconciling these needs necessitated widening the employment available to women.

Secondly, the July 1915 Munitions of War Act created the Ministry of Munitions (MOM), which was staffed at senior level by captains of industry and led initially by David Lloyd George. His appointment was inspired, and the ministry continued to be led by highly capable people until it was disbanded in 1919. The MOM's aims were to increase capacity, reduce costs and improve quality (a particular problem in shell production). The army was costing £2 million per day and the navy £550,000 per day in 1914,[4] and the troops deserved improved quality and supply for that money. The Act gave the MOM control over the workforce and sanctioned what was called the 'dilution of labour'. Companies were allowed to employ women to do unskilled and semi-skilled work, the skilled labourer was not permitted to do work that an unskilled or semi-skilled person could do, and controls placed on trades unions made strikes much more difficult (for detailed discussion of the wartime role of women in Surrey's industry, see Chapter 5). As a result, more unskilled and semi-skilled male labour could be released to the armed forces. The Act also allowed subcontractors to be engaged by main contractors and, from this, Surrey's small manufacturing and engineering businesses really benefited. Businesses involved in military contracts could apply for loans to expand factories and defray the costs against excess profits.

At the start of the war there were just four government-run factories in the UK – Farnborough (aircraft), Waltham Abbey (gunpowder), Enfield Lock (rifles) and Woolwich (munitions) – but, by the end, there were 309.[5] Ultimately, the MOM took over much large-scale manufacturing nationwide by constructing National Factories, particularly from 1917. These factories were usually new-builds on vacant land, but some were existing factories that the government took over or compulsorily purchased if the owners were failing to meet the military contracts they had been awarded. The biggest National Factories were the shell factories (some of which became new towns). The MOM geared up industry for a war that was expected to last until 1919. The Armistice in November 1918 came as a surprise to many, and well-funded and fully galvanised industry was unprepared for the massive slump in orders that ensued.

So, how did all of this affect Surrey and its relatively small industrial infrastructure? Surrey in 1914 was strongly agricultural but had pockets of industry that had developed along the Thames, Wey and Wandle Rivers, at Brooklands racetrack in Weybridge (opened in 1907), or simply thanks to the presence of certain

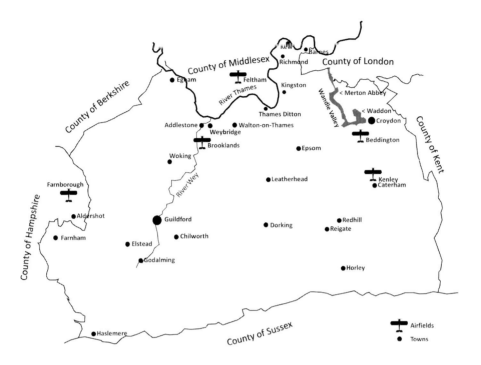

Map showing airfields and sites of significant industrial activity in Surrey
(© Martin Stilwell)

skills (an example of the last is an engineering community close to Kew Gardens Underground station). The heavier and dirtier industries were based along the Wandle Valley, but some small towns, such as Thames Ditton, also had foundries and manufacturing.

Across Surrey, engineering companies were contracted to make metal fabrications, shell fuses, electrical equipment, gauges and optical instruments. The county also manufactured vehicles at AutoCarriers (AC Cars) in Thames Ditton and at Dennis Brothers in Guildford, the latter having an excellent reputation for lorries and fire engines. Dennis received immediate orders for its 3-ton and 4-ton lorries, in chassis form. These vehicles shared the same reliable engine design, supplied by White & Poppe of Coventry (a company Dennis purchased in 1919). By autumn 1914, Dennis was supplying to the military an average of fifteen 'Type A' (4-ton) lorries a week, with a peak in one week of thirty-four. These were built to military standard and became one of the 'subvention' lorry designs made nationwide. (Subvention lorries could be purchased by private buyers who were paid a subsidy of £110 over three years in return for the government having the option to buy back the vehicle 'at times of war' at a depreciated price.) All of this made Dennis a profitable business and its lathes were already working twenty-three hours a day by December 1914.[6] Another Guildford-based firm was Drummond Brothers Ltd, makers of medium-sized lathes. Throughout the war, Drummond's entire production was tailored to meet military orders, which its staff worked multiple shifts to fulfil. The factory burnt down in 1915 but was quickly rebuilt and production resumed.[7]

The sector of wartime manufacturing that was to become synonymous with Surrey – aviation – had a slow start. This industry was centred on Brooklands airfield, within the racetrack circuit, where low numbers of relatively flimsy aircraft were already being made by small companies, including Blériot Manufacturing Aircraft Company Ltd and Martin & Handasyde. Before war broke out, the Sopwith Aviation Company had already expanded beyond its hangar space at Brooklands and was manufacturing dependable aircraft (initially for the Royal Naval Air Service [RNAS]) at its Kingston factory, although all final assembly and flying of land-based aircraft was from Brooklands.[8] At the start of the war, the RNAS's demand for Sopwith aircraft already filled the company's order books and the War Office did not place large orders with it until 1916.

Control of Brooklands airfield itself was generously handed to the Royal Flying Corps (RFC) by owner Hugh Locke King at the outbreak of war. The RFC took over all of Brooklands' flying schools but allowed the manufacture, assembly and testing of aircraft to continue. No evidence of clashes between the military and private companies at Brooklands has been found. This dual use of Brooklands continued until 1917. The airfield was also, until 1916, the centre of successful airborne wireless development.[9]

In the first months of the war, most aircraft engines were French designs, by companies such as Le Rhône and Clerget, and were of the rotary type in which the whole engine spun around the crankshaft (to aid cooling) and the propeller was fixed to the engine, rather than to the crankshaft. These were made and serviced in England under licence, and a Mercedes car dealer in Addlestone, Gordon Watney, turned over his company to aircraft engine repairs, thereby initiating Addlestone's long connection with the aviation industry.

Throughout 1915, Surrey's industries continued to develop apace. The county came under the jurisdiction of the Metropolitan Munitions Committee, which also controlled London; military contracts could therefore be co-ordinated across the Home Counties. Most factories were now on full-time working but had few female employees, although the employment of women in the aviation industry to sew the cloth onto aircraft wings and fuselages was well established.

New businesses opened to meet military demand – for example, entrepreneur and self-publicist John Whitehead opened a small aircraft factory in residential Richmond to make B.E.2b and Shorthorn aircraft. His company purchased land

Dennis Brothers' 30hp War Office subvention 'A'-type lorry, supplied in large numbers to the British Army (SHC 1463/PHTALB/3/1)

Dennis Brothers' subvention model undergoing its War Office tests, 1914 (SHC 1463/ PHTALB/3/1)

at Feltham in Middlesex as its final assembly base and thus established Feltham Air Park, which remained an airfield until 1947. The Sopwith Aviation Company expanded by purchasing land and housing adjacent to its existing factory in residential Kingston. Its orders were still predominantly from the RNAS, but the RFC had also become interested in ordering Sopwith's proven designs. Aircraft manufacturing at Brooklands and Kingston continued to benefit local companies working in related fields, such as Lang Propeller Ltd, founded by Arthur Lang in 1913 for the manufacture of metal- and fabric-tipped wooden propellers. Lang propellers were fitted to aeroplanes designed by many of the leading manufacturers, including Sopwith, Martinsyde, Armstrong Whitworth, De Havilland and the Royal Aircraft Factory at Farnborough. Wartime demand meant Lang's base at the Riverside Works in Weybridge soon reached full capacity and the company moved to larger premises in Addlestone. The manufacture of propellers remained a skilled woodworking industry throughout the war.[10]

It was not only Surrey's aviation-related industries that thrived during 1915. Accurate gauges were needed in their thousands by Britain's industry and military. One of the early National Factories formed by the MOM was the National Gauge Factory in Croydon. The MOM appropriated a German-owned gauge factory, Pintsch's Electrical Manufacturing Company, in November 1915 and, to avoid awkward questions over the funding of what might still be seen as a German business, created the Vidal Engineering Company to take over the factory, finance it and

Manufacturing at Lang Propeller Ltd (courtesy of Chertsey Museum, CHYMS.2954.017)

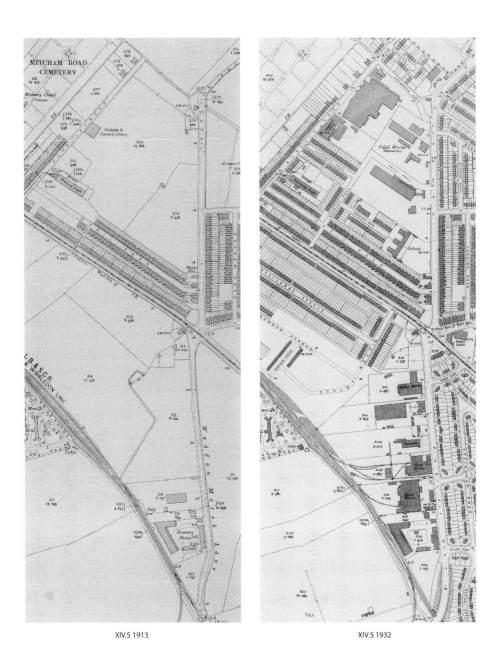

XIV.5 1913   XIV.5 1932

Ordnance Survey 25-inch maps of 1913 and 1932 (sheet no. XIV.5) showing industrial growth at Waddon, Croydon. The Vidal Engineering Company's buildings are shown top right.

operate it as the National Gauge Factory on the ministry's behalf. The factory ran successfully as a private business, but under the very close scrutiny of the MOM.[11] Vidal moved to a new purpose-built site in Waddon in 1917.

The centuries-old gunpowder factory at Chilworth (making cordite) and the lime works at Brockham and Betchworth, between Dorking and Redhill, also worked flat out to meet orders. Interestingly, the Chilworth factory had been owned by German company Vereinigte Rheinisch-Westfälische Pulverfabriken AG since 1885 but was taken over by Nobel's Explosives Company in 1914 (Vickers owned a 40% interest in the latter). In 1915, a cordite factory for the Admiralty was opened on an adjacent site and became the main producer of propellant there.[12]

In 1916 there was a considerable increase in manufacturing across Britain to meet the requirements of the country's fast-expanding war machine. The armed forces wanted men, the MOM wanted munitions, manufacturers wanted orders, and the people wanted food. These needs had to be managed and so central control by the government became even more pronounced. Companies were encouraged to employ women and thereby release fit men for the services, and this helped to drive the move to automation and production-line methods. With the introduction of conscription, men who worked in a trade judged to be vital for the war effort could apply for exemption certificates to avoid being called up. The list of exempt trades was large and included many in the engineering industries prominent in Surrey.

Finance was available to fund factory expansions and the government con-structed more National Factories. One of the more obscure of these was the Box Repair Factory at Beddington, near Croydon, which was converted from a cement store and opened in February 1917 under the management of the MOM's Trench Warfare Supply department.[13] The factory repaired salvageable grenade and bomb boxes. Of its 308 employees, 89% were women. This very efficient factory managed to reduce the cost of repairing a box from 10d in 1916 to 5d by April 1917.[14] The ministry also built a Tin Box Manufacture & Repair Factory at Walnut Tree Close in Guildford in 1918, one of seven such factories it built and managed directly.

In Guildford, Dennis Brothers erected new factory buildings on Woodbridge Hill. In May 1916, the MOM asked the company to fulfil an increased order of twenty-five lorries per week and promised an order of thirty-five vehicles per week from June 1917. In return, the MOM contributed to the cost of expanding the Woodbridge site.[15] (Dennis was careful to ensure that the funding of growth could be met from any excess profits on military orders. This financial management paid off handsomely post-war.) To counter problems finding and keeping a labour force, Dennis built twelve houses for skilled workers in nearby Woking Road and sought to employ women in its less-skilled trades.

Dennis remained a very profitable company that did not forget its civilian customers during the war, knowing that the eventual cessation of military orders was inevitable and would leave it with a large factory to utilise. Dennis vacated its original Guildford offices in Onslow Street at the end of 1917. The vacated offices were taken over by Drummond Brothers' office staff, thereby freeing up space at Drummond's own lathe factory. Dennis and Drummond collaborated to make a special version of the Dennis 4-ton subvention lorry that was a portable workshop with its own power supply. This vehicle was highly regarded by maintenance teams in France.

Into the aviation history of Surrey then arrived a company synonymous with Brooklands: Vickers Ltd. Prior to 1916, Vickers had built its aircraft at its machine-gun factory at Crayford in Kent. In that year, it purchased the vacant Itala car factory alongside the racetrack at Brooklands. This purchase marked the beginning of the move of all of Vickers' aircraft manufacturing to that site, on which it remained until the 1980s.

The Blériot Manufacturing Aircraft Company Ltd, also based at Brooklands, was forcibly wound up in 1916 because of financial irregularities by some key shareholders.[16] The extent to which Louis Blériot himself had control over this situation is unclear, but orders from the government for his aircraft enabled him subsequently to open a factory in nearby Addlestone under the name Blériot & SPAD Ltd.[17] (He had already purchased the land for this in 1915, but did not then have the orders to fund the move.)

Vickers Ltd factory at Brooklands late in the war (courtesy of Brooklands Museum)

SPAD aircraft at Brooklands airfield (courtesy of Brooklands Museum)

Blériot's new factory was built in 1916, funded by the MOM, and made the SPAD (Société pour L'Aviation et ses Dérivés) VII fighter, designed by Louis Béchereau of Deperdussin, another Blériot company. For reasons that remain unexplained, the factory had to dismantle and reverse-engineer a French-built SPAD VII to create the engineering drawings from which to build (which may be why pilots reportedly said that the French-built aircraft flew better!). Altogether, 100 SPAD VIIs were built.[18] Blériot might have expected that prestigious orders from the government would follow, but he was given an order to build the Avro 504 biplane that was used at Brooklands for pilot training.

Martin & Handasyde, which had been renamed Martinsyde Ltd in 1915, also needed to expand and purchased the former Oriental Institute buildings at Woking, 5 miles from Brooklands, where it produced its own single-seat aircraft. Martinsyde retained most of its Brooklands hangars for construction, but would eventually, like all of the companies, move manufacturing elsewhere and keep only hangars for final assembly and flight testing at Brooklands airfield.[19]

Elsewhere in Surrey, the Whitehead Aircraft Company (Ltd) and the Sopwith Aviation Company expanded as new military orders came in. Whitehead remained unique in Surrey in only ever making aircraft of its own design.

To support airframe manufacture, Lang Propeller Ltd started to expand its new Addlestone factory. The shaping of the blades of the wooden propellers by hand required skilled woodworkers and Lang therefore continued, exceptionally in Surrey's aircraft industry, to have an almost male-only workforce. Nearby, Gordon Watney also expanded his engine building and refurbishment business. He still concentrated on rotary Le Rhône and Clerget engines, but also began to refurbish the in-line Beardmore engine.

Smaller companies continued to spring up around the county to satisfy military orders and to take on subcontracted work from the aviation industry. The relatively few foundries in Surrey worked to the full on government orders for munitions and engine components; the parts of the county in which they were situated, such as Thames Ditton, Merton Abbey and Waddon, must have been unpleasant environments.

Not all companies were in Surrey's recognised engineering or manufacturing locations. In very rural Elstead, between Guildford and Farnham, the Weyburn Engineering Company made engine components, using, by the end of the war, much female labour. The company went on to be a major manufacturer of such components, particularly camshafts, only closing in 2008.[20]

All of this was still on a relatively small scale in comparison to the massive expansion of manufacturing that occurred in 1917. Industry in general, but particularly aviation, benefited greatly from Winston Churchill's appointment as Minister of Munitions in July 1917. Having served briefly on the Western Front after the Dardanelles fiasco, he had returned to government. Under David Lloyd George and his successors, the MOM's organisation had become top heavy, with too many departments; upon his appointment, Churchill immediately rationalised its seventy departments into ten larger ones that were led by capable civil servants rather than captains of industry (who were seen to have conflicts of interest). A committed supporter of aerial warfare, Churchill initiated a major air force expansion programme that resulted in the RFC increasing from eighty-five squadrons in December 1917 to 200 in December 1918. To achieve this, Britain had to build a massive 3,500 aircraft and 4,000 engines per month.[21] The effect on Surrey's aircraft and related components industries was dramatic.

Churchill also forced Britain's two military air services, the RFC and RNAS, to liaise in order to co-ordinate their requirements and avoid competing against each other, working with the reorganised Air Board. (The Board would be replaced by the Air Ministry in early 1918, under the leadership of the very capable Sir William Weir.) One of the Air Board's first decisions was to reduce the number of government-approved aircraft types from fifty-one to, by September 1917, just thirteen.[22] One of the types retained was the Farnborough-designed S.E.5a fighter, which came to form a major part of Surrey's aircraft production.

The Air Board also rationalised the way in which aircraft were accepted by the military and in 1917 created RFC Aircraft Acceptance Parks to receive and inspect newly built aircraft. Each park usually handled just one type of aircraft. The two parks created in Surrey were at Brooklands, which henceforth no longer handled pilot or observer training, and Kenley. Brooklands was a dedicated S.E.5a Acceptance Park (with Sopwith Salamanders added in 1918) and Kenley managed deliveries of Airco DH.4 and DH.9 two-seaters. Surrey's aircraft factories were also henceforth usually dedicated to building only one type of aeroplane at a time, with Vickers, the Air Navigation Company Ltd (an incarnation of Blériot) and Martinsyde building the S.E.5a (the last named also built smaller numbers of its own designs) and Whitehead building the Sopwith Pup and then the DH.9. The Sopwith Aviation Company continued to build its own designs, particularly the famous Sopwith Camel, but production of these was also rationalised by the Air Board. The increase in aircraft orders and decrease in aircraft types in 1917 enabled local industry to rationalise and to focus on producing components for specific aircraft and engines.

Engine types were also streamlined and in this field one Surrey company suffered a notable failure. ABC Motors of Walton-on-Thames had designed a small engine called the Wasp. This engine was one of the first radial types, in which the cylinders remained static and the crankshaft spun along with the propeller. The engine was designed to be easy and cheap to make. It looked good too. Despite some problems, particularly with the air cooling of the cylinders, the company designed a larger version called the Dragonfly. This had a better power to weight ratio than the ubiquitous contemporary Bentley BR2 rotary engine and was expected by many factories nationwide to be considerably cheaper to make. Ronald Charteris, the owner, sold the Dragonfly engine to the Air Ministry and Sir William Weir decided to rationalise all aircraft engines to just two types, the Dragonfly radial and the Rolls-Royce Eagle V8. The Dragonfly was a disaster. It overheated quickly and suffered very bad torsional vibrations. Engines rarely lasted more than twenty hours. Even the benefits of low production costs did not materialise, and it cost more to make than the Bentley BR2.[23] Farnborough's engineers were unable to resolve the problems and the engine was withdrawn in 1918, leaving new aircraft still on the drawing board to be hastily re-engineered to take existing engines, such as the Bentley.[24]

Although Surrey had no national-level munitions factories, the county's foundries and engineering shops continued to make small quantities of specialist shells and many fuses for all shell types. In the Merton Abbey area, the Eyre Smelting Company produced considerable volumes of soft metal for local casting companies.[25] Lagonda Cars in Staines eventually employed nearly 900 women to make fuses for shells and small aircraft components. The shortage of skilled labour continued to be a problem, as many firms found it difficult to adapt to using less experienced women workers.[26]

It was not only engineering companies that moved over to military contracts. Well-respected house builder Walter Tarrant of Byfleet (adjacent to Brooklands) turned over his workforce to building wooden and Nissen huts, using mainly

S.E.5a aircraft at Brooklands Airfield (courtesy of Brooklands Museum)

ABC Motors' troublesome Dragonfly radial engine (courtesy of The National Archives of the UK, AIR 1/702/27/3/689)

Women carpenters working at the Tarrant hut workshops, 3 miles from Calais, 26 June 1918 (© IWM, Q6767)

female workers. Under his leadership, around 150 women went to France as carpenters to erect the huts. It was reported, on their return in January 1919, that Tarrant's 'lady carpenters' had erected 37,000 huts (15,000 of his design and 22,000 Nissen huts) over two years. Despite being situated close to the Front, there had been no casualties among Tarrant's workers.[27] (For further discussion of Tarrant's scheme, see Chapter 5.)

Around the turn of 1917–18, the government planned to establish a National Aircraft Factory at Ham, a short distance from the Sopwith Aviation Company's Kingston facility. However, the new factory never actually became a 'National' factory: Sopwith persuaded the MOM to let it run the factory, which it leased from the ministry in early 1918, as an assembly shop to its existing factory. Sopwith's manufacturing capacity consequently received an immediate boost.

Meanwhile, Vickers, Martinsyde and the Air Navigation Company were, by the start of 1918, almost entirely dedicated to building the S.E.5a. Vickers started to build the large Vimy bomber at Brooklands just before the Armistice (Vimy production having hitherto been at Crayford), but the resulting aircraft were too late to see action in World War I.[28]

Two new aircraft factories were built in Surrey during the war's final year. National Aircraft Factory 1 (NAF1) was built on 198 acres at Waddon, adjacent to

RFC Beddington in Croydon, by Messrs Holland and Hannen and Cubitts, who were also tasked with managing it. It was operational from March 1918 and was designed to build forty DH.9 aircraft and 600 machine-gun interrupter mechanisms per week, but it never came close to achieving those numbers.[29] Poor industrial relations and management plagued the factory and by October 1918 it was producing only nine aircraft per week.[30] At its peak in November 1918, NAF1 employed 3,600 workers, of whom 46% were women, a lower proportion than had been intended (according to plans for skills 'dilution', women should have accounted for approximately 60% of the workforce). It seems that building a factory working on production-line principles in an area without familiarity with such methods, and with a management lacking relevant experience, was a poor decision. The second new factory was built in Kew by the Glendower Aircraft Company, which was already building DH.4 aircraft to government contracts in South Kensington. The Armistice came just as that factory was getting into its stride.

The following table shows the number of aircraft built by Surrey factories in 1918:[31]

Glendower Aircraft Company, Kew	77
NAF1, Waddon	241
Air Navigation Company Ltd (Blériot), Addlestone	318
Martinsyde, Woking	486
Whitehead Aircraft Company, Richmond	596
Vickers Ltd, Brooklands	1,357
Sopwith Aviation Company, Kingston upon Thames	1,363

However, these figures do not give the whole picture of production: in the same year, a further 6,008 Sopwith aircraft were built under licence across the UK, plus approximately 1,400 in France.[32] Viewed alongside the total number of Sopwith aircraft built between 1913 and 1919 (3,494 at Kingston, 11,169 under licence elsewhere in the UK, and approximately 4,200 in France),[33] the rate and efficiency of production during 1918 are clear. Nationwide licensing similarly increased the number of Lang propellers that could be manufactured. While there are no definitive figures for total production, Lang itself made 5,426 propellers from 1 June 1918 alone and submitted royalty claims for over 16,000 that had been built by other companies over the course of the war. It is estimated that the war saw in excess of 25,000 Lang propellers made to military orders.[34] Arthur Lang himself had left the company. Delays in negotiating its royalty payment agreement with the government caused a cash flow problem that forced Lang to sell the firm to Thomas Sopwith in 1917. He then moved across the Atlantic, where he established a new

S.E.5a aircraft parked at Brooklands airfield (courtesy of Brooklands Museum)

propeller business. The level of aviation-related production in 1918 can be gauged further from a statement by the Air Ministry that the cost of supplies to the air force in that year was £113 million.[35] This huge amount of money illustrates the evolution of the relatively small RFC of 1916 into the substantial air force of 1918.

Gordon Watney's successful engine refurbishment factory in Addlestone burnt down on 9 June 1918 when its petrol store exploded, killing the night watchman on his rounds. The watchman was believed to have struck a match in the store to light a cigarette. The MOM made a claim against Watney for £47,430, the estimated value of the lost engines, which were government property. Watney fought long and hard with his insurers, who said that the factory was destroyed by an 'explosion' and not by a 'fire'. The outcome of the claim is unknown, but Watney's business survived, albeit with a reduced output.[36]

The Armistice came sooner than the government had planned for. Orders for munitions and aircraft came to an abrupt halt, although contractors were allowed to complete orders that were in progress. Most of the smaller companies that had been created to process war orders, or had expanded to do so, did not survive long. All of the National Factories closed. The troublesome NAF1 in Croydon was one of the first to shut its doors; its workers were summarily dismissed, resulting in local civil unrest.[37]

The Sopwith Aviation Company faced a large tax bill on its excess profits and voluntarily liquidated to avoid payment, rendering 1,400 workers idle.[38] It immediately re-formed, using the name of its chief pilot (Harry Hawker), as Hawker Engineering. The company had no further need for the rented factory in Ham, which was taken over by Leyland Motors to service and civilianise its subvention lorries. Thus, perhaps by some dubious business methods, was Sopwith's aircraft production in Kingston able to continue after the war, albeit on a much smaller scale.

The Whitehead Aircraft Company's factory in Richmond had to close due to high debts, as did the Glendower factory in Kew (the building became a Chrysler/Dodge vehicle factory). ABC Motors voluntarily liquidated and re-formed as ABC

Motors (1920) Ltd. Its directors went to court in 1921 with a massive claim of £609,000 against the government for the design of the failed Dragonfly engine (which they claimed was fit for purpose). The government response stated that only fourteen engines had been delivered by the time of the Armistice and £2 million of taxpayers' money had been spent trying to make the engine fit for service. The claim was thrown out.[39]

Lang Propeller Ltd did not long survive the war: in June 1918, the company secretary and general manager wrote to the MOM that the directors 'feel very strongly that the demand for aeroplane propellers after the war is likely to be very considerably reduced and that in consequence it behoves us to consider what trade it is possible for us to take up to supplement the reduced post-war output of propellers'. It was proposed that the firm should diversify into cabinet making and permission was sought for the factory to produce some sample pieces of furniture 'with a view to keeping our staff fully engaged after the war'. Permission was refused, although it was observed that it was a typical case, 'illustrating the difficulties of facilitating the preparation for post-war industry – particularly by reason of the general labour shortage'.[40] By comparison, Dennis Brothers had managed its finances and production very well and continued to thrive post-war, its fire engines achieving near legendary status.

Of the 150 Surrey companies known to have carried out war contracts, by the time of the centenary of the Armistice in 2018 just two survived using their Great War era name. Dennis Brothers was part of Alexander Dennis Ltd, makers of bus chassis in Guildford. Gillett & Johnston, a small Croydon foundry making bells and large clocks, which in World War I had turned over its business to munitions work, was still maintaining public and tower clocks from premises in Kent.[41]

4

A COUNTY AT WAR

MICHAEL PAGE

'A Long and Arduous Struggle'

Herbert Brockman, a cashier for a cement company, and his wife Isabel lived at Eaton Cottage in Thames Ditton with their two children, Miles and Nancy, and the children's nurse, Elsie May Taylor. During 1916 at least, the children put together an illustrated newsletter, the 'Eaton Cottage Herald', to keep family and friends up to speed with events in the Brockman household. The newsletter paints a charming picture of a comfortable middle-class life on the banks of the Thames, enlivened by seaside holidays, camping and cooking in the garden, messing about on the river and amateur theatricals. Yet the reader is always aware that the children's escapades were taking place against the backdrop of a war that had come to permeate almost every aspect of their lives – their snowmen took on the guise of the Kaiser and the United States' President's wife; homemade jigsaws were sent to the local war hospital; mother sold flags for the British Red Cross (BRC) while father served as a Special Constable enforcing air-raid precautions. An illustration of 'the ladies of the house knitting … very industriously for the soldiers while Nancy sits and sews' is captioned 'Sister Susies!', a reference to the popular song 'Sister Susie's Sewing Shirts for Soldiers'. A mournful depiction by Nancy of pre-war Easter eggs and the eggs they faced in 1916 reflects the developing food crisis. Even the children's jokes reflect the conflict and the animosities it had stoked up: 'Teacher to very small girl in Sunday School class, "Now, what would you say if Satan were to speak to you?" "I don't speak German" came the cutting reply.'[1] (See Chapter 2 for the Brockman children's illustration of their father in his uniform, and for Special Constables.)

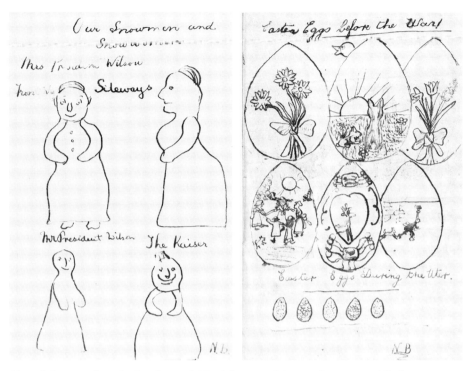

Above left: a page from the Brockman children's homemade 'Eaton Cottage Herald' of 1915, depicting the Kaiser and US President Wilson's wife as snowmen (SHC 9497/1/1)
Above right: a page from the Brockman children's homemade 'Eaton Cottage Herald' of 1916, depicting Nancy Brockman's comparison of Easter eggs before and during the war (SHC 9497/1/4)

The war could be experienced everywhere – in shops, churches and cinemas, on the roads and railways, in schools and on farms. Advertisers rapidly adapted their messages to the new situation: Ven-Yusa oxygen face cream was promoted as 'the faithful ally of war workers'; Spirella Corsets were marketed opportunistically as 'For War Time and All Time. Unbreakable'.[2] As 1918 dawned, Cobham business-man Frederick Robinson wrote in his diary, 'People no longer talk of the war, they are saturated with it, they live with it, they sleep with it, it enters into their every thought and action, it is part of their flesh and of their bone.'[3] It could be experienced in the silence of church bells and striking clocks (in case their sound alerted Zeppelins) and in the rumble of the far distant guns of the Western Front, which could be heard across Surrey when weather conditions were favourable. Vera Brittain, in Kingswood, 'felt the sinister shudder of guns from the Belgian coast shake the Caterham Valley like a subterranean earthquake',[4] while Eric Parker, guarding the Chilworth Gunpowder Works, recalls standing by St Martha's Church, high on the Downs, while:

… close to my ear were the sounds of battle, field guns, heavy guns, the shaking boom, the rattle of musketry, as if we were fighting Germans in the next parish. All came to me in repercussion of sound from the oak door behind me. I stepped a yard to the side and I was in the silence of Surrey; a step to the right, and I was in France.[5]

For Rose Macaulay, in her beautiful poem 'Picnic: July 1917', the sound of 'the great guns' had become a familiar backdrop to summer rambles in Hurt Wood: '… we drowsily heard and someone said,"They sound clear today."'[6]

The bombardment of London was also audible and visible. In September 1917, Frederick Robinson was alarmed to see 'numberless shells' exploding over London, though it was 20 miles away, and commented, 'To have actual hostilities going on within earshot and within sight brings it home as nothing hitherto has done.'[7]

Even time was affected: on 21 May 1916, British Summer Time was inaugurated and it was ordered that clocks be put forward an hour. Not all approved, some calling the new summer time 'All fools' day' and others refusing to adjust their clocks.[8]

Frederick Arthur Robinson, indefatigable Cobham diarist (courtesy of IWM, Docs.11335)

Though many people did believe that the war would be short and sharp, more thoughtful observers realised that it would be a conflict like no other. James Chuter Ede, a member of Surrey County Council's Education Committee, wrote, 'Here, as in all places, we move in the shadow of the Great War … The dislocation of the world as we knew it forces itself upon us at every turn.'[9] The Rector of Godstone reflected in the September 1914 parish magazine, 'With a suddenness that is difficult and almost impossible to realise, we find ourselves to-day engaged in a war that has no parallel in the history of the world, and of which none of us can foresee the end … It will be a long and arduous struggle.'[10] The Rector of Byfleet wrote, 'The greatest war ever waged: the largest hosts ever mustered: and between the Christian nations! It is appalling and it is horrible.'[11] The Bishop of Winchester in Farnham Castle advised, 'It is sober truth that in its

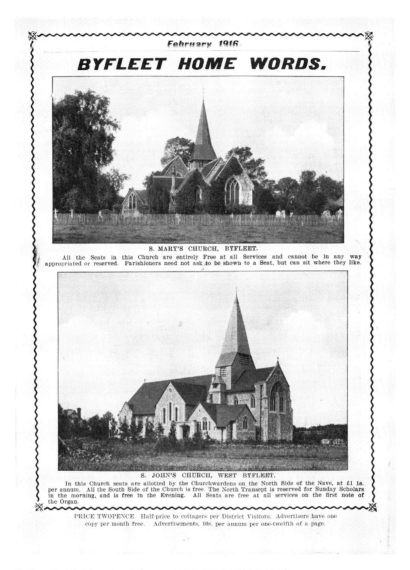

February 1916

BYFLEET HOME WORDS.

S. MARY'S CHURCH, BYFLEET.

All the Seats in this Church are entirely Free at all Services and cannot be in any way appropriated or reserved. Parishioners need not ask to be shown to a Seat, but can sit where they like.

S. JOHN'S CHURCH, WEST BYFLEET.

In this Church seats are allotted by the Churchwardens on the North Side of the Nave, at £1 1s. per annum. All the South Side of the Church is free. The North Transept is reserved for Sunday Scholars in the morning, and is free in the Evening. All Seats are free at all services on the first note of the Organ.

PRICE TWOPENCE. Half-price to cottagers per District Visitors. Advertisers have one copy per month free. Advertisements, 10s. per annum per one-twelfth of a page.

Byfleet Parish Magazine, February 1916 (SHC 1786/6/1/6)

scale, in the numbers whom it will touch, in the amount of suffering it may cause, there has been nothing like it in the history of Europe.'[12]

People desperately sought reliable news about the war, but newspaper reports were often out of date, censored or one-sided. Frederick Robinson immediately began a diary in which he recorded the latest events as reported in a great variety of newspapers and magazines and attempted to discern, through the half-truths and rumours, a sense of how the war was really going. Increasingly, he came to believe, 'it is a war of lies as well as of arms and one literally does not know what to believe'. On complaining to an officer friend that British and German reports of the same action were hopelessly divergent, he was advised that 'if you take the two reports and mix them up together you get the approximate truth'. Rumours and conspiracy theories spread when hard facts were absent and Robinson could never quite decide whether any truth lay behind them: that Russian troops had landed (a story endorsed by a bishop from the Cobham pulpit), that the Germans were extracting glycerine from corpses, that an 'Unseen Hand' was at work in high places for Germany, and that the drowned Kitchener was alive and well and a prisoner of war – another story convincingly verified by a Cobham informant. With the official war film *The Battle of the Somme*, he felt he was getting close to the truth: 'One is able to realise the immensity of the operations and the marvellous organisation, and to drink to the full the gruesomeness and cruelty of it all.' It left him 'mentally and physically exhausted', although he hated that it was shown alongside 'screaming farces of the Charley [*sic*] Chaplin type'.[13]

A Place of Refuge

From the very start of the war, the county mobilised itself to support those who flocked there. Surrey not only provided a temporary home to the thousands of raw recruits in training camps and billets but also shared in offering support and accommodation to the many refugees from occupied Belgium. Dora Black of Sutton spent her 1914 summer vacation from Cambridge University commuting into London to volunteer with the Women's Emergency Corps as it laboured to organise temporary homes for the hungry, exhausted and frightened Belgians flooding into Victoria Station.[14] Towns and villages across Surrey established committees to co-ordinate the local reception of Belgians allotted to them.

In April 1915, Guildford was providing a home for ninety-three refugees; in September 1917, Reigate Borough was housing 122 and £1,698 had been subscribed to the local Belgian Refugee Fund since the start of the war; the local newspaper, the *Surrey Mirror*, offered the refugees a '*Colonne des Refugies Belgiques*' to provide them with news in French for a period.[15]

The Walton, Hersham and Oatlands National Emergency Committee patted itself on the back in a report in the *Surrey Times* of March 1916, describing how over £900 had been raised and houses converted into hostels and furnished for the reception of refugees, of whom 150 had passed through the committee's hands. Finding employment for many of the refugees had, however, proved difficult, as most were from the 'upper Belgian classes' and unused to manual labour.[16] In Richmond, a large Belgian community was established and employed at the munitions works across the Thames in Twickenham. It was founded by engineer Charles Pelabon, who had fled Antwerp before its capture by the Germans, and had a workforce of around 2,000 at its height. A veritable community in exile, Walloon-speaking for the most part, grew up around the factory, filling the local Catholic churches, sending children to the two schools that Pelabon set up for them in Richmond, and flocking to Belgian shops, clubs and societies. In Richmond itself there was a Belgian patisserie, a tobacconist and toymaker and two cafés, one of which also served as a brothel.[17] Dehon, Godar & Co., engineers, was another Surrey-based,

Index record cards for two Belgian families who formed part of the community of 123 refugees in the Weybridge district (SHC Ac1321/7/11/6)

Belgian-established munitions firm, with a factory in Barnes employing in 1918 nearly seventy exiled Belgians in making shells.[18]

Soldiers and Belgian refugees were not the only people to enjoy Surrey's hospitality: air raids on London, particularly towards the end of the war, brought those who were fleeing the capital and sleeping wherever they could. Halls and churches were made available, but many ended up sleeping outside. In September 1917, Frederick Robinson wrote from Cobham: 'The trains from London are crowded again and the village hall has been thrown open for people to sleep in, who would otherwise spend the night under the hedges.'[19] They were not always welcome. A letter in the *Surrey Mirror* lamented the influx of refugees into the Caterham area and characterised them as 'pauper aliens, criminals and outcasts from the whole world', many of whom appeared to be Jewish.[20]

Doing One's Bit

From the very first weeks of the war communities sought, in a ferment of patriotism, to do their bit in support of the war effort. Committees sprouted up across Surrey to organise the making of comforts for the men overseas or supplies for the local war hospital or convalescent home, churning out vast quantities of garments. In Byfleet, in December 1914, the headmaster of the church school reported that his scholars had made 189 pairs of socks, 92 scarves, 4 vests, 12 body belts, 124 pairs of mittens, 111 pairs of cuffs and 2 helmets (a grand total of 534 articles) and proudly observed that the boys had given their football subscriptions to the wool fund.[21] A similar story was replicated across the entire county.

The Chertsey Women's War Work Association mobilised volunteer collectors, subscribers and workers from its Windsor Street base to make comforts for the troops, both those overseas and those in the Grange War Hospital, Chertsey. In a poem published in the *Surrey Herald* on 1 September 1916, the association proudly asserted that, like the men at the front, it too was 'keeping the line' and doing its bit to overcome 'the hosts of the powers of darkness', and its members had shown themselves 'worthy of helping a man!' (see Chapter 5 for more about the Women's War Work Association).[22]

In Guildford, the Queen's Comfort Fund, led by Mrs Elias Morgan, whose husband commanded at the regimental depot, looked to the needs of both the men in the front line and the prisoners of war of the Queen's (Royal West Surrey) Regiment (QRWS). It was held up by the War Office as a model until a more centralised organisation was adopted with the creation of the Queen's Regiment and the East Surrey Regiment Prisoners of War Relief Fund in 1917.[23] Godstone Church, like so many others, sent Christmas gifts to all those on its roll of honour: in 1915, the parcels contained plum pudding, sausages, Oxo cubes, potted meat, cocoa, bullseyes and chocolate.[24]

Some initiatives were on an ambitious scale, looking beyond the immediate locality, such as Evangeline Lady Farrer's War Hospitals Supply Depot in Dorking, which supplied war hospitals at home and overseas, and casualty clearing stations and ambulances at the Front.[25] The demand for medical supplies was immense: in March 1917 an urgent appeal was made for readers of Stoke D'Abernon parish magazine to collect the naturally antiseptic sphagnum moss growing by Black Pond at Oxshott, which had 'wonderful healing properties and [was] used for dressing wounds in place of cotton wool'.[26]

"Keeping the Line."

Are we "Keeping the Line" in Chertsey?
 We Mothers, and Sisters, and Wives!
Are we worthy to call them "Kinsfolk"?
 These Men who are giving their lives.
Are we "Keeping the Line" in Chertsey?
 And fighting the same grim foe—
The Hosts of the Powers of Darkness—
 Who are plotting our overthrow!

For we each of us can do something
 In a hundred different ways,
And the one who helps with her fingers
 Does as much as the one who pays.
We must "Keep the Line" in Chertsey
 By working as hard as we can,
And prove by our "Women's War Work"
 We are worthy of helping a man!

Chertsey Women's War Work Association poem, reminding members of the importance of 'Keeping the Line' at home as the men served at the Front (SHC P2/7/2)

Paying for the War

Collecting tins and flag sellers for war-related good causes were encountered everywhere ('a perfect nuisance' grumbled Frederick Robinson[27]), raising money not only for British causes but for the country's French, Russian and Serbian allies who, in the early part of the war, bore the brunt of the conflict. In Guildford, there were eighteen flag days between August 1915 and November 1918.[28] Of course, paying for the eye-watering cost of the war was not just a matter of voluntary donations. Frederick Robinson again offers a jaundiced commentary. As early as November 1914 he was complaining of the doubling of income tax and the raising of indirect taxes on beer and tea, 'The income tax payer is always the milch cow. One is prepared to make sacrifices, but one is at liberty to doubt whether the course proposed is the best.' In the latter stages of the war, Robinson had even more to grumble at: the basic rate of income tax stood at 5s in the pound on earned income (25%) and 6s on unearned income, and super tax and excess profits tax further soaked the wealthy. He was particularly exercised by the scandalous hike in the cost of sending a letter: 'Today to this country's disgrace the 1d post is abandoned and the three-halfpenny post takes its place.' He was prepared to concede 'that it is after all better for the British Government to take a third or a quarter of one's income for a year or two than for the Germans to come and take the lot', but when the details of a proposed (but never implemented) luxury tax were published, he exploded: 'Of all the egregious folly and nonsense this is the limit. Practically everything that makes life worth living is to be subject to the tax collector's rapacious maw.'[29]

Vast sums were also raised by the government through voluntary subscriptions to war loans and war savings certificates. Advertisements urging people to subscribe, in however small a way, as their patriotic duty, were ubiquitous. Robinson found their strident tone 'aggressive, not to say offensive'.[30] Local War Savings Associations were formed, War Savings Weeks were staged across Surrey and the 1917 Victory Loan promoted vigorously. At a meeting in Guildford, Doctor T.E. Page of Godalming called on the public to put every penny they had into the loan, as 'they would then sleep easy of nights because they would possess two of the most reposeful things in the world – a good conscience and a good investment'. The town held a War Plane Week in March 1918 that raised £237,000 through the sale of war bonds and war savings certificates, investors inspired by slogans such as: 'Guildford buys the war planes gladly; Willie gets the wind up badly.'

Even more spectacularly, Guildford's Feed the Guns Week in October 1918 recreated 'Flanders by Moonlight', with a 6-inch howitzer, sandbags and a Red Cross dressing station in the burnt-out ruins of a draper's shop, and raised £280,197.[31] On a smaller scale, the War Savings Association for Nutfield,

Opening of a recreated scene from the Western Front in Guildford High Street for
Feed the Guns Week, October 1918 (SHC 1946/box 7)

Bletchingley and Godstone, inaugurated in July 1917, called on people to
contribute 6*d* a week towards the cost of a collectively purchased war savings
certificate (15*s* 6*d*). Once an individual had contributed the full price, one of the
association's certificates would be transferred to his ownership. The association
raised £6,185 in the War Weapons Week of June 1918, this success earning it the
right to have a gun, aeroplane or tank named 'Godstone' – an example of one
of the ways in which the government sought to incentivise and personalise its
money-raising efforts.[32]

Schools Go to War

Schools of all levels were drawn into the patriotic endeavours. Logbooks and
school magazines from all parts of Surrey relate a similar story. For example, the
logbook of Maple Road School, Whyteleafe, tells of the children being 'very
restless and disinclined to pay attention to work … they are obsessed by war
excitement' and of the distracting effect of the Fusiliers quartered at nearby
Court Farm. The pupils' energy was diverted into making shirts for soldiers,
collecting eggs for the BRC hospitals at Burntwood Lane in Caterham and
Purley, putting on an entertainment to raise funds for cigarettes for serving old
boys, collecting horse chestnuts for dispatch to King's Lynn for the extraction
of acetone (which was used in the manufacture of the explosive cordite), and
picking blackberries (which were sent to Kingston to be made into jam for the

troops).[33] The last activity had to be halted because of the severe shortage of teachers. This was a common theme as male teachers enlisted or were conscripted. The Surrey Education Committee reported in February 1918 that the average size of classes had increased to 37.2 children, although some were over sixty, in part due to the influx of people fleeing London.[34] As early as 13 October 1914, Perry Hill Council School, Worplesdon, had only two teachers and the head to supervise 139 pupils. On 25 January 1915 there were two staff members for 132 children in seven standards.[35] The exigencies of the war forced the Royal Grammar School, Guildford, to appoint its first woman teacher in 1917.[36] Education was further disrupted by an Education Committee scheme, introduced in April 1918, under which boys (and later girls) who had reached the age of 13 could be excused from school attendance if they were needed to work on the land. It was reported in November 1918 that 1,401 children had left school prematurely under the scheme.[37]

Older students were still further engaged. Amid reports on sports team and examination successes, the magazines of Sutton High School for Girls are crammed with patriotic poems, reports on the activities of the War Savings Association and stirring tales of old girls and the former gymnastics teacher now working in munitions factories or with refugees.[38] All pupils had to learn to knit so they could provide comforts for troops and the school also contributed to Lady Smith-Dorrien's campaign to make bags in which wounded soldiers could keep their possessions

Miss Margaret Bell and students at Sutton High School for Girls, 1910 (courtesy of Sutton High School for Girls GDST)

while in hospital. 'Lonely' soldiers were adopted as penfriends and their letters of thanks printed in the magazine. Many of the old girls were VADs at Benfleet Hall, a large local house transformed into a military hospital, and in 1916 forty of the injured men visited the school for tea and games, causing the school hall to ring 'with the deep-toned voices of the British Tommy'. As part of an economy drive, prize winners had to be satisfied with certificates rather than books, and those taking exams had to write on both sides of the paper.[39]

The boys at the Guildford Junior Technical School were involved even more directly in the war effort, making metal fittings for use in the Royal Aircraft Factory in Farnborough.[40] More traditional schools, such as the Royal Grammar School (Guildford) and Reigate Grammar School, lovingly chronicled the exploits of their Officer Training Corps (OTC) and their alumni serving overseas. The Reigate Grammar School magazine introduced a roll of honour as a regular feature and an ever-increasing number of obituaries filled the pages. The boys were left in no doubt as to their duty and in April 1916 the headmaster praised the OTC for its zeal (although in 1914 members of the corps had attempted to arrest the milkman as a German spy out to steal their rifles) and for preparing its members to be ready even 'to defend those ignoble people who would hamper our efforts to make ourselves efficient and would profit by our sacrifices, and live secure hiding behind our backs'. He reserved particular opprobrium for 'those despicable people who are opposed to national military service'. Fifty-three old boys fell (17.3% of those who served).[41]

The death rate among the alumni of Charterhouse in Godalming, where military training was made compulsory during the war, was still higher – around one in five. Among Surrey's public schools, only St John's School, Leatherhead, and King's College School, Wimbledon, had a marginally higher rate.[42] Two Guildford schoolmasters, Edwin White at the Royal Grammar School and Albert Smith at Abbot's School, stood out against the prevailing climate: both appeared before the Guildford Borough Military Service Tribunal as conscientious objectors in February 1916 and both were given absolute exemptions, but White was subsequently convicted and fined for distributing literature of the No-Conscription Fellowship.[43]

An Age of Austerity

As the war dragged on so the food supply worsened.[44] Prices rose relentlessly and by the end of the war most staples cost at least twice as much as they had done, with sugar up over 200% and fresh eggs four times as expensive.[45] Food Control Committees were established across the county in August 1917 to conserve food supplies and to control prices, particularly of such essentials as milk, meat and bread.

Each committee had to include a representative of Labour and a woman to broaden the range of opinion and help to 'hold the balance fairly between consumers and retailers'.[46] Even so, long food queues had to be endured, particularly during the winter of 1917–18, before the introduction of compulsory rationing.

In Kingston, it was reported that queues of 500–800, mostly women and children, were besieging the Maypole Dairy Company shop in Clarence Street to buy margarine, 'many of whom have waited for hours in the bitter cold in the hope of securing a little of the coveted fat'.[47] Kingston's Executive Food Officer, Mrs Bumstead (seemingly the only woman in the country to have held this position), interviewed in 1921, recalled facing down 'a great crowd of women' who threatened to seize the margarine stored at the local supply depot.[48]

Some families sought to buck the system by installing more than one family member in a queue; others sought to obtain more than they needed to sell on at a profit.[49] Distribution was also erratic, with villages losing out to towns in securing what foodstuffs were available.[50] Conflicts between Food Control Committees and provision merchants broke out, and the imposition of maximum prices helped drive cattle away from the market and caused butchers to reduce their opening hours.[51] The influx of Londoners added to the pressure. Rose Ponting wrote to her sweetheart, 'Last Tues: they passed 200 for the shelters, never seen Dorking so crowded, everybody's house full up seems a job to buy food, can't get tea, butter, bacon, lucky if one can get hold of a bit, some of the bakers have got special permission to sell new bread, so much wanted, couldn't cope with it.'[52]

Rose Ponting of Dorking (SHC 9496/3/4)

Frederick Robinson's diary again provides a deeply felt response to the worsening situation. Hotels and restaurants were placed under ever more elaborate regulations, restricting opening hours and the number of courses and introducing regular meatless days. On 3 January 1917 Robinson had to endure 'a most unsatisfactory and unpleasant meal, both in choice and quantity' at his club and groaned, 'The fear of eating one mouthful more than the legal allowance and so committing a criminal offence is not conducive to good digestion.' In April, he complained that people were being fined for sprin-

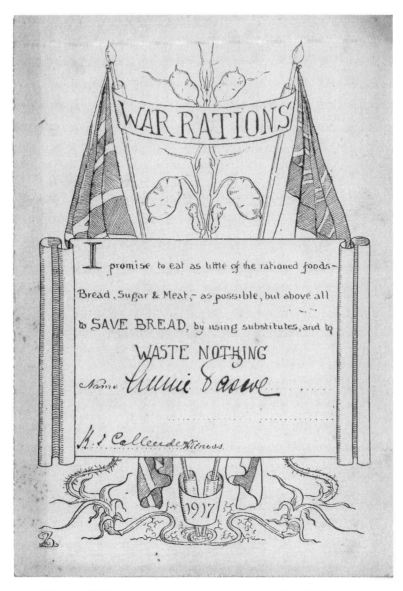

WAR RATIONS

I promise to eat as little of the rationed foods ~ Bread, Sugar & Meat, ~ as possible, but above all to SAVE BREAD, by using substitutes, and to WASTE NOTHING

Name *Annie Pascoe*

H. S Callender Witness.

1917

Annie Pascoe of Woking promises to eat less and waste nothing, 1917
(SHC 6932/7/3/11)

kling sugar on cakes or buns, and at the end of the year catastrophe hit when it was announced that 'there is to be no more ice cream'. The price of that vital staple, bread, was controlled, yet the resultant subsidised but adulterated 4lb loaf (costing 9*d*) Robinson decried as 'beastly'.[53] Rose Ponting reported that the people of Dorking felt the same: 'Folks about here are all saying they don't think the bread has so much nutriment [*sic*] in it, as they all seem to be getting thinner.'[54]

Letter from Rose Ponting to her sweetheart Will Chapman, 23 August 1918
(SHC 9496/3/4)

A voluntary rationing scheme introduced in 1917 and endorsed by the King failed to control the situation. Offences against the 1917 Food Hoarding Order increased in number. In January 1918, Lady Mabel Gore Langton of The Glade, Englefield Green, was fined £80 for hiding away 125lb of tea and 35lb of coffee; most notoriously, in February of the same year, a Member of Parliament, William MacCaw, of Rooksnest, Godstone, was fined £426 15s for hoarding rice, sugar and tea, among other items.[55] In Guildford, a private Food Vigilance Committee was set up to promote equitable distribution and report suspected hoarding.[56]

The threat of compulsory rationing alarmed many. Rose Ponting told of the forthright views of an old lady lodging in the Dorking apartments owned by Rose's father:

Poor old soul she is worried about this food rations, she will starve and I don't know what … Sat eve she got in such a wax, she wouldn't be compelled to do anything if compulsory rationing came in she wouldn't have anything to do with it, we asked what she would do then, she said she'd sooner starve than be forced to present a card at each shop.

Rose could see the social justice of the measure:'I told her it would be a good thing in one way if food is so short it will give the poor people a chance of getting a bit, as well as the rich, those that have the work to do need the most food.'[57]

Despite popular fears, sugar rationing went ahead late in 1917 and it was becoming obvious that a more extensive compulsory scheme was inevitable. Pre-empting compulsion, Guildford introduced a local rationing scheme from 4 February 1918, under which each person was limited to 4oz of butter or margarine and 8oz of butcher's meat a week. The meat ration was soon increased to 1lb per head when it was argued that those doing hard, manual work needed more nourishment. The ever vigilant Guildford Borough Food Control Committee also complained to the Food Controller that local prisoners of war were receiving a daily allowance of ½lb of meat (although the allowance had in fact been reduced to 6oz a day).

On 25 February 1918, a complicated compulsory rationing system came into force, with the weekly rations per person set initially at 4oz of butter, margarine or lard, and 8oz of sugar and a maximum of three coupons (i.e. 1s 3d) worth of butcher's meat such as beef, mutton, lamb or pork (cooked or tinned meat, game, rabbits and bacon were more easily obtained).[58] The system was subject to constant tinkering by the Food Controller. In May 1918, Frederick Robinson noted, 'The weekly joint … is now reduced to 10oz of meat including bone, per person,' and 'jokes in regard to this are going the rounds as to telling the butcher to "slip the joint under the door" or "put it in the letter box" etc.' A fastidious man, he, perhaps unsurprisingly, did not greet with enthusiasm the Food Controller's concession in July that the 'eye pieces from pigs' heads' might be acquired without coupons to supplement his diet.[59]

Nutritious wartime recipes were promoted in government leaflets and extolled in local papers. The *Epsom Advertiser* published a series of weekly menus by Mrs Windsor, 'the cookery expert'.[60] 'The Pudding Lady', Miss Florence Petty of the National Food Reform Association, lectured the people of Stoke D'Abernon on war cooking, so they could 'learn how to be happy though rationed',[61] and a Weybridge Urban District Council pamphlet promoted such delicacies as sheep-head pie and dripping pudding. The same pamphlet also condemned beer and spirits as expensive luxuries that should only be taken by doctor's orders.[62]

Luxuries or not, opportunities to consume alcoholic drinks were, in any case, severely restricted during the war so that drunkenness did not interrupt munitions production. In 1915, under the Defence of the Realm (Liquor Control) Regulations, drinking hours were limited to 12–12.30 p.m. and 6.30–9 p.m. in the Metropolitan Police Area (which included large parts of Surrey) and these restrictions were extended to west Surrey the following year.[63] Treating other people was forbidden, and spirits and beer were progressively diluted until Frederick Robinson complained that whisky, now costing three to four times the pre-war price, was mostly water, and beer was reduced to a 'mild almost tasteless fluid'. He was, however, forced to concede that convictions for drunkenness had plummeted and that perhaps after the war the restrictions should be maintained, at least for pubs (gentlemen's clubs should be exempted as their members, he felt, were not in the habit of getting drunk).[64]

From 1917, to ensure that children, in particular, could obtain nutritious meals, the Minister of Food Control promoted the establishment of National Kitchens, providing ten-year interest-free loans to local authorities to fit them out. The kitchens were staffed mainly by volunteers, particularly well-to-do women anxious to 'do their bit'. Customers brought their own bowls and utensils and could obtain a

---

The Government is safeguarding Food Supplies, and excessive prices will not be permitted, but

The women of the United Kingdom can help their country by spending Every Penny wisely, and to the best advantage.

Foods may be regarded generally as being of three kinds. Some of each should be included in the daily supply.

The three kinds are :—

(1) Starchy and sugary food ; such, in the main, are potatoes and sugar.

(2) Fatty foods, such as dripping or butter.

(3) Body building foods. The body building substances are present in large proportions in all lean meat, in fish, in eggs, in many kinds of beans and peas and nuts, and in Cheese. Rice and flour also contain a considerable proportion of body building substances mixed with much starchy food.

The first two kinds of food are of great value in helping the body to carry on its work, but some of the third kind of food is essential for the growth and repair of the body.

In addition to the three kinds of food forming the bulk of the diet, certain salts and substances that are in vegetables and fruit are necessary if the body is to be kept healthy.

A sufficient quantity of water must of course be taken.

Fresh milk is a remarkable food, as it contains every necessary kind of food substance.

It is important to remember that food must not only contain the right amount of the necessary substances, but these substances must be in such a form that they can be digested in the body and then absorbed in the blood.

The real (strength giving) value of ordinary food materials by no means corresponds with their cost. By sensible buying and good cooking it is easy to prepare a meal which is pleasing and palatable and of high food value at a much smaller cost than if no care and intelligence were exercised in choosing.

HERE ARE SOME FACTS ABOUT FOODS.

A mixed vegetable and meat diet suits most people best.

VEGETABLE FOODS.

DRIED PEAS, HARICOT BEANS and LENTILS contain as much flesh-forming material as MEAT, and are very much cheaper.

BREAD and PASTRY made from " SECONDS " FLOUR, although less attractive in appearance than that made from white flour, is more nourishing.

OATMEAL is a very rich food, but requires thorough boiling to make it digestible.

POTATOES are best value when cooked in their skins, or steamed.

ONIONS, BEETROOT and CARROTS are more nutritious than CABBAGES, but greens and fruit are valuable as they keep the blood in good condition.

BANANAS, RAISINS and DRIED CURRANTS are cheap and nourishing.

SUGAR and TREACLE are useful foods, but Jam is not nearly such good value as Margarine or Dripping.

ANIMAL FOODS.

HERRINGS, BLOATERS and KIPPERS are most nourishing.

CHEAPER CUTS of Butcher's Meat contain as much nourishment as the best meat ; excellent stews may be made from them with cheap vegetables.

FRESH FOODS are better than canned foods.

DRIPPING and MARGARINE contain as much food value as the best butter ; dripping is well worth buying. It is an extremely valuable food for children, who will take it readily with bread or toast or as dripping pudding. SUET PUDDING should be given to children who dislike fat meat.

CHEESE is one of the cheapest and best of foods, and is rich in nourishment.

WHAT TO DRINK.

COCOA when taken with milk and sugar is a food, and is more beneficial than tea or coffee.

BEER and SPIRITS have small food value and, at the best, are expensive luxuries for anyone in hard times, except under doctor's orders. Intemperance in time of War cannot be too severely condemned.

SKIMMED MILK is a good drink for children, provided some dripping is given as well to supply the fat taken from the milk.

Food advice leaflet issued by Weybridge Urban District Council (SHC Ac1321/7/3)

portion of soup for 1*d* and a main course with potatoes and vegetables for 4*d* to 6*d* (depending on the amount of meat it contained). If a meal contained meat off the bone, customers were still required to use their precious ration coupons. By the end of 1918, most towns of any size in Surrey had a National Kitchen, some more than one (Epsom opened its third in October 1918; Richmond ended up with four).

A few schemes met with opposition. Weybridge opened a small National Kitchen in the Technical Institute in February 1918, but a more ambitious plan met with objections that it would not make a profit unless it sold 700 portions a day and would be a burden on the rates, and by the time the council was ready to proceed, the armistice had intervened.[65] Increasingly, the kitchens provided meals *in situ*, rather than to take home, and Woking opened a restaurant on its premises, hoping to attract the custom of the many Royal Air Force (RAF), Army Pay Corps and munitions workers in the neighbourhood.[66] One newspaper wondered if such establishments might become an enduring feature, given the changes the war had brought about, commenting:

> It seems certain that the present shortage of domestic workers will not be greatly abated in the future: housewives will, therefore, have to consider in what ways they can reduce the work of their households. One obvious way is to have less cooking done in the home. We have long been accustomed to the idea of having our washing done outside our homes; why not the cooking too?[67]

Austerity extended beyond the food in the shops and on the table. Coal rationing was introduced in 1917, the amount allocated dependent on the number of rooms in a house. A pamphlet issued by the Board of Trade spelt out the implications: 'To save Coal … means fewer hot meals, fewer hot baths, smaller fires, earlier to bed, no reading in bed …'[68] When the Robinson family's coal allowance was reduced by three-quarters, Frederick wondered: 'Are we to sit shivering in the cold or are we to sit and have our meals in the kitchen with the servants?'[69]

Travel was also affected. Petrol rationing meant private cars could be used less and less and coach outings disappeared. The railway network was taken over by the state at the outbreak of war and the transportation of troops was prioritised. Some branch lines and stations were closed. By December 1916, Frederick Robinson, a daily commuter from Cobham to the City, reported: 'The trains this Christmas are running hours late, and everything on the railways is confusion twice confounded.' The following year, he lamented that while fares had gone up by 50%, the service had declined, with no refreshment cars, very few porters to carry luggage, 'and the ticket collectors and in some cases the guards are women'.[70] Even walking as a mode of travel became more difficult as boots

COAL–URGENT

Except among the poorest houses there will not be a house with as much coal as it would like to have during the coming winter.

All must save, but those, who have most, must also save most. A fire for all; but not two fires for one person. That is the rule to burn into the memory.

To save Coal—what does it mean

It Means — fewer hot meals, fewer hot baths, smaller fires, earlier to bed, no reading in bed.

It Means — not starting fires until the cold weather really sets in, not continuing fires when once the spring weather has come.

It Means — only using one light in a room when one light will serve—as it generally will— giving up the decorative lights and the shaded lights in the drawing-room and elsewhere, stopping lights in halls and passages.

It Means — living in fewer rooms and not dining in one, sitting in another, working in another, and entertaining in another.

IT DOES NOT MEAN HARDSHIP.

It may mean inconvenience. It may mean having breakfast in the kitchen. It may mean having to live together more than usual. But compare these little things with life in the trenches or life on the seas in the small boats that are out at all hours in all weathers and you will see it is no real hardship.

YOU CAN SAVE COAL ON YOUR RATIONS

[P.T.O.

Board of Trade leaflet advising residents how to save coal in the face of shortages, September 1918 (SHC 6520/28)

and shoes rose in price and declined in quality, the inevitable consequence of the commandeering of leather for the army.

As restrictions bit, so tempers grew shorter and deference declined. Frederick Robinson complained:

> Shopkeepers – or their flapper assistants – seem rather to pride themselves on being 'out' of things. In most cases you have to take what you can get, and any complaint is generally met with impertinence and possibly by you being asked 'do you know there is a war on?' which is a favourite and most offensive form of repartee.[71]

At least bureaucracy blossomed. Numerous regulations controlling the food supply were issued, 'the breach of any one of [which], either from ignorance or from a want of understanding, constitutes a crime, punishable by imprisonment, even with hard labour'.[72] Reigate Grammar School magazine published a humorous anonymous letter on the difficulties of obtaining extra margarine through the local Food Control Office:

> 'Oh, you want a form for Edible Fats', said a middle-aged and placid individual … 'There seems to be a lot of forms', he muttered vaguely … 'and none seems quite to fit your needs … Ah! here's a form that looks as if it might do. Try this, and if you can't get it with this come round to me again and I'll see if I can help you.'[73]

Despite salvage campaigns, paper was in ever shorter supply, as shipping was monopolised for soldiers and food. Even so, the government continued to 'deluge the country with their never ending buff coloured forms for the wretched stay at home civilian to fill up … Really, as someone remarked the other day, "the war is becoming quite a nuisance."'[74] Rose Ponting put the same sentiment more pithily in a letter to her sweetheart: 'It's war time isn't [it] dear, we must save paper for the Government to waste.'[75]

A ditty doing the rounds captures the atmosphere of the winter of 1917–18 perfectly:

> My Tuesdays are meatless
> My Wednesdays are wheatless
> I am getting more eatless each day
> My stove it is heatless
> My bed it is sheetless
> They're all sent to the YMCA
> The bar rooms are treatless

My coffee is sweetless
Each day I get poorer and wiser
My stockings are feetless
My trousers are seatless
My! How I do hate the Kaiser.[76]

The Church at War

Morale was at a low ebb by this stage and social cohesion fraying. The churches, through regular services of intercession and charitable activities, had striven to maintain public confidence that victory would go to the righteous and that public suffering and the terrible death toll would ultimately be rewarded, but the message of hope was wearing thin. As 1918 dawned, the Rector of Godstone wrote: 'It is impossible to do more than keep going.'[77] The relative optimism of the start of the war had dissipated. Few people may have begun to doubt the justice of the war and most continued to see it as, in essence, a battle between good and evil, yet the losses, deprivations and disquiet over the direction in which the conflict was leading the country were having a profound impact.

The authority of the churches and public willingness to look to them for spiritual solace had, perhaps, been compromised by the contradiction within the churches' message: on the one hand, the war was embraced as a just and sacred cause, on the other, it was characterised as divine judgement on a sinful world – 'our life with all its luxury, pleasure-worship and money-worship, all its forgetfulness or contempt of God, all its unequal pressure on the poor', as the Bishop of Winchester put it.[78] The Anglican Church had generally accepted the morality of the cause and threw its weight behind the recruitment drive. The Rector of Byfleet left no room for doubt as to how the young men in his parish should respond: 'Every man with a spark of patriotism or manly feel or even sympathy in his nature must long to be at the front helping his comrades.'[79]

The Nonconformist churches were similarly committed, even if conscription, with its rejection of the voluntary principle, later caused them disquiet. The Pastor of Godalming Congregational Church wrote:

We are fighting for freedom, civilisation, democracy and Christianity, against an evil and remorseless barbarism, and against a nation whose conduct has already shown itself to be worse than that of savages. If the War Lords of Germany prostrate Europe it were better for us to die.[80]

There were exceptions: the Vicar of Woodham was, at least, prepared to criticise Sir Arthur Conan Doyle's call for 'fiercer hatred' of the Germans.[81] Gilbert Sadler, Pastor of Alwyne Road Congregational Church in Wimbledon, was prepared to resign in July 1915 rather than allow a roll of honour in his church, arguing that 'soldiers fought in an army for the determination of who should rule a land … This was a political matter, but Christ says "My Kingdom is not of this world" … If we begin with a roll, it might mean "King and Country" posters next.'[82]

Some of the smaller denominations maintained a pacifist stance. As is well known, most Quakers refused to fight, although some were prepared to serve at the Front with the Friends' Ambulance Unit. Members of the little-known sect of the Society of Dependents or Cokelers, which had some adherents in south-west Surrey, remained committed to the cause of peace.[83]

The Church of England, in particular, seems to have misjudged the popular mood by launching a National Mission of Repentance and Hope in 1916 to bring about true Christian renewal. Surrey churches participated, holding mission services and meetings throughout October 1916, but results were disappointing. The Rector of Godstone wrote:

> No one can ever be satisfied with those results which we are permitted to see; and of course there is the wish that more had availed themselves of the opportunities that are given in such a week; but we cannot doubt that the prayers made and witness given will have their effect.[84]

Frederick Robinson, a member of Cobham Parish Church, thought the mission, particularly its call for repentance and soul searching, was misconceived at a time 'when the Country and every individual more or less is making supreme sacrifices to uphold the right and put down the wrong'.[85] Several lay members of the Farnham Ruri-Decanal Conference also argued that a demand for national contrition and, still worse, any claim that the war was a punishment for sin, were inappropriate when the country was engaged in a desperate fight in a just cause.[86] As the editor of the *Dorking and Leatherhead Advertiser* wrote at the Armistice, the war had almost displaced formal faith:

> This war has absorbed our energies and centred our thoughts. Even to talk of anything else has bored us. We have breathed it as an atmosphere, worked for it as a life purpose, sacrificed for it as a religion, and if called to give our best love have felt as if we were giving them to God. It has been unlike all other wars in the world's history.[87]

The End

The end almost took people by surprise. Through the spring of 1918 the news from the Western Front was terrible as Germany, benefiting from its victory in the east, launched waves of attacks and the Allied line buckled. Defeat seemed imminent. When, through the summer and autumn, French, British and, increasingly, American troops surged forward and the German armies began to fall back, Frederick Robinson refused to allow himself to believe that the tide really had turned until the news came that Germany was prepared to negotiate. Still fearing his hopes would prove false, he wrote:

> We can hardly believe that this may mean peace. Is the war suddenly coming to an end? Is this awful nightmare, this dreadful thing that we have lived with night and day for the last four years to suddenly become a hideous memory of the past? We can scarcely believe it.[88]

Popular joy that victory was in sight was tempered by the fear and disruption caused by the terrible Spanish Influenza epidemic. The first wave struck Surrey in the summer, but the autumn/winter outbreak was far more deadly: deaths from influenza, 179 in 1917, soared to 1,541 in 1918 and still numbered 603 in 1919, before dropping to 136 in 1920. The 'flu, unusually, was particularly virulent among those in the prime of life: in 1917 nineteen people aged between 15 and 45 died from influenza; in 1918, the figure was a staggering 876. Spanish 'flu, which could kill with horrifying speed, often led to pneumonia, and deaths from that disease also rose significantly.[89]

Rose Ponting wrote fearfully to her sweetheart: 'The Flue [sic] is very bad here I never remember so many deaths in Dorking before.'[90] Schools were closed, cinemas and theatres disinfected after each performance and people warned to avoid overcrowding and 'indiscriminate expectoration [spitting]'.[91] Popular remedies, including whisky, cinnamon and tobacco, were useless or worse.[92] Makers of soaps and disinfectants had a field day and Dr Williams' Pink Pills for Pale People were relentlessly promoted as a cure-all (just as they had been for neurasthenia and digestive disorders).[93]

The Armistice was signed at 5 a.m. on 11 November and over the following hours the news seeped through. The Rector of Witley, travelling into London by train to go shopping, reported 'windows and roofs … full of cheering men and women' and a 'joyous frolicking crowd' in Trafalgar Square.[94] Impromptu street celebrations and church services broke out across the county despite the dismal weather. Frederick Robinson's relief is almost tangible. In the penultimate entry in his diary, which now filled an extraordinary 3,474 pages, he wrote: 'A day never to be forgotten! The day has come at last which we have lived for these long four years and three months. The horrible thing is over!' As he made his way home, he passed the Houses of Parliament. With lighting restrictions lifted, the clock face was illuminated, and he rejoiced in the 'thundering tones of Big Ben reverberating the great fact of peace'. At that moment of joy he was sure it had all been worth it: 'We have the satisfaction of feeling that the enormous sacrifices made have not been in vain, that the ends for which we went to war have been attained.'[95] The following years would reveal ever more clearly what the true cost had been.

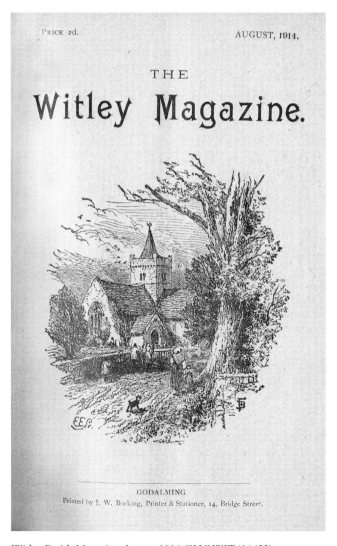

Witley Parish Magazine, August 1914 (SHC WIT/16/33)

WOMEN IN WARTIME

SUE HAWKINS

Women in Surrey before World War One

Only a third of the female, working-age population of Surrey was in employment in 1911, and half of those worked in domestic service, with others employed in traditional female spheres such as dressmaking, shopkeeping, laundry work, teaching and nursing.[1] However, war caused this picture to change drastically. As men left their jobs in 'civvy street' to join the forces, gaping holes appeared in some of the country's key workforces, and when government and industry bosses looked for solutions they came to the reluctant conclusion (and in the early days it was very reluctant) that there was only one obvious answer: to mobilise the country's women. Propaganda pressure on women to contribute to the war effort became intense. Newspapers were full of pleas, bribes and threats to persuade women to support 'the boys at the front'. Women across the country responded.

Women on the Land?

Despite agriculture being an important part of Surrey's economy, very few women worked on the land.[2] Victorian values persisted into the twentieth century, dictating that outdoor work was not respectable for women, so few women did it.[3] But, as men joined the forces, the agricultural workforce became depleted to dangerous levels and a crisis in feeding the nation loomed. In September 1915, the Board of Agriculture (BOA) finally took action, calling on County Councils 'to increase production of food' by encouraging women to move onto the land.[4]

Noeline Baker MBE

Noeline Baker (1878–1958) was a suffragist and activist in Surrey during the Great War. Born in New Zealand, she settled in Guildford in 1905. She was a founder member of the Guildford branch of the National Union for Women's Suffrage Societies (NUWSS). On the outbreak of war she worked with the London Society's Women's Services Bureau, helping women to find voluntary war work and assisting working women made unemployed by the failing economy. She returned to Surrey in 1915 and after attending a meeting during which the issue of agricultural labour shortages was discussed, she (alongside other women) formed the Surrey Committee for Women's Farm Labour (SCWFL). She threw herself into her roles as SCWFL's secretary and treasurer, travelling incessantly across Surrey and beyond attending meetings, persuading farmers to employ women and interviewing potential recruits.

Her influence grew and in February 1917, when the Women's Land Army was formed, she became organising secretary for the Surrey branch. In 1918 the pressure overwhelmed her; she described herself as 'dead tired', but after a day in bed she resumed her duties!

Noeline continued her work after the war; she was appointed as the only female member of the Surrey Agricultural Executive Committee, representing women's views and issues, and was appointed honorary secretary of the Surrey branch of the National Association of Landswomen (which replaced the WLA). In 1920, in recognition of her services, Noeline was awarded an MBE.[1]

Noeline Baker (far right) and staff of SCWFL, Guildford, 1918 (Noeline Baker papers, MS-0619-9, courtesy of Hocken Collections, Uare Taoka o Hākena, University of Otago)

The women of Surrey were ahead of the game. In spring 1915, the Dorking and Leith Hill Women's Suffrage Society (a branch of Millicent Fawcett's National Union for Women's Suffrage Societies [NUWSS]) appealed to women to volunteer for agricultural work. 'Every woman who can work and is free to work should come forwards,' it urged.[5] In Guildford, Noeline Baker took matters further, establishing a committee to recruit women for land work.

The Surrey Committee for Women's Farm Labour (SCWFL) became a body of women highly influential in the county, spearheading the move to employ women in agriculture by recruiting and training them, arranging their accommodation and identifying farmers willing to employ them. By summer 1916, nearly 100 Surrey villages had set up registers containing the names of 1,756 women prepared to work on the land.[6] Because of their initial reluctance to embrace the idea, appeals were made to women's patriotism. A letter to the editor of the *Surrey and Hants News* urged: 'Farnham men have come forwards so splendidly to enlist … we feel sure Farnham women will be equally patriotic and help to keep "the home fires burning".'[7]

Persuading farmers was harder, but the SCWFL had influential supporters in the county, none more so than Lord and Lady Onslow of Clandon Park. Violet Onslow spent much time cajoling her husband's tenant farmers to support the scheme: Mr J.M. Kelly thought local women were 'very expensive, when cost is set against amount of work they are able to do', while George Ewing was concerned about the reaction of his remaining male labourers: 'My experience of [women] is that they do not get on with the men.'[8] Both farmers finally agreed to co-operate with the scheme.

By mid-1916, the obstacles had mainly been overcome. Women came forwards in large numbers and during 1916 over 600 women across the county received government armlets, in recognition of at least thirty days' work. The armlet was a very precious award, a public acknowledgement of the work women were doing.[9] Farmers, 'whose prejudices were supposed to be insuperable', also revised their views, acknowledging the experiment as a success.[10]

On 18 April 1917, all talk was of SCWFL's day of competitions at Cross Farm, Shackleford, with female land workers from across the county converging to demonstrate the skills they had learnt. The milking competition provided quite a sensation. It was won by 10-year-old Mary Soutar of Limpsfield, who beat her mother to the first prize. Her mother must have been overwhelmed with pride but somewhat mortified, as she managed the dairy at Titsey Place (one of the largest manor houses in Surrey).[11] Joan Cleverly of Ripley was probably the unluckiest competitor. In the ploughing competition she struggled to control 'a couple of lively horses' and consequently lost out on the prizes. The same horses then caused problems in the harrowing competition; just as she was nearing the finish, they bolted and overturned the harrow.[12] The day was a great success and the women workers received many plaudits in the press.

The Women's Land Army

The SCWFL had been doing splendid work in Surrey for nearly two years when the Women's Land Army (WLA) was formed. Its quasi-military organisation was reflected in the first paragraph of a handbook issued to all recruits: 'You are now in the Women's Land Army, serving your Country just like the Soldiers and Sailors … and your work is quite as important as theirs.'[13]

The SCWFL (by now renamed Surrey Women's Agricultural Committee [SWAC]) managed recruitment for the WLA in Surrey. Selection was tough and many applicants were rejected for poor references, unsuitability or health reasons. Between February and July 1917, of 670 candidates interviewed, only 193 were accepted.[14]

Finding suitable accommodation for female workers proved much more difficult than recruiting or finding them jobs, especially as many came from comfortable homes and were not used to rural living. Miss Close, of Montpelier Square, London, asked for help in placing three of her servants in farm work, saying she would accompany them and was prepared to 'camp out or live in a hut or caravan … to be near my little gang'.[15] But later she expressed horror at the accommodation: 'At several farms mere … sheds are offered, leaking all over & filthy, totally unfit for anything'. She added: 'We want to go where there are some cows, not merely hay and arable.' Clearly Miss Close had a rather romanticised idea of farm work.[16]

Not all recruits were happy with their new lives and some rebelled, complaining too vociferously or even absconding. Adams and O'Mara, two

Land Girl harrowing (courtesy of Guildford Borough Council Heritage Services, LG1520–13)

Florence Winifred Hooker of the Women's Land Army

Florence Hooker was one of several thousand young Surrey women who joined the Women's Land Army (WLA). Her Land Army Handbook (SHC 8488/1) provides details of her service. She was the daughter of a washerwoman and an agricultural labourer, and she enrolled in the WLA on 29 May 1918 at the age of 18. Perhaps she had been waiting excitedly to reach the minimum age and joined up as soon as she could. Her first outfit consisted of two overalls, one pair of breeches, a hat, mackintosh and jersey, one pair of boots and one pair of clogs. These were updated twice during her service, replacing items that had worn out.

Details of Florence's training are not recorded but the map of England at the back of her handbook shows how the WLA girls were moved around. She was sent to several places in East Anglia and Somerset, and also spent time near Guildford. For a young woman from a poor background, this must have been a great adventure.

Her last uniform update was in June 1919, so she may have remained in the WLA until it was demobilised that November. In 1920, Florence married George Thompson; they had a son, Kenneth, in 1924. By 1939 she was still living in Surrey (in Guildford), both she and her husband working: he as a tile-maker in a brickyard and she as an assistant school caretaker. Florence lived to the ripe old age of 87.

Florence Winifred Hooker in Women's Land Army uniform (SHC 8488/1½)

members of the Surrey WLA, were sent to work on farms in Kent as threshers. They absconded. The committee moved them to gang work, but they ran away from that too, at which point they were dismissed. To make matters worse, they stayed a night at the Girls' Friendly Society in Aldershot, telling the manager to send their bill to SWAC. When O'Mara had the temerity to ring HQ in Guildford 'for instructions', she was told in no uncertain terms to return her uniform (and that of Adams) and repay the bill, which the committee had honoured.[17]

Despite the initial doubts and unrealistic expectations, SWAC and the WLA were a great success. By mid-1918 there were nearly 2,200 women working on the land in Surrey.[18] The conclusion of the war brought most of this activity to an end. The WLA was disbanded in November 1919 and the women of the SWAC were increasingly sidelined and starved of funds. They held their last meeting in June 1920.[19] The return of servicemen from war, combined with a general agricultural depression, reduced the need for women's labour. Women, who had been instrumental in keeping the country fed, began to be forced back into their pre-war lives.

Learn to Make Munitions!

As in agriculture, the rush of women into manufacturing marked a significant shift from the pre-war era. In 1911 only 400 or so women in Surrey were employed in such work, but by 1918 the figure had risen to a staggering 13,000 plus.[20] Some types of manufacturing work were considered particularly suitable for women, especially intricate jobs that required a delicacy of touch; women's more nimble fingers were thought to be particularly well adapted to such work.

Aviation attracted many women workers and was one of the county's key industries. The Sopwith Aviation Company, based in Kingston upon Thames, had 3,500 employees, about a third of whom were female.[21] The women were quickly trained in one or two repetitive tasks, perhaps making small components for engines, sewing fabric to the frames of wings, or painting the roundels on the planes.[22] There were at least fifty companies connected to the aviation industry in Surrey, together employing around 6,000 women.[23]

The presence of women in traditionally male spaces did not go unnoticed and they were not always welcomed. Despite the depletion of the male workforce, those men who remained fought their own battles to preserve the integrity of their work. The introduction of women could seriously devalue a job because the accompanying 'dilution' (changes in work practices that broke highly-skilled jobs into semi-skilled tasks that could be learnt with minimal training) removed the skilled element. It was therefore constantly challenged by trades unions.[24]

Women workers put the finishing touches to a Sopwith Salamander, Ham Works, 1918 (courtesy of Kingston Heritage Service)

Surrey did not have any enormous munitions factories, but it did have several medium-sized concerns, and these also employed women. The largest was Gillett & Johnston of Croydon, employing nearly 1,000 women making fuses and ammunition boxes, while AutoCarriers of Thames Ditton had 650 female workers (60% of the workforce).[25] Munitions work, despite its dangers, was very attractive. It paid well and was associated with the 'glamour' of making armaments for 'our boys'. Companies played on this heavily in their recruitment. Caterham Munitions Works advertised for wives of serving soldiers to work in its factories.[26] The implication was clear: help us to make weapons for your husbands. Women were also lured by promises of 'Good earnings, cheap hostel accommodation. Several hundred wanted at once.'[27]

Working in factories required a rethink of women's dress. Flowing skirts and blouses with lace and flouncy bows were completely impractical, and uniforms soon began to appear. The image of Sopwith workers shows the women dressed in plain dark-coloured overtunics, while those working in munitions factories donned short tunics over breeches, such as those worn by Nellie Peters from Chilworth Gunpowder Works.

The Ministry of Munitions issued a pamphlet advising women how to dress when working in munitions factories.[28] It was only common sense really; factories could be hazardous places. At AutoCarriers, a young female worker tripped and fell against a machine. Her blouse was caught in the machinery but a quick-thinking fellow worker grabbed her, 'preventing her from being whirled round the lathe

Vickers' Virgins!

Joyce Read, an old girl of Sutton High School for Girls, became a 'munitionette', working at a Vickers factory in Erith, Kent. 'Girls work the lathes, mark and view the shells, and there are even women labourers,' she wrote. They wore blue overalls and a brass 'V' for Vickers on their collars, which earned them the nickname 'Vickers' Virgins'! The girls worked in three eight-hour shifts, 'and everywhere you turn ... there are shells, shells, shells'. The factory was filled with the 'grinding roar of thousands of revolving wheels and of steel cutting steel'. It must have been a completely new, exciting and perhaps a little overwhelming experience for a young graduate from a polite girls' school.[1]

Hilda Collins was a teacher at the same school. In 1916, she must have caused quite a stir when she resigned to work at a munitions factory in Lancaster, one of the country's largest. Her shift lasted from 7.30 a.m.–6.30 p.m. with breaks for lunch and tea. She was most upset by the rule that insisted they stand to work. 'Did you ever hear anything so scandalous?' she wrote in her account to her old school. Later she drove a van to 'fetch and carry from ... the explosive factory and the Naval construction works'. Although she preferred driving in the 'sun and fresh air' to the din of the factory, she 'wouldn't have missed [those] three weeks [working inside] for anything'.[2]

War workers at Vickers factory, Brooklands (courtesy of Brooklands Museum)

Nellie Peters, worker at Chilworth Gunpowder Factory, in uniform. Nellie had spent much of her childhood in Dorking Workhouse (courtesy of Dorking Museum)

head'.[29] Were it not for his speedy actions, she probably would have been killed.

The death of one female munitions worker scandalised the coroner. Rose Wells died suddenly on 2 October 1918 from acute laryngitis. At her inquest she was described as a 'strong healthy girl'. The shocking thing about Rose's death was not the manner of it but her age – she was only 14. When the coroner heard that she worked from 7 a.m. until 8.30 p.m., he could not contain himself. 'From 7 in the morning to 8.30 at night for a girl of 14? Ridiculous hours, even if we are at war!' he exploded. When someone interjected that she did not always work those hours, the coroner replied, 'I don't care if she only worked that time two or three days a week, the hours are altogether too long for a young girl.'[30]

Tarrant's Lady Carpenters

In July 1917 a surprising advert appeared: 'Women immediately wanted for service in France.' But these women were not to be nurses, they were to be trained as carpenters by Surrey-based builder W.G. Tarrant and work in France constructing huts for the military. The adverts promised good wages.[31] Tarrant had launched his scheme in late 1916 and by February 1917 had recruited twenty women, mostly from Byfleet. Once in France they would live together 'in a little camp ... [where] they will be in the care of a lady superintendent'.[32] The 'plucky little band of carpenters' settled quickly into their work and were joined by more as war continued.[33] A lady who visited the camp in 1918 described it as a 'truly wonderful sight ... women of England – young and enthusiastic daughters, bright, smiling, healthy and happy ... with fearless spirit and right goodwill,

W.G. Tarrant's 'Lady Carpenters' at work near Calais, 30 June 1917
(© IWM, Q2459)

[working] no great distance from the sound of the enemy's guns'. She watched as '… two girls … sawed, chiselled, planed and hammered', producing huts for 'war-worn soldiers of the king'. In total, approximately seventy women took up the challenge.[34] They finally returned to Byfleet in January 1919, to be lauded as heroes, having built 37,000 huts using '23 tons of nails per week'.[35] (For further discussion of Tarrant's scheme, see Chapter 3.)

Women in the Military

As the war continued, opportunities opened up for women within the military itself. 'Hundreds of thousands of positions now held by men [in the army]' could be done by women, announced one newspaper.[36] An advert for the Women's Army Auxiliary Corps (WAAC) claimed that 5,000 women every week were needed, as storekeepers, cooks, waitresses, drivers, etc. The recruits would receive good wages, accommodation and rations.[37]

Women rushed to join. Across the country more than 57,000 came forwards, and this success led to the establishment of the Women's Royal Naval Service (WRNS) in late 1917 and the Women's Royal Air Force (WRAF) in April 1918.[38] Surrey women responded. Netta Broad of Kingston upon Thames and Rose Kate Overington from Godalming were both members of the WRAF, both in their early twenties and from similar working-class backgrounds. Rose joined the WAAC as a cook in 1917 and was posted to Denham Camp in Buckinghamshire. When the WRAF was formed she transferred, remaining in her role at Denham, where she met her husband-to-be, James Lumley.[39] Rose was demobilised in October 1919 with the rank of Chief Section Leader, and married her sweetheart in 1922.

Netta worked in the WRAF as a 'regular member' at the First Motor Transport Repair Depot. Sadly, she died in February 1919, aged 22, from pneumonia, and was buried in Kingston Cemetery; her simple headstone bears the WRAF insignia and a cross.[40] Doris Luker also died in service. She enlisted with the WAAC after the death of her brother James at the Somme, and in early 1918 she was posted to France. Twelve months later she also contracted pneumonia and died in the General Hospital at Étaples. Both Netta and Doris were probably victims of the Spanish 'flu pandemic of 1918–19, as victims often contracted pneumonia following the 'flu. Doris was buried in the war cemetery in Étaples, her grave bearing the inscription 'She nobly answered her country's call'. She is the only woman to be remembered on the Woking Town Memorial, alongside her brother.[41]

Rose Kate Overington, proudly wearing her WRAF uniform (SHC SGW/9, courtesy of Sheila Lumley)

Woking Town war memorial. Inset showing Doris Luker and her brother's names. Doris is the only woman listed on the memorial (© Kirsty Bennett)

Flora Sandes (1876-1956)
Britain's Female Soldier

Surrey lays claim to Britain's only official serving female soldier of World War I. Flora Sandes (whose family lived in Thornton Heath) had always shown a propensity for adventure. She joined the First Aid Nursing Yeomanry but found it too tame, and in 1912 she went to Serbia with the Women's Sick and Wounded Convoy.

When war broke out in Europe, she applied to the War Office but was rejected because she was not a trained nurse. Refusing to be thwarted, Flora returned to Serbia, joined the Serbian Red Cross, and worked as a nurse. But she found herself drawn to combat and realised a long-held ambition when invited to enlist as a private in the Serbian Army. In 1916 she was badly injured in close-combat fighting. Not fit enough to re-join the troops, she returned to caring for her Serbian soldiers.

Her contribution to the army was recognised by promotions to sergeant major and then lieutenant, and she was awarded one of the Serbian Army's highest decorations. After the war, Flora married a fellow officer. When he died in 1941 she moved back to the UK, where she died in 1956, aged 80.[1]

Flora Sandes while serving with the Serbian army (© IWM, Q91136)

War Work Rooms: Hives of Activity

The war spurred women of all classes and ages to throw themselves into work. While some entered occupations previously closed to them, others chose more familiar work. Such women turned up at workrooms across the county, come rain or shine, sewing, knitting and crafting for 'their boys'. They organised themselves (or were organised by local ladies) into work parties making comforts and medical supplies. Their output was prodigious.

Chertsey Women's War Work Association first opened in November 1915 and throughout the war it met twice weekly. It had over 800 subscribers who gave donations to buy supplies, or gifts of materials, but its main funding came from its 'celebrated 2*d* teas', which generated substantial profits.[42] By February 1916 it had eighty-nine workers and in September it appealed for more, promising: 'We will publish a complete list of all those who have worked for us or donated. Do not let your name be missing.'[43] In December, the threat of exposure was replaced by a bribe: 'Surely [you] can spare an hour or two, and … at any rate enjoy a most delicious tea, which still remains at the marvellous price of 2*d*.'[44] Women tempted by promises of cake (thus contributing at least to the coffers) could then be shamed into doing some work while they were there. Pretty canny!

By the end of the war the association had made an astonishing 11,140 items, including socks, vests and treasury bags.[45] Similar groups sprang up all over Surrey. Throughout the war, Dorking War Hospital Supply Depot specialised in making

Members of the Chertsey Women's War Work Association outside its headquarters at the end of the war (SHC P2/7/1-22)

Items Made by Chertsey Women's War Work, Jan 1916-Jan 1918

935 Shirts	26 Hot water bottle covers
818 Socks	25 Handkerchiefs
859 Vests	21 Belts
799 Treasury bags	20 Pairs of mittens
500 Munition bags	17 Arm muffs
229 Pairs of slippers	12 Pairs of pyjamas
216 Nightshirts	11 Pairs of pants
216 Sulfur bags	11 Bed jackets
126 Scarves	10 Hessian Bags
74 Red ties	9 Pairs of gloves
57 Pillows	4 Helmets
54 Bolster cases	3 Towels
54 White day shirts	1 Dressing gown

A list of 'comforts' produced by the Chertsey Women's War Work Association between January 1916 and January 1918 (SHC P2/7/1, author's image)

bandages, dressings and other medical supplies for hospitals, casualty clearing stations and ambulances. Its work was much appreciated, as a letter from a war hospital in Italy testifies: '[We have] a group of eye cases, which have received great benefit from [your] excellent eye pads. I don't know what we would have done without them.'[46] Like the Chertsey group, its output was prolific. In six months alone it produced nearly 53,000 individual items.[47]

Road Sweepers, Post Office Workers and Tram Conductors

Women stepped into the breach in a wide range of roles. Farnham Urban District Council decided to replace road maintenance men with women in the winter of 1916–17, noting that although they were undertaking a 'none too pleasant task', they did it in 'a most business-like manner'.[48] Post offices also saw the potential of women employees in positions previously closed to them, in sorting offices, running counters and delivering letters. In Kingston, as early as June 1915, the experiment of employing women sorters was 'found to work admirably'.[49]

Guildford was just one council among many that issued tram conductor licences to women.[50] Of course, not everyone was pleased with the development. One man wrote, '[The women] will never make conductors. [They find] the art of … issuing tickets while the vehicles are in motion is not an easy one to acquire,' although he acknowledged that they 'look quite smart in the official overcoat, peaky cap and

Mrs Rose of Westcott on her Dorking Post Office delivery round (courtesy of Dorking Museum)

– ahem – blue puttees'.[51] In August 1918, Surrey's women conductors went on strike and the trams stopped running for five days. The dispute was over a war bonus. Male tram conductors would receive an extra 25s to compensate for the increased cost of living, whereas women would get only 20s. The Committee on Production explained that '[the cost of living] falls more heavily on men than on women'. The women disagreed and despite being accused of being unpatriotic, they stuck to their guns. After several more days of strikes the committee caved in to their demands.[52]

Khaki Fever and Women Patrols

More women in work also meant more women out in public, which suddenly seemed crowded with young, unchaperoned women. Add to this throngs of khaki-uniformed young men and it was a dangerous mix, considered by the *Daily Express* to be 'a grave menace to morality'.[53] It was suggested that women were suffering from a sort of hysteria; the excitement elicited by the sight of men in uniform was driving women to immodest behaviour. 'Khaki fever' was blamed for a rising tide of immorality and a growth in illegitimacy.[54]

The National Union of Women Workers developed a solution to declining morality among workers, establishing a network of 5,000 voluntary 'women patrols' across the country 'to prevent and protect women from immoral behaviour'.[55] There was no women's police service on the outbreak of World War I, but the war-time women patrols were sanctioned by the police and members carried cards of authorisation and wore a uniform and an armlet bearing their registration number.

Rhoda Brodie MBE
Women Patrols Leader

Rhoda Brodie was the daughter of a retired headmaster of Whitgift High School and educated at Croydon Girls' High School (CGHS). When war broke out, she was 40 years old and living with her parents. She threw herself into voluntary war work. Most notably, she was patrol leader of the Women Patrols in Croydon, one of the first to be established in Surrey. She commanded a troop of around forty women who patrolled in pairs between 8 and 10 p.m. The patrols were entirely voluntary, with the exception of a few who were asked to work an extra hour a night and received 'the police rate'. The women wore heavy blue coats and carried a police whistle and lantern. They were disbanded in September 1919.[1]

Rhoda was also honorary secretary of the Croydon Association of Voluntary Organisations and secretary to the Croydon War Refugees Committee.[2] In 1918 she was awarded the MBE for her war service.

Other alumnae of CGHS included Kathleen Leeds, a member of Rhoda's women patrols, and Kate Luard, whose wartime exploits as a trained nurse in France and Belgium are recorded in her memoir, *Unknown Warriors*. Kate received the Royal Red Cross and Bar, a rare distinction, for her services during World War I.[3]

Rhoda Brodie, Patrol Leader, Croydon Women Patrols
(courtesy of Museum of Croydon)

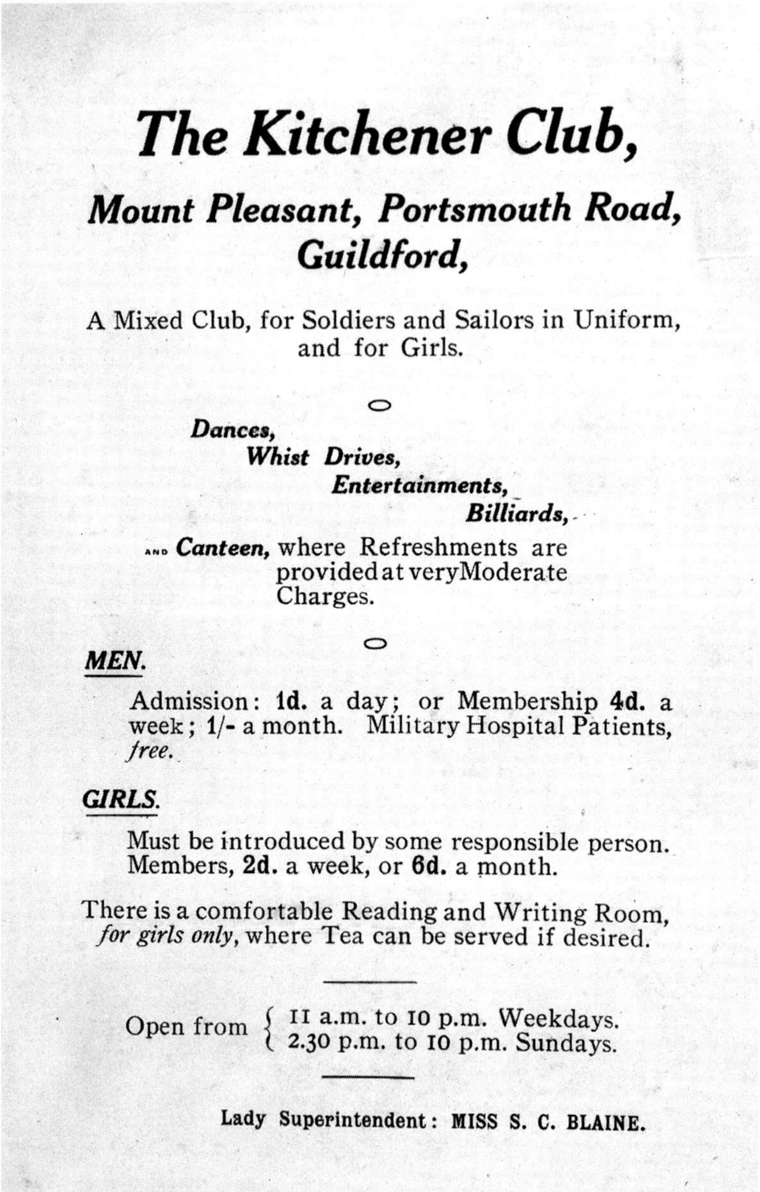

The Kitchener Club,

Mount Pleasant, Portsmouth Road, Guildford,

A Mixed Club, for Soldiers and Sailors in Uniform, and for Girls.

○

Dances,
Whist Drives,
Entertainments,
Billiards,

AND **Canteen,** where Refreshments are provided at very Moderate Charges.

○

MEN.

Admission: **1d.** a day; or Membership **4d.** a week; **1/-** a month. Military Hospital Patients, *free.*

GIRLS.

Must be introduced by some responsible person. Members, **2d.** a week, or **6d.** a month.

There is a comfortable Reading and Writing Room, *for girls only,* where Tea can be served if desired.

———

Open from { 11 a.m. to 10 p.m. Weekdays.
          { 2.30 p.m. to 10 p.m. Sundays.

———

Lady Superintendent: MISS S. C. BLAINE.

Flyer advertising the Kitchener Club, Guildford (SHC QRWS/30/ELIAA/2)

Patrols were set up in towns across Surrey. Their role was explained at a meeting in Godalming:

> We walk about the streets and lanes at night … make friends with [girls] and, if necessary, urge them to go home. We are not out in any way to prevent innocent enjoyment … What we want is to create a moral atmosphere in the streets by our silent presence.[56]

Wimbledon took a different approach, employing two women as police officers.[57] They focused especially on problems relating to the 'large camps on the Common … [where] the girls seemed to contract a kind of khaki fever'. Their job was 'to stop assignations being made with men' when the latter came across girls in the streets.[58] Later, eleven women patrols were recruited to assist the policewomen, who were finding it hard to cover the whole district.[59] The two policewomen were stood down in 1917 (due to lack of official support), but the women patrols continued to provide moral policing for Wimbledon's streets.

A year after Wimbledon's experiment ended, the Chief Constable of the Surrey Constabulary, Captain Mowbray Lees Sant, recruited two officers from the Women Police Service's headquarters in London 'for the purpose of dealing with females at the camps in the vicinity of Frimley'.[60] He also suggested that policewomen could usefully be employed in each of the eight divisions in Surrey. However, by March 1919, with demobilisation, the two women police officers were no longer needed at Frimley, although one continued to work in Godalming. The idea of employing policewomen in each of Surrey's divisions was not mentioned again.[61]

Another approach to the morality problem was to provide alternative activities for young women, which kept them off the streets and out of the pubs. Girls' clubs, offering safe places for respectable young working women to meet, were established in towns by groups of local ladies.[62] Some, such as those in Woking and Guildford, were mixed clubs where soldiers and young women 'of good character' could meet 'in comfortable surroundings and in a good social atmosphere'. The club was overseen by a Lady Superintendent, to ensure that propriety was maintained.[63]

6

WORKING THE LAND

MARTIN STILWELL

The story of farming in World War I is one to admire. Despite labour shortages, poor harvests and difficulty importing grain and meat, servicemen and civilians alike were fed, and only towards the end of the conflict were some foodstuffs rationed. Campaigns of the battlefields and the high seas are well known, but the battle to feed the people was just as important in contributing to the Allies' eventual success. Surrey played a significant role.

Britain entered World War I with agriculture in recession and the country importing cheaper wheat and meat than it could produce itself. Germany, by contrast, entered the war with a very strong farming industry. However, Britain was prepared. Academics had in 1914 set the national target calorie intake at 3,000 calories per adult per day: 1,800 from carbohydrates, 800 from fat and 400 from protein. They then calculated the cost per person per day of obtaining the share of calories from each crop type. For carbohydrates, oatmeal only cost 4*d*, wheat 6*d* and potatoes 8*d*. Milk and cheese were also very cost-efficient, but meat and eggs were very expensive in providing their share.[1] The government decided that arable land would be much more cost-effective than pasture in keeping the nation fed.

However, there was a problem: manpower. By the end of 1914, the government estimated that one in eight skilled farm workers had joined up, along with a larger proportion of valuable casual farm labourers. The resulting labour shortages were particularly noticeable at harvest time and from 1915 soldiers could take four weeks' leave to help with the harvest. To increase food supply, the government encouraged the use of allotments, estimating that as much as 7% of food came from holdings under 1 acre.[2]

In 1916 matters took a turn for the worse. The armed forces had grown greatly in size and needed to be fed, with the added logistical complication that food for troops had to be transported overseas to the fighting fronts. Furthermore, German submarines were starting to take a toll on shipping crossing the Atlantic, preventing crucial imports of food reaching Britain, and the North American wheat and UK potato harvests were poor. A telling statement from the Board of Agriculture and Fisheries set the scene for the future direction of government-controlled agriculture: 'The United Kingdom had 34 m[illion] acres of land under grass and 13 m[illion] acres under other crops; per acre of land the latter area was providing at least four times as much food as the former.'[3]

In December 1916, Prime Minister David Lloyd George created the Ministry of Food, headed by the Food Controller. One of its tasks was to oversee county War Agricultural Committees (WACs). The ministry agreed to pay fixed prices for the food it wanted; in return, the WACs were to survey the land in their county and instruct farmers as to what to do with it. The result was a considerable increase in productive land, but a corresponding need for more farm workers. This clashed with the armed forces' requirements: they wanted 30,000 more labourers to join up. The armed services and the government therefore reached an agreement on the use of servicemen in agriculture. Agricultural Companies (ACs) were formed within the army to manage the allocation to farms of soldiers of lower medical grades.

Events moved quickly, and the Labour Corps was formed in February 1917 and absorbed the ACs. The particularly acute problem of a lack of skilled ploughmen was resolved by the temporary transfer of 18,000 soldiers until the 1917 harvest was complete. Many of those temporarily transferred were Category A men who were surely missed by their units. New sources of workers were also valuable: German prisoners of war (POWs) were found to be very hard-working and many had farming skills that were also put to good use. The agricultural labour force was further enhanced by women volunteers, some of whom were absorbed into the Women's Land Army (WLA) in January 1917 (see Chapter 2 for further discussion of POWs in Surrey, and Chapter 5 for women in agriculture). These arrangements continued successfully into 1918, which turned out to be a bumper harvest year.

The deployment of enlisted, yet unfit or battleworn, soldiers to work the land was crucial – had such men been discharged, many would have found employment in the well-paid munitions industry and consequently have been lost to agriculture.

Reduced imports of food led the government to implement, in December 1916, Regulation 2L under the Defence of the Realm Act. This allowed local authorities to force landowners to use all available land for food purposes and to take control of unoccupied, badly managed, fallow and common lands for the same. This heralded the start of something that some landowners, headmasters and club secretaries would come to dread: Ploughing Orders. Underused land, whether field, pasture, lawn, cricket pitch or tennis court, was to be put to the plough. 'Total war' was coming to the people.

The Board of Agriculture and Fisheries' Food Production Department, the Ministry of Food and the county WACs had every right to be very pleased with their war work. Britain started the war with a farming industry weaker than Germany's but emerged with one that was strong and profitable. Germany badly overestimated the 1916 harvest forecast and this, allied to poor control of food allocation, created a crisis that resulted in large reductions in food supplies to towns and cities in 1917. The urban population experienced famine conditions by summer 1917 and a rapid drop in morale; circumstances did not improve in 1918.[4]

Surrey's Agriculture

At the outset of the Great War, agriculture was one of the main employers in Surrey and crucial to the county's economy. Yet Surrey's farms were relatively small and fragmented. This was chiefly because its proximity to London made it valuable for housing, but also because much of the county was hilly and those parts that were flatter (e.g. the north-west or the Wealden areas, south of the Downs) provided poor-quality or hard to work soil.

The outbreak of war brought few immediate changes to Surrey's agriculture. In this, the county followed the national pattern: the harvest and overseas food supplies at that time fulfilled the country's needs and there was no initial urgency to increase production. Indeed, the productivity of Surrey's mainly arable agriculture could easily be improved merely by enlarging the amount of land that was under the plough. Wheat, for example, was grown extensively on both pre- and newly-ploughed land, including on some surprisingly small plots of only a few acres. Farmers whose land was unsuitable for growing wheat or oats had to grow potatoes.

In late 1915, Surrey County Council (SCC) formed a WAC to implement the instructions from the Board of Agriculture and Fisheries. Subcommittees at district level were also set up. In 1917, the pace of agricultural production in Surrey accelerated. The lack of urgency until then is indicated by the fact that the Surrey WAC had purchased just one tractor for the whole of the county – and even that proved troublesome!

Of concern to Surrey's WAC in 1917 was that the county was falling short of the target set for it by the Board of Agriculture and Fisheries of ploughing up an extra

18,000 acres of land. It had managed to add only 10,000 acres by November. Efforts were made to remedy this. In addition to compelling farmers to plough all available low-productivity land (through Ploughing Orders if necessary), an extension of the amount of land used for allotments was encouraged, utilising land deemed unsuitable for large-scale farming. This was organised at district and borough level. By November 1917, there were in Surrey just under 25,000 allotments, covering nearly 1,900 acres, for cultivation in 'spare hours' by residents.[5]

Percy Webb, Clerk to Walton-on-Thames Urban District Council, proudly summarised the achievements in his district by the end of 1917:

Another opportunity of service was given us by the Cultivation of Lands Order. The Council and their Surveyor took up the matter with energy and with surprising results. Applications for land poured in and were granted, with the result that not less than 1,300 allotments, varying from 10 rods to 12 acres, were cultivated in the parish with considerable success. Over 53 acres were set out under the Orders, comprising 22 pieces of land in various places. In addition many gardens of empty houses were cropped by neighbours with good results. It was a cheering sight to see men and women of all classes, many of them unaccustomed to such labour, digging away in the bitter cold of the spring. The excellent show of produce exhibited at the Central Schools was eloquent of their achievement. Thirty seven tons of seed potatoes and twenty tons of lime were sold to cultivators and 247 gardens and allotments were treated by the potato sprayers.[6]

There were also improvements to the supply of labour to work the land in 1917. When, in that year, the Labour Corps was formed, Surrey gained one Agricultural Company (425th AC) to manage those soldiers allocated to farming in the county. It was based at Stoughton Barracks in Guildford. In March 1917, 125 men of the Home Defence Force and 160 men of Army Class W Reserve (i.e. in reserved occupations) were working in agriculture for 425th AC.[7] In November, it was reported that 837 soldiers were then allocated to agriculture in Surrey, a significant increase over the eight months since March and one that resulted in the 680th and 694th ACs being formed at Stoughton to supplement 425th AC.[8]

Soldiers working in agriculture were often posted close to their homes, as the farmer to whom they were allocated was responsible for their board and lodgings or for ensuring they were able to get to and from their place of work. Living at home saved everyone time and money and also provided a psychological boost for the soldier and his family. In many cases, being away from the front line and in relatively healthy employment near home was just what a downgraded soldier needed, and his health improved.

Miss Boxall, Land Girl (courtesy of Guildford Borough Council Heritage Services, LG1520-14)

Women were also, by that time, making a significant contribution to Surrey's agricultural labour force. By July 1917, there were 869 women working full time on the land in the county, plus 994 part time and 261 willing but not employed (see Chapter 5 for a detailed discussion of women in agriculture).[9] By late 1917, mechanisation had also advanced: the one (troublesome) tractor of March had been supplemented by twenty-two more of different and more reliable designs.

Surrey was getting into its stride and the effects were very visible in 1918. The WAC reported in May 1918 that it had added 24,000 acres of ploughed land and now had 35,000 acres of new arable land, which was a seventh of the total arable and grass-land in the whole county. The WAC was pleased to report that only two other counties could better this. The main crops across the county were still wheat and grass, with potatoes on smaller plots. The expansion continued through the year. Allotment holders received 700 tons of seed potatoes and the fleet of tractors had grown to seventy-nine by September: a mix of Fordson 22hp, Titan 20hp, Parrett 20hp and Samson 20hp (all of them from America and run on kerosene).[10] By November 1918, the 837 soldiers working in agriculture had grown to 1,371, assisted by 110 POWs. The majority of Surrey farmland was still allocated to pasture and mowing (providing stock feed), but any land that was not good pasture and could be better used would have been allocated to ploughing by the District WAC.

Two Surrey Districts Compared

Each year, the District WACs required farmers to provide returns on how their land was being used (including fallow land not in use and temporary grassland created as part of crop rotation). This data is now held at The National Archives on a parish-by-parish basis.[11] The data for two differing districts are here presented for comparison. The Kingston and Wimbledon District was a relatively populated area and so might be expected to have grown more market garden crops, while the Reigate District included part of the Weald and so might be expected to have had more wheat and grazing lands. It might also be anticipated that the amount of land available would increase significantly over the course of the war, particularly in 1918 and 1919, thanks to measures to increase the amount of productive land by ploughing up spare land, recreation grounds and sports grounds. What the statistics show is a little surprising.

In the Reigate District, the acreage of land used for agriculture increased, especially between 1918 and 1919, but not by as much as might have been expected. The rise was just 1.75% between 1914 and 1918 and 3.6% between 1918 and 1919 – a period when there was a great deal of pressure on landowners to use all available land. Note, however, that the report's statistics were collected from farmers and landowners and not from allotment holders or owners of large houses or estates whose land had been turned over to agriculture. Individually, such private lands were relatively small, typically 5 acres, but cumulatively they could be significant. For example, the Chertsey District WAC had 1,100 acres under Ploughing Orders in December 1918; these were mostly fields and gardens attached to larger houses and small farms.

Statistics show a surprising consistency in the nature of land use in the Reigate District over the course of the war. This consistency indicates that farmers were already using the land well and growing crops that were needed. The proportion of land used to grow wheat was small compared to that used for pasture and mowing, which indicates that this part of Surrey was used more for stock (cattle, predominantly) and horses than for crops.

It is interesting to compare these figures to those from the Kingston and Wimbledon District WAC's reports. Here, the farms were relatively small, but the area included Richmond Park and Wimbledon and Ham Commons. While these could be ploughed or grazed, they were also valuable as locations for military camps. Indeed, the District WAC must have found it difficult to meet usage targets because some of its parishes experienced a notable drop in land availability after 1914, as land was taken for military use. Yet certain of its parishes notably increased their agricultural land. For example, Kingston and Long Ditton parishes both showed a reduction of 50% in the availability of agricultural land between 1914 and 1918, yet Claygate and New Malden parishes increased their availability by nearly 40% over the same period. The net result was that the amount of land available for agriculture remained fairly static.

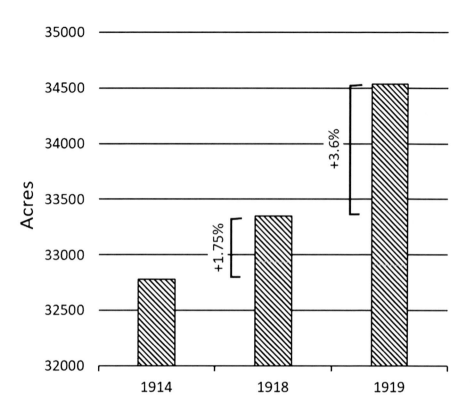

Reigate District acreage under cultivation, 1914–19

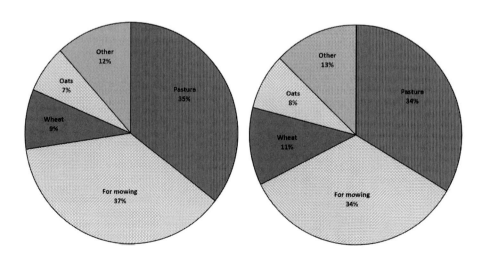

Agricultural land usage in Reigate District in 1914 (left) and 1919 (right)

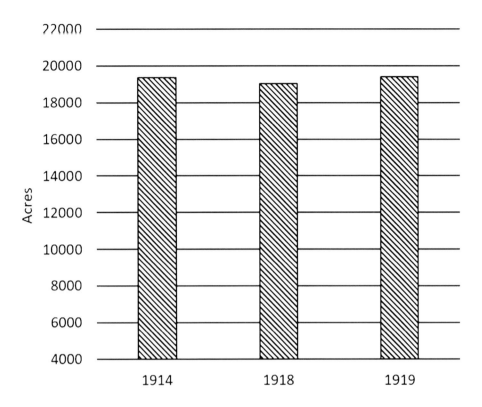

Kingston and Wimbledon District acreage under cultivation, 1914–19

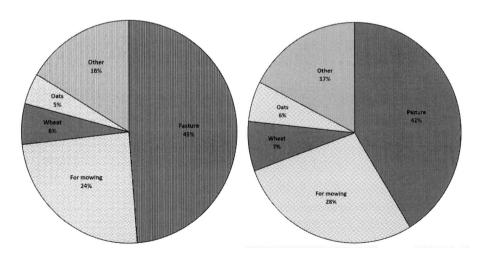

Agricultural land usage in Kingston and Wimbledon District in 1914 (left) and 1919 (right)

The crop type figures for Kingston and Wimbledon District mirror the Reigate figures, with a relatively small change in the district's land usage across the period. By 1918, there would have been a large increase in Ploughing Orders relating to land belonging to large houses and manors in the district, but the statistics do not reflect this, as such parcels of land were often too small for data on them to have been gathered. The proportion of pasture is surprisingly high but reflects the large number of parks (and golf courses) that would have been allocated to grazing rather than ploughing. There were a large number of army camps in the parks, and their horses needed pasture and silage.

The statistics for these two districts go somewhat against the rhetoric and perceptions relating to wartime land use. Although the amount of land used for agriculture in Surrey did increase during World War I, the increase in these districts was much less than might be expected at a time when it is easy to imagine not a yard of grass left untouched by the plough. However, what did improve (and is not reflected in the statistics) is the efficiency of the usage of the land. Surrey's tractors were in constant toil and were moved from one plot to another daily. That the level of land cultivated was maintained and extended and the efficiency of its use improved were remarkable achievements given that so much skilled and experienced labour was lost to the armed forces.

Many small plots of land were handed over to local farmers to manage. Some landowners had nonetheless to pay for their ploughing, planting and harvesting, although in return they received income from the sale of the resulting produce. It must have been difficult for some landowners and schools to have seen their pristine lawns and fields ploughed up, and not everyone was compliant. Lady Cheylesmore of Queenswood Lodge in Englefield Green, for example, was found to have used the three soldiers from the Agricultural Company allocated to her estate to lay turf on her lawn.[12] This was soon stopped, and the District WAC inspected her estate and immediately slapped a Ploughing Order on it.

The Battle of the Golf Courses

Surrey reportedly had seventy golf courses at the time of the Great War, most of them, on the face of it, on good grassland that would be a prime target for food production. However, between the WAC and the cultivation of that land stood the golfing community. By 1917, many golf clubs were already in trouble, with falling membership and tight finances. To reduce the size of a course by cultivating some of its land would further lower membership and imperil finances. Most clubs' membership consisted of wealthy and influential people – and many were less than patriotic when their golf was threatened.

For Surrey, this story starts in the spring of 1917 when the county's WAC was planning the autumn harvest against an aggressive target set by the Board of Agriculture and Fisheries. All golf clubs in Surrey were invited to a meeting in June 1917 to establish what of their land could be allocated to food production. The minutes and report from that meeting have not survived, but from it seventy golf courses were identified.[13] Twenty-three of those were deemed unsuitable for agriculture, among them nearly all of the top courses in Surrey. These included Walton Heath Golf Club (GC), owned by newspaper magnate George Riddell, where his close friend, Prime Minister David Lloyd George often played, plus St George's Hill GC, Weybridge, situated within one of the most expensive and prestigious estates in Surrey, and Combe Hill GC, where royalty and Winston Churchill played. Walton Heath GC did allocate some spare land beyond the course for agriculture and St George's Hill GC was also used as a large Red Cross hospital (whose officer patients could play on the course as part of their recovery). A contemporary newspaper report on Walton Heath's course noted that its land had not been ploughed for cultivation because it was 'all heather and stone, is unproductive and has no depth of earth anywhere'.[14] Were that true, it would have been a very poor golf course rather than one of the county's more prestigious ones! A couple of further courses that were situated within large, high-status parks such as Old Deer Park, Richmond (Royal Mid-Surrey GC) and Richmond Park (three courses) had a lot of land and could comfortably accommodate grazing, ploughing and allotments while retaining eighteen holes for their members.

Of the remaining forty-seven clubs, just nine had land suitable for ploughing, while the rest were given grazing and hay production targets. The grazing of sheep on courses was common because it caused less damage to the greens and fairway than ploughing. In all, the WAC managed to obtain from golf courses only about 500 acres of agricultural land, about 10% of the total they occupied.

Eight of the nine courses that were required to plough up some land have been identified: Beulah Hill GC (near Croydon), Bleakdown GC (now West Byfleet GC), Bramley GC, Farnham GC, Guildford GC, Royal Wimbledon GC, Shirley Park GC and Wey Manor GC, Byfleet. There is no obvious common denominator to explain why these eight were selected. Beulah Hill, Bramley and Guildford courses are on hilly land. The story of Bleakdown GC could give a clue, though. The course was owned by Hugh Locke King (who built nearby Brooklands racetrack) and was a private members' club. It lay mainly on sand, had never been farmland and would not seem an obvious target for ploughing. However, neither Locke King nor the club secretary attended the Surrey WAC's meeting in June 1917. Nor did they, as requested, attend any subsequent meetings. As a result, a Ploughing Order was placed on the club, which consequently had to reduce its

Golfers on Reigate Heath in 1913. The golf course escaped the plough during the war (SHC 7828/2/122/182)

course to its more undulating nine holes. Perhaps representatives of the other eight courses allocated for ploughing also failed to attend the June meeting and fight their case.

Bleakdown GC survived the war without difficulties and was renamed West Byfleet GC in the 1920s, but not all of the others did. The fates of the other clubs ordered to plough were as follows:

Beulah Hill GC, founded in 1913, was ordered to plough 30 acres but only managed 10, and requested permission to allocate the remaining 20 to cattle grazing. The WAC insisted it plough all 30 acres. The club did not survive the war.

Bramley GC had to plough just 3 acres (it is a hilly and wooded course). The resulting reduction to fifteen holes put strain on its membership, and therefore its finances, and the club all but closed in 1917. The whole course was then used as a nursery for ewes, and 400 lambs were reared there in 1918. The club reopened after the war under member ownership and has been successful ever since.

Farnham GC allocated a number of holes to food production. It suffered the same falling membership fate as Bramley and was wound up in 1917, its assets sold by auction, and the land ploughed. The club re-formed in 1923.

Guildford GC was asked to reduce its course to no more than twelve holes, with the land released to be ploughed. The club had no funds or manpower to do this and was in considerable financial trouble in 1918. The club survived the war, just, and a second 'artisans' club was formed in 1919 to use the same course.

Royal Wimbledon GC was in the enviable position of owning Warren Farm within its land. Eight-and-a-half acres were under the plough and a further 3 acres allocated for grazing. There are no records of the membership levels suffering.

Shirley Park GC was reduced to nine holes. No records indicate any hardship to the members or finances.

Wey Manor GC in New Haw, Byfleet, was formed in 1913 by barrister Bramwell Davis KC, on land that was originally Wey Manor Farm. The whole course had been given over to cultivation by February 1918 – voluntarily, evidence suggests. That month's WAC minutes record that it had received an invoice from Davis on behalf of the club for £921 19s 2d compensation and £220 out-of-pocket expenses for just six items.[15] The committee sent a surveyor to the course to assess the claim. Unfortunately, the results remain unknown as the subsequent records are lost. There is more than a hint of profiteering in this.

The ninth course that Surrey's WAC allocated for ploughing may have been Beckenham GC. Although the course was in Kent, its clubhouse was in Surrey and so it came under the jurisdiction of Surrey's WAC. The club allocated for cultivation 15 acres of unused land and 6 acres 'between holes'. Croydon Corporation used 20–30 acres of this for allotments.[16]

Surrey Agriculture after the Armistice

The Armistice did not bring a sudden halt to the pressure on landowners and authorities to produce food. In contrast to industry, in which the cessation of the conflict caused orders for armaments and equipment to be cancelled with a stroke of a pen, Ploughing Orders continued, albeit at a reduced level, until the spring of 1919. Agriculture experienced more an 'easing off of the accelerator' than a sudden 'putting on the brakes'. It must have pained many owners of large houses and sports clubs to see a horse or tractor ploughing up their lawn or tennis court despite the war being over. The 1918 harvest was successful, but the Board of Agriculture and Fisheries still had to provide food for troops and civilians and ensure that the winter food supply was maintained until supplies from overseas returned to normal (which took a year). The half-yearly meeting of the Surrey WAC took place on the day after the Armistice, but such was the continued pressure on food production, the report of the meeting scarcely refers to the end of hostilities and the return of peace.

Conclusion

Britain and Surrey could be satisfied by their work to manage and increase wartime food production. In agriculture, as in industry, the war accelerated improvements. By 1918, German cities, after four years of blockade, were running out of food, which placed great pressure on their armed forces to try to win the war quickly. By contrast, the Allies, by maximising domestic food production and keeping the vital Atlantic supply line open, suffered fewer and less severe food shortages and kept their populations fed. The importance to the war effort of an efficient and self-sufficient system of agriculture was evident; moreover, the experiences of World War I would be crucial come the outbreak of a second war some two decades later.[17]

7

TREATING THE WOUNDED

SUE HAWKINS

The British Red Cross in Surrey

When war broke out in August 1914, the Surrey Branch of the British Red Cross (BRC) was well prepared. There were already forty-two women's and fourteen men's detachments, organised into nineteen divisions, with over 3,000 members.[1] When the War Office called on the BRC to help supply the massive numbers of beds that would be needed to deal with surges of wounded soldiers arriving from the battlegrounds, Surrey's response was almost instantaneous. By the end of 1914 at least thirty-five hospitals had opened across the county, staffed by Red Cross Voluntary Aid Detachments (VADs).[2] The VADs undertook all types of hospital work, from nursing to administration, cleaning and cooking, and a host of other duties without which a hospital cannot function.

The hospitals ranged in size and function. Two of the largest were Clandon Park (with 134 beds) and the Red Cross Annexe at the Royal Surrey County Hospital (over 100 beds). Both were 'front-line' hospitals, receiving casualties in convoys by train, directly from the ports. However, the vast majority were small 'auxiliary' hospitals, which cared for the less seriously injured, and convalescent hospitals, which provided rehabilitation. The smallest was a nine-bed convalescent home at Pennyhill Park in Bagshot. Amazingly, almost all were established in private houses, donated by their owners, in full or in part, for the war effort.

War Comes to Brooklands

On 22 June 1914 *The Times* reported a fierce battle taking place near Weybridge. Planes whirled high in the sky while troops fought valiantly but were beaten back by enemy invaders. What was this – an invasion by German troops, before war had even been declared?[1] No, it was Surrey Red Cross volunteers demonstrating their preparedness for invasion, at Brooklands racetrack.

Organised by Ethel Locke King (vice president of Chertsey Red Cross Division), the 'war games' of June 1914 saw local Red Cross detachments erecting a clearing hospital, rest stations, an advanced stationary hospital and a base hospital in the grounds of Brooklands, to receive and treat the 'wounded'. The racetrack had become a battleground, and the hospitals were so realistic that 'the whole area ... presented a scene that brought war conditions vividly to the eye'.[2]

Over 600 Red Cross members took part in the exercise, which was attended by Queen Alexandra. Aeroplanes spotted the 'wounded' and directed ambulances to them, which ferried them up the chain to the clearing hospital and, by way of a rest station, to the base hospital. The event was acclaimed a great success, receiving nationwide coverage. It was the first demonstration of Red Cross war work the country had seen. Little did the participants know how soon they would be doing this for real.

The Red Cross Stationary Hospital, Rest Stations and Clearing Hospitals from the edge of the Royal Enclosure, Brooklands, *Red Cross Journal*, July 1914 (courtesy of British Red Cross Museum and Archives)

A Family Affair

The MacDonalds of Woking are an excellent example of a family's support for the British Red Cross. Leslie, the younger daughter, joined first, in September 1914, as a VAD nurse at Beechcroft Hospital, Woking, later serving at Netley Hospital. In early 1918, she moved to northern France, where she worked as an ambulance driver. Leslie resigned from the VAD in March 1919 to marry her American sweetheart, who had also been working in northern France.

Mother, Katharine, was next. She enrolled in March 1915 as quartermaster of Beechcroft, rising to commandant in November 1916. When the hospital began to close in August 1918, not wanting to give up her war work Katharine joined the Women's Royal Naval Service (WRNS). She had postings in both the UK and France before the service was disbanded in 1919.

Ione, the elder daughter, joined in November 1916 and was posted to the 2nd Eastern General Hospital in Brighton, where she worked for thirteen months as a VAD nurse.

Poignantly, Katharine's husband, John, was killed in France in March 1916 whilst working for the Graves Registration Committee. It is telling of their dedication that all three women continued their war work despite (or perhaps spurred on by) John's death.[1]

Leslie's marriage to Valentine Burkhart Lee. Ione is front left, Leslie is next to her, with Katharine to Leslie's right, wearing her WRNS uniform (by kind permission of Katharine, Leslie and Ione's descendants)

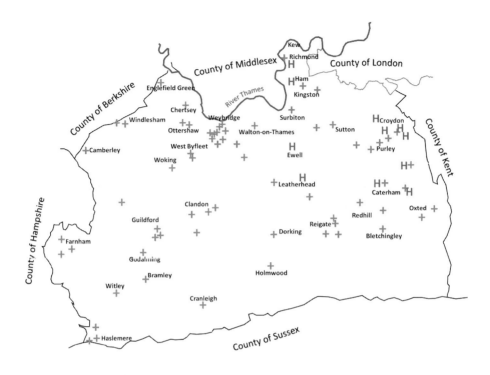

Map of Surrey showing location of Red Cross hospitals (+) and military hospitals (H)
(© Martin Stilwell)

Of course, the military also ran hospitals to treat the wounded. Two of the main military hospitals in the South-east were in Woolwich and Waterloo, while the Cambridge Military Hospital was attached to the army base at Aldershot. It had close ties with west Surrey's newly opened auxiliary hospitals, including the convalescent home at Thorncombe Park, Bramley, another of Surrey's large private residences.[3] By the end of the war, Thorncombe had cared for nearly 2,300 soldiers.[4]

Clandon Park

Clandon Park Military Hospital opened on 6 October 1914 with 100 beds. Lord and Lady (Violet) Onslow were determined it should treat soldiers arriving directly from the Front; in fact, it was claimed to be the only private hospital in the district to receive direct convoys of soldiers. The Onslows spent a considerable amount of their own money rearranging accommodation in their home and equipping it as a fully functioning hospital, with operating room and X-ray equipment. The private nature of the hospital caused problems; the authorities were not quite sure what to do with it. Lord Onslow was particularly firm that it should not be a convalescent home. 'Do not attempt to turn [it into] a convalescent home,' he wrote to his wife, 'as the men would get into awful trouble with the women'.[5] Onslow spent much of the war in northern France and wrote daily to his wife, worried about the great responsibility he had left her to bear. When the hospital was accepted as a front-line hospital in summer 1915, Violet was made commandant and ran it herself.

Her first batch of wounded, a convoy of 103 Belgian refugees, arrived on 15 October 1914, at 3 in the morning, 'shattered and half-starved'.[6] An astonishing assortment of 100 private cars and carriages moved patients from Clandon Station to the hospital. Many were seriously wounded and two died almost immediately. Violet's hastily drawn together staff of ten fully trained nurses from the Red Cross and thirteen VADs worked tirelessly on their first ever batch of wounded. By early December, most patients had been discharged.

However, new arrivals were few and far between and the hospital stood empty for weeks at a time. Violet's staff became restless, 'disappointed at having nothing but domestic duties to perform, the grumbling and lamentations were unceasing'.[7] Mary Pike had joined Clandon 'to learn the nursing' but as 'interesting' work dried up, she was moved to scrubbing. In her resignation letter she wrote: 'I find it impossible to undertake the work as "scrubber"… I am afraid [I must resign] if

Violet, Countess of Onslow, in uniform (centre) with wounded soldiers and a Red Cross nurse, c. 1918 (© National Portrait Gallery, London, 138984)

Ethel Locke King DBE

Ethel Locke King was a leading light in Surrey's British Red Cross long before the outbreak of war. She and her husband Hugh, a wealthy businessman, lived at Brooklands House and according to one account, they 'owned half of Weybridge'.[1] Ethel shared her husband's passion for motor cars – he constructed the first motor-racing track in the world at Brooklands – and she could often be seen whizzing around the track in her smart Itala sports car. She even took part in the first 'ladies' race held there.[2]

Ethel was an activist in the Red Cross, involved in the Weybridge group as early as 1911, increasing her sphere of influence in 1912 to be vice president of the North Surrey Division and in 1915 becoming Assistant County Director. She was a pioneer in the establishment of auxiliary hospitals, setting up at least sixteen institutions in north Surrey, many in properties owned by her husband, in locations ranging from New Malden in the east to Chertsey in the west.

Ethel was a woman to be reckoned with, prepared to stand her ground even when her opponent was a member of Surrey's landed aristocracy, as evidenced by her run-ins with Lady Onslow. She was a formidable woman who in 1918 was made a Dame of the British Empire.

Ethel Locke King (right) in her Red Cross Commandant's uniform, talking to a nurse at Brooklands Hospital (courtesy of Brooklands Museum)

nothing but scrubbing is what I'm considered fit for.'[8] But things picked up in mid-1915, as convoys started to arrive more frequently, and Onslow congratulated his wife ('I am so glad to hear that you have plenty of operations and I hope the nurses are satisfied'), but he warned again about taking convalescent cases. 'I should pass on as many [convalescent] cases … as fast as you can – they are only a nuisance and get the girls in the family way!'[9]

Initially, the Red Cross was overwhelmed by volunteers, but as the war continued demand outpaced supply. Competition between local VAD units for recruits became intense. Violet and Ethel Locke King locked horns over VADs many times over the course of the war. In one exchange, they quarrelled about who should 'have' Cobham. Ethel suggested that Violet's 'smaller division' might offer the Cobham detachment more work; Violet's response to this demeaning description of her own detachment does not survive.[10]

There were problems finding doctors too, as more volunteered for service. Violet eventually decided to 'fall back on what to most of my staff seemed a new idea, and not an altogether welcome one, namely a woman Resident Medical Officer'. The experiment was a success, and despite initial misgivings about women doctors treating male soldiers, the men responded well. 'They were on their honour to see that all went well', she reported.[11]

Clandon became a key front-line hospital in Surrey. Some 5,000 patients passed through it during the war. The hospital closed in April 1919, and the Onslows got their home back. But as Violet mused, the house was full of ghosts:

> Almost every corner of it has a tale to tell … Often there seem to enter at the main door (where the step is worn quite thin by the incessant tread of so many feet) the khaki-clad figures, their wounds bandaged, their faces tired and worn… the stretchers passing up and down … the sitting room peopled with patients … and sometimes whilst I sit by the fire and the telephone bell rings suddenly, I almost wonder if the message will be this … 'To Commandant, Clandon Park Hospital, Guildford. Prepare to receive 98 cases other ranks … time of departure will be notified later.'[12]

Asylums as Military Hospitals

In early 1915 the War Office needed more hospital capacity and turned to the networks of asylums for a solution. These large institutions, already equipped with beds and staff, could be quickly reconfigured into military hospitals.

Horton Asylum near Epsom was the first in Surrey to be converted into a military hospital. There was the little matter of what to do with its existing patients, but that was resolved by simply moving them to other asylums in London.[13] This was incredibly traumatic for the patients, some of whom had spent most of their lives at Horton. The authorities commented: 'The sorrow exhibited by many of the patients … and the regret shown by members of staff in parting with them, were pathetic.'[14] At Horton, patients begged to be allowed to stay '[to] assist in the work of the new hospital … the more rational [offering] to undergo any hardship in the way of accommodation if they could only stay for this purpose'. Their pleas were ignored, and 'many touching scenes [were] witnessed … on the separation of the patients from the members of staff whom they have grown to love and rely upon'.[15]

Over 2,000 patients were cleared from Horton in a matter of weeks and the work of converting it into Horton (County of London) War Hospital began. 'No effort will be spared to make "Tommy" happy and comfortable,' the authorities reported.[16] The most important alteration was the removal of any signs of the former use of the buildings: 'shutters and locks, padded rooms, hot water control valves …', all had to go.[17] The asylum's female nurses were kept on, but as probationers working under a new team of hospital nurses, which must have caused some resentments since experienced asylum nurses now had to defer to new staff in wards in which previously they had ruled the roost.

Women distributing cigarettes to soldiers assembled in a hall at the Horton (County of London) War Hospital (SHC PC/58/84)

Horton's asylum neighbours, the Manor and the Ewell Epileptic Colony, went through a similar process as war progressed. Occupants of the Manor were moved twice! In 1916, its mainly female patients were cleared to the Epileptic Colony (the latter's own patients being moved to Hanwell Asylum), only to be moved again in early 1918 when Ewell was also taken over by the military.[18] This must have been hugely distressing for such vulnerable patients.

Horton and the Manor treated nearly 60,000 soldiers during the war, with only 389 deaths between them (0.7%), while Ewell cared for 1,731 with shell shock.[19] Across the country, the converted asylums treated nearly half a million patients, or one-sixth of the total number of sick and wounded men, from all fronts.[20]

While the soldiers received the best care possible, it isn't clear that the same can be said for the asylum patients. Death rates in asylums rose dramatically during the war, and while the authorities were quick to claim this was not the result of over-crowding, it is difficult to believe this was not a factor. These vulnerable, mentally ill patients are among the forgotten victims of World War I.[21]

Kenry House

True to the ethos of the military, regular soldiers and officers were as far as possible treated separately. Special wards were put aside for officers, as happened at Horton, and whole institutions were assigned as officers-only. Kenry House on Kingston Hill was lent to the Red Cross by Lord Dunraven as a hospital for convalescing officers from the 3rd London Military Hospital at Wandsworth. It was run by Eveline Anstey Drummond Hay, the wife of Francis Drummond Hay, a senior diplomat. A couple of trained nurses and a small group of local VADs supported her. A photograph album from the hospital shows soldiers enjoying the grounds at Kenry House, lounging on the terrace, playing tennis and taking part in fancy dress activities.

Convoys

Wounded soldiers had a tortuous journey from the trenches back to Blighty, passed along what became known as the 'casualty chain'.[22] Field ambulances evacuated soldiers from the trenches to casualty clearing stations, hospital trains took them to base hospitals in northern France, and from there they crossed the Channel to military ports, before being transferred by train to hospitals around the UK. The arrival of convoys of wounded at railway stations became a common sight.

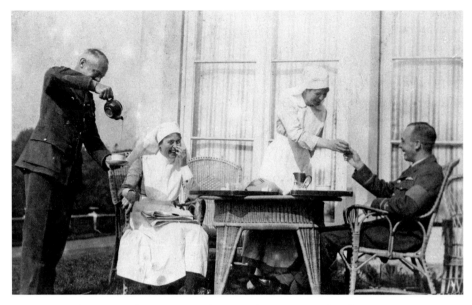

Captain Clough, Sister Tomlinson, Miss Nicholson and Lieutenant Wills off duty after breakfast, on the terrace of Kenry House (courtesy of Kingston Heritage Service)

Thorncombe Park Auxiliary Hospital ambulance (courtesy of Bramley History Society)

In Surrey, Guildford was a major receiving station for the wounded, being hand-ily placed for the Military Annexe to the Royal Surrey County Hospital. Local newspapers reported on trainloads of injured as they arrived. One Sunday in April 1915, a convoy of 100 wounded arrived at Guildford. A great crowd gathered to watch them emerge from the train, and for many, the sight of gallant soldiers 'moved them as nothing else could have done'. The group was cheery and making jokes. 'Where is the war?', one Irish soldier apparently quipped. 'We have heard a lot about it!' Various Red Cross detachments were on hand at the station to help with the detraining and the onward journeys. The crowd cheered and waved handkerchiefs as the soldiers left, while groups of young ladies distributed daffodils or gave out oranges to the departing soldiers.[23]

Some weeks later the scene was not quite so optimistic. This convoy was packed with wounded from Ypres. It was 'a distressing and pathetic spectacle', as 100 'blood-stained and mud-bespattered' soldiers were carefully offloaded into waiting ambulances and cars. They were by far the most serious cases yet to arrive at the station. Many were wounded in both legs and others had shrapnel wounds to the head or chest. Six suffering from gas poisoning presented 'a ghastly spectacle', their flesh yellow from the effects of the gas. The reporter was amazed by the patients' stoicism as they were moved, 'never murmuring … occasionally there was twitch-ing of flesh, a biting of lips or a clenching of the hands'.[24]

Patients

Although most casualties were wounded, some were suffering from typhoid and typhus, and specialist hospitals emerged to treat them. In Surrey, a cluster of 'enteric' hospitals opened around Croydon, while the Manor became a specialist centre for malaria, experimenting with many new approaches.[25] Locals were not entirely happy with this; concerns were raised, when mosquitos were discovered in the grounds, that malaria could spread into the community. Fears were unfounded, and no cases of malaria were ever identified in the neighbourhood.[26]

At Horton, nearly half of patients presented with bad fractures and horrible penetrating wounds of their internal organs, resulting from gunshots, bombs and shrapnel. The wounded benefited from the expertise doctors acquired as the war continued. Techniques were honed, even in operations that were simple but 'exten-sive in character', while those that involved the heart 'could only be described as wonderful'. Operations to repair damaged nerves enabled surgeons to develop 'extensive anatomical knowledge [and] considerable mechanical ingenuity'. Antibiotics had yet to be discovered, and operations to remove septic tissue from

Thomas Rountree, 1st Australian Imperial
Force, at Horton War Hospital, 1917.
His double amputation was the result of
trench foot (courtesy of Philippa Scarlett,
Indigenous Histories [indigenoushistories.
com], originally in the possession of Les
Hackwood of the 1st AIF)

festering wounds became more common
and more heroic in nature: the cleaner the
wound, the more likely the soldier would
be to recover enough to be sent back to the
lines – which was the main objective. Later
in the war, building on this growing expertise, Horton became a specialist centre for
eye, ear, nose and throat injuries.[27]

Despite the dreadful injuries, accounts
of soldiers in war hospitals frequently por-
tray them as cheerful – Australian soldiers
were often cited by nurses as their 'favour-
ites' because of their good spirits and sense of
humour. Margaret van Straubenzee, a VAD
nurse at Clandon Park, declared she preferred
the Australians because they were a 'cheery
crowd', even though they were hard work to
keep in order. She became particularly close
to one, who she called 'Loney'. Margaret
'liked him very much, but not to the extent of
being followed round, waiting for me to come
off duty'. She feared his intentions were too
serious. After he was discharged, he sent her
'suggestive picture post cards', but nevertheless,
she agreed to meet him in London before he
went back to the Front. Some years later, he
wrote to her from Australia to tell her about his
'delightful wife, three daughters and one son'.[28]

Shell Shock

Not all casualties had physical injuries. The term 'shell shock' was thought to be
demoralising, and hospitals preferred medical terms such as neurasthenia, but shell
shock remained rooted in the popular mind. It was an insidious disease. Outwardly,
patients showed no physical sign of trauma, but they were every bit as damaged
as their comrades with missing limbs and bandaged heads. Many were accused or
suspected of shirking and cowardice, but the reality was that many hospital beds
were occupied by soldiers suffering from psychological problems. Springfield Asylum

in Tooting became one of the largest centres in the country for the treatment of 'mental and nervous cases' among soldiers,[29] and in early 1918, the Ewell Epileptic Colony was commandeered as a centre for the treatment of shell shock patients. Of patients treated in ex-asylum hospitals in Surrey, nearly 6,000 were suffering from psychological conditions.[30]

Some also ended up in poor law asylums. To protect them from the ignominy of being confused with 'pauper' inmates, military cases were designated 'service patients', which gave them special privileges. Brookwood, one of Surrey's main poor law asylums, accepted at least 200 military patients during the war, transferred from military hospitals after their initial diagnosis. Records from Brookwood provide some insight into the nature of the conditions from which they suffered.

GA was 28 years old when he was brought to Brookwood in April 1915. He had recently returned from the Front, where he had been for three months, and was described on arrival as 'rather dull & stupid, answering questions very slowly'. He appeared to be suffering from delusions that 'rats [were] gnawing at his insides and sometimes they come out of his mouth'. Nearly a year later, nothing much had changed; he remained deluded and at times was very abusive and threatening. After sixteen months at Brookwood he was discharged to Hampshire County Asylum.[31]

Gunner AEG (25 years old) had been in France for about eight months when he was admitted to Brookwood in July 1915. He was hearing voices urging him to commit violent acts. On admission, he was 'in a confused and incoherent state unable to give an account of himself'. He continued to be troublesome and violent towards other patients and staff; by October his general health was also declining, and he became anaemic, wasted and feeble. His general health deteriorated further, and he oscillated between mania and melancholia, until in May 1918, he died. The cause of death was given as exhaustion due to mania.[32] AEG was buried in Brookwood Military Cemetery with a Commonwealth War Graves Commission headstone.

The War Ends, but the Work Goes On

Even though peace was declared in November 1918, the hospitals of Surrey continued to care for wounded and sick soldiers, but as 1919 progressed, most of the buildings that had served as hospitals were handed back to their owners. The displaced asylum patients were moved back to their old homes, and the valiant volunteers of the Red Cross picked up the pieces of their old lives – although things for most were probably never quite the same again.

Remembering VADs and Nurses

Servicemen who died during World War I are famously memorialised, but less so women who died. A memorial to the twenty-five Surrey VADs who died in service stands in the grounds of the former Royal Surrey County Hospital (now the Farnham Road Hospital), Guildford. Many died from infections contracted on duty. Florence Adds, Muriel Spiers and Ida Hamilton Wood died from flu caught in the pandemic of summer 1918. Elizabeth Gordon died in Salonika from malaria, while Margaret Arnold caught pneumonia and died at Le Tréport, northern France. Both Elizabeth and Margaret were buried in military cemeteries near where they died.

Phyllis Pearce's life is not commemorated on a Surrey memorial. Phyllis, from South Norwood, was a nurse in Queen Alexandra's Imperial Military Nursing Service (QAIMNS), posted to Rouen in northern France. Her brother had been killed near Ypres in November 1914. News of his death hit Phyllis hard, and by April 1915 her superiors were concerned for her state of mind. She was sent to Le Havre and given a bed in the hospital while she waited for a ship home. Sadly, it was too late: she threw herself out of a third-floor window and died, her death certificate citing acute neurasthenia as the cause.[1] Phyllis was buried in a Commonwealth War Graves Commission (CWGC) cemetery at Le Havre, her headstone bearing the inscription 'Beloved daughter'.[2]

Surrey Red Cross VAD Memorial, erected in 1922 at the Royal Surrey County Hospital, Guildford (courtesy of Vivienne Bennett)

8

PEACE, VETERANS AND REMEMBRANCE

KEITH GRIEVES

Rolls of Honour and Peace Celebrations

At church and chapel porch doors, places of work, post offices, council offices and parish shrines lists of men and women serving overseas were updated constantly during the Great War to demonstrate pride in those in peril far from home. Weybridge's beautiful, handbound roll of voluntary attestations prior to November 1915 is entitled *Liber Amicorum* ('book of friends'). A local artefact of Lord Derby's scheme, civic pride in the volunteer was a central theme in remembrance and is reinforced in the book's chosen text: 'All these were honoured in their generations and were the glory of their times' (Ecclesiasticus 44:7).[1] Names of volunteers who had died are identified in red ink.

In the Great War, of unforeseeable duration and scale of sacrifice, rolls of honour became living documents of kinship, friendship and community. Their formulaic underlining and annotations starkly reflected news of the wounded, missing, prisoners and, with dates, those killed in action or who had died of wounds. At Coldharbour, 'Our Roll of Honour' was compiled in 1919. Eighty names are given, in rank order, with the fallen identified in red. This working document, with torn edges and pin holes, has the patina of having been displayed before the community's permanent memorial was erected.[2]

The enormous scale of service and sacrifice was reflected in lists that identified the fallen and those who served, such as the parish war shrine that listed 874 'Hale men and residents'.[3] In Godstone, it was 'a matter of pride' that in February 1916, 202 names were on the list of local men serving.[4] By November 1916, the same list was 'very difficult to keep … accurate and up to date'.[5] Lists of ex-servicemen were compiled relentlessly and in Ham, in 1920, comprised their names, addresses and units.[6] The scale of the co-ordination needed to maintain local records during a vast, attritional war was unprecedented. Information for the memorial volume *Croydon and the Great War* was co-ordinated by the Borough's Libraries Committee. The list of names to be included arose from poster appeals, advertisements, circular letters and exhibitions; it was provisionally published in the 'Peace' souvenir issue of the *Croydon Times* on 26 July 1919.

Five years after the Armistice, the Bishop of Kingston recounted: 'Almost unexpectedly we realised that the long strain was over; the awful suffering and the toil of human life had drawn to an end.'[7] News of the Armistice was often brought by sound. The diarist George Sturt wrote: 'On hearing the bells I almost broke into sobs.'[8] Church bells, which had been silent since the precipitate rejoicing of the Cambrai advance in October 1917, rang soon after 11.30 a.m. on 11 November 1918, followed by 'excitement' in Farnham.

National markers of remembrance and thanksgiving for victory were delayed until the peace treaty had been signed, and in the meantime, programmes for 'welcome home' events held for returning servicemen varied greatly between communities. In March 1919, the peace pageant and victory ball at Addlestone included tableaux representations of the Allied nations, which culminated in the depiction of 'The Nation's Hope' by a 'much alive baby'.[9] Two months later, Colonel Piggott and Lord Abinger, representing the army and the navy, hosted a celebratory 'homecoming' for seventy men at Ewhurst Village Hall, which was bedecked with Allied flags.[10] The 'welcome home' for Kingston's servicemen took place at Baths Hall much later, on 13 November 1919.[11] The Horsell 'welcome home' at Woking Skating Rink was attended by 350 ex-servicemen on 6 December 1919.[12]

The National Festival, or Peace Day, on 19 July 1919 brought an urgent response in Cranleigh, where a subscription appeal to fund the celebrations had been issued just seven days earlier. A public meeting decided that the programme would comprise a tea for children under 15, lunch for ex-servicemen, sports, entertainments and a firework display in Knowle Park.[13] The welcome home event for Godalming 'Citizens' took place at the Drill Hall on 26 July 1919; the mayor's address at the event was accompanied by a meal and concert.[14] The main Peace Day site at Croydon was Duppas Hill, but councillors also attended celebrations at South Norwood, Pollards Hill, Wandle Park and Addiscombe to endorse borough-wide expressions of the National Festival.[15] The Act of Remembrance and Thanksgiving on 31 October 1920 at St John the Baptist Church, West Byfleet, reflected the

Hale (Surrey) Parish War Shrine.

DEDICATED DECEMBER 30th, 1916.

The two side Panels contain the names of 821 Hale Men and Residents in Hale (25 per cent. of the entire population) who are serving, or have served, voluntarily in the Great War.

The centre Panel gives the names of those—53 in number—who have already made the supreme sacrifice.

Hale parish war shrine postcard, *c.* 1917 (SHC PC/64/ALB2/87)

presumption that the Sunday nearest All Saints' Day was more appropriate than the celebratory Armistice Day.[16]

The Comrades Movement

In 1917 the 'Comrades question' vexed Lords Onslow, of Clandon Park, and Midleton, of Peper Harow. Lord Onslow feared that if the 'wrong hands' acquired control of the Comrades of the Great War (the anti-socialist ex-servicemen's organisation, formed in late 1917 to protect the rights of discharged ex-servicemen and women) 'much mischief might be done'.[17]

The initial subscription list included Sir Jeremiah Colman of Gatton Park, Mary, Countess of Lovelace of Horsley Towers, Mr A.H. Lancaster of Send, and £500 from the Lord Lieutenant's County Fund, and aspired to provide meeting places for discharged servicemen in Surrey. February 1918's appeal to 'Join the Comrades' revealed that its 3,000 members in Surrey were a small proportion of the county's 40,000 ex-servicemen and women.[18]

In Surrey there were ten town branches and twenty-two village 'posts' in 1919. A public meeting in Hersham led to the formation of a post there.[19] The Molesey post was invited by the vicar to use St Andrew's Hall as a social centre; ladies of the parish lent furniture, games and other equipment.[20] County families sought reassurance that local welcome home events and war memorial schemes would demonstrate the patronage of the traditional social elite and counter political agitation, but their social leadership sometimes met resistance.[21]

Place-Related Identity in Local Worlds

In Norbury Park, where a peace bonfire was built, three trees were planted so that future generations might know how Mickleham Parish Council celebrated the Treaty of Versailles.[22] The 'Welcome Home' invitation card from All Saints' Church, Kingston, featured a pencil drawing of an outsized church tower.[23] These examples demonstrate that local *patria* was highly visible in memorialisation processes. Committees were intensely possessive of remembering *their* fallen and honouring *their* 'returned' men and women. Listing the fallen; site and design decision-making processes; the circulation of subscription appeals and invitations to unveiling ceremonies — all employed collective memories of focal points and boundary markers to help to define home districts as 'small and remarkably self-sufficient worlds'.[24]

The first meeting of Holmwood War Memorial Committee deplored the news that the names of Holmwood's fallen might be inscribed on Dorking's town memorial.[25] Horsell's parishioners were told not to subscribe to fundraising for Woking's war memorial. In case of doubt about where a name should be inscribed, Horsell's vicar stated, 'I would suggest that the decision should rest with his nearest relative; but that the name should be put on one Cross, not both.'[26]

Unusually, the 'Churt men' defined themselves at their meeting of 'Returned Service Men', for which subscribers to the village's war memorial fund waited before planning their war memorial. These ex-servicemen decided that their community's commemoration should include men beyond the parish, from an additional four roads eastwards to Frensham Common.[27] By contrast, inscriptions on Horley's memorial were to be 'confined strictly' to the names of the fallen of the parish.[28]

Invitation from All Saints' Church, Kingston, to a Welcome Home, 13 November 1919 (SHC 3148/9/4)

Battlefield Crosses

During the construction of permanent war cemeteries in France and Flanders, most of the temporary wooden battlefield crosses that originally marked the graves of the fallen were burnt near the old front line. Cracked, discoloured and damaged, battlefield crosses were sometimes returned to relatives when requested. A few survive in British churches. In St Mary's, Byfleet, twenty-two wall-mounted grave markers surround the war memorial tablet. These include regimental grave markers, standard Graves Registration Unit (GRU) crosses and an Imperial War Graves Commission (IWGC) wooden cross for Private F. Beer, Queen's (Royal West Surrey) Regiment. This memorial collection of grave markers was the initiative of Frederick Cornelius Stoop (1855–1934) and Agnes Macfarlane Stoop (1859–1935), of West Hall. Their extensive philanthropy in Byfleet included a 1918 thanksgiving of £5,000 in gratitude for the survival of their sons and sons-in-law, and they were part donors of the recreation ground in 1921.[29]

Battlefield crosses at St Mary's Church, Byfleet (© Martin Starnes)

Private F. Beer's battlefield cross (© Martin Starnes)

The battlefield crosses at St Martin of Tours Church, Epsom, contain further layers of memory. Faded medal ribbons adorn the GRU marker there; its zinc tag names Lieutenant H.H. Grundtvig MC. The battlefield cross for 2nd Lieutenant C.J.W. Alderton, Gordon Highlanders, who died on 20 November 1917, has a later brass commemorative plaque. It may have been affixed when his mother, Sarah Eliza, left Epsom in 1927.[30] Of St Barnabas Church, Ranmore, Arthur Mee noted: 'On the chapel door is a simple wooden cross from the grave of the eldest brother.'[31] This is one of two GRU crosses there honouring Henry Cubitt, eldest son of Lord and Lady Ashcombe of Denbies, respectively Lord Lieutenant of Surrey and President of the Surrey Branch of the British Red Cross. Originally intended to commemorate Henry, the beautiful fresco in St Barnabas was eventually dedicated to the Ashcombes' three fallen sons.[32]

Naming the Fallen on Wall Tablets

Despite his interest in useful memorials, Lawrence Weaver, architectural editor of *Country Life* 1910–16, acknowledged the need for monuments that served 'no purpose but remembrance'.[33] Names and inscriptions were a memorial's most important elements. No longer pictorial or sculptural, the wall tablet was a framed inscription with 'restrained detail'.[34] For example, in a foliate-bordered frame, the wall tablet 'The Men of the Holmwood who fell in the Great War 1914–1918' lists twenty-nine alphabetically arranged names with regiments. With aesthetic restraint and solemnity, the crisis of the Great War is shown by the text: 'They were a wall unto us both by night and day' (The Bible, I Samuel 25:16), rather than by a pictorial representation of modern war.[35]

At Farnham Methodist Church, the memorial's central panel records the names of fourteen who fell, with one panel either side remembering fifty-nine who served. The simplicity, diversity and economy of plain wooden boards and sparing use of motifs suggest that text outweighed image in local commissions. There was no corporate template for the design of General Post Office wall tablets. The 'Croydon Postal District Roll of Honour 1914–1918' comprises an undecorated metalled list, without alphabetical order, of employees who fought. A framed, coloured scroll with floral border lists the names, with regiments, of Epsom Post Office workers who enlisted from delivery round and office counter.[36]

Elsewhere, the fallen were remembered, in resonant settings, by their surviving friends and teammates. In the pavilion of Banstead Cricket Club, a plain wooden board 'Roll of Honour 1914–1918' holds the names of twelve men who did not return to the crease at the Lady Neville Recreation Ground. The wooden board

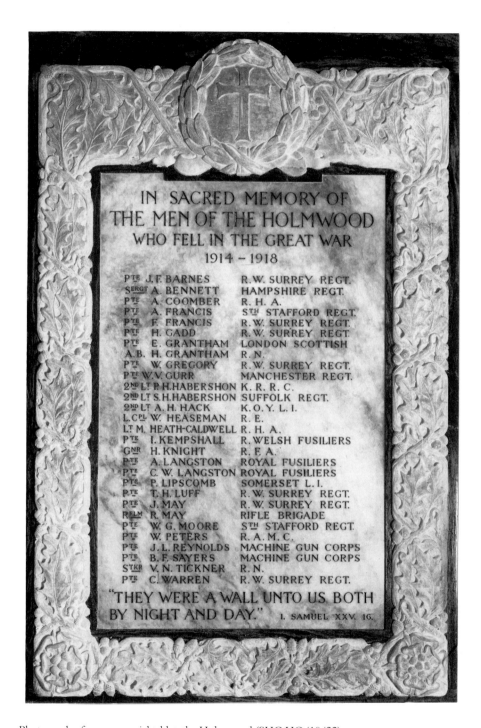

Photograph of war memorial tablet, the Holmwood (SHC HO/10/22)

at Epsom Downs Golf Club depicts, under the club's cypher, a wreath enclosing eleven names. The wall plaque in Wonersh and Bramley Liberal Club, now the Village Club, lists six members who fell in the Great War. A grey alabaster shield uses the Scouting sign for 'Gone Home' to commemorate three fallen leaders and eight Scouts of the 9th Guildford Congregational Scout Troop. It was at Centenary Hall, Chapel Street, and is now at Holy Trinity Church, Guildford.[37]

Wayside and Churchyard Crosses

In support of the erection of a wayside cross, a parishioner who had lost a son stated: 'I take it that the war memorial is to be essentially a tribute to the fallen. Therefore, I think, the benefit of the living should be quite a minor consideration.'[38] The language inherent in a cross's design responded to a sorrowful need for traditional devotional art and a new (post-Reformation) landscape of standing crosses.[39] These prominent monuments varied in design, material and size according to available funds. At Christ Church, Brockham, the inscription on a tall churchyard cross reads: 'Ye who pass by remember the gallant dead/Men of this village who gave their lives in/The Great War 1914–1919.'[40]

Horley's war memorial cross is at the junction of the roads to Charlwood, Reigate and Crawley. In these ways, the 'mark of the Great War' was visible in every place.[41]

There are numerous examples of the encircled Celtic cross, or wheel cross, in Surrey. Erected in 1915, the Clandon Park Hospital Cemetery Memorial in the churchyard has an elaborately carved Celtic cross, with characteristic interlace pattern. A second Celtic cross was erected outside St Peter and St Paul Church, West Clandon.[42]

A plan for the Celtic cross for St John's churchyard, Dormansland, reveals the plinth and steps to be of Hopton Wood stone and the shaft of Portland stone.[43] Notes on the plan

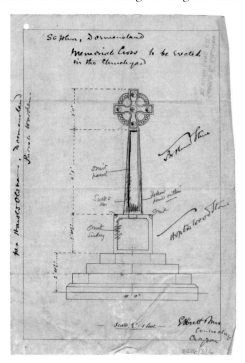

Plan of proposed memorial cross for St John's churchyard, Dormansland (SHC 8026/3/6)

suggest some simplification of the design, which retained a substantial four-step feature, built by Messrs Ebbutt & Sons of Croydon. The circle of eternity was extensively used in war memorial design, including at Kingswood, Ewhurst, East Clandon and Westcott. Proposals for a Celtic cross near Banstead's village well eventually took the form of a quatrefoil cross, associated with the medieval St Brynach's Cross at Nevern, Pembrokeshire.

The medieval cross of tall shaft and wide spreading base, with panels of tracery and crocketed gabled heads, profoundly resonated with antiquaries.[44] Bletchingley's Gothicised cross was designed by P.M. Johnston, known then to readers of *Surrey Archaeological Collections*, and cost £500, raised by public subscription.[45] The churchyard cross at Ripley has an octagonal cross, shaft, plinth and three-stepped base. Crosses with tall shafts on wide bases are found at Holmwood Common, Horsell, Great Bookham, Thames Ditton, Shalford and Epsom. At the churchyard extension of St John the Baptist, Kingston Vale, the crucifix cross once stood among fields, conspicuous and visible from the London Road. The plinth of this 16-foot-high cross bears twenty-six names: 'In memory of our dead, 1914–1918.'[46]

The Lutyens War Cross

Most of the war memorials designed by Sir Edwin Lutyens (1869–1944) were for parishes known to him. At St John the Baptist, Busbridge, for example, he had earlier designed a Jekyll family gravestone and the chancel screen. His cross there has a tapering shaft with short cross arms. The 'simple cross of great dignity' impressed Arthur Mee, whose thoughts turned to Lutyens' Cenotaph in Whitehall.[47] Of Lutyens' forty-four free-standing memorials, whose listed status demonstrates their great significance, fifteen war crosses were designed in the years 1920–25.[48]

Margaret Lewin gifted Abinger's Lutyens short-arm tapering war cross, in the 1917 churchyard extension, in memory of her son. It was inscribed 'In honour of those who fought and conquered' and was badly damaged by a V1 flying bomb on 3 August 1944. In an initialled note, John Gibbs, churchwarden and antiquarian, wrote: 'Lutyens' War Memorial Cross has been cut off from its base, and lies on the ground in five pieces.'[49] The cross was rebuilt, and rededicated in 1949 in memory of Mrs Lewin and her daughter, Mabel Farrer, and acquired a sword of sacrifice on its west face.

At Shere, Lutyens had designed the lychgate. He offered a war memorial design in November 1919, it was rejected in favour of a shaft-on-steps type, simply inscribed '1914–1918'.[50]

Blomfield's Cross of Sacrifice

The war memorial crosses at Abinger, Horley, West Byfleet and Leatherhead are surmounted by the Cross of Sacrifice, which Sir Reginald Blomfield (1856–1942) designed as the IWGC's national war cross. The Thames Ditton parish cross bears a variation – a relief stone laurel wreath for the sword handle. Blomfield's cross was a precisely-proportioned bronze sword in different sizes affixed to an unornamented stone shaft. Intended to be 'abstract and impersonal' and free of historic styles, it was identifiable with war.[51] Over-age for military service overseas, Blomfield joined the Inns of Court Volunteers in 1914 and dug a trench line at Woldingham in defence of London.[52]

An IWGC Cross of Sacrifice was unveiled and dedicated at St Jude's Cemetery, Englefield Green, on 10 November 1929, to the memory of sixty-two fallen buried there (thirty of whom were from the Canadian Forestry Corps, whose hospital was nearby).[53] In Church Walk, Reigate, a small IWGC Cross of Sacrifice was erected to mark the fifty-two war graves in the cemetery adjoining St Mary's Church.[54] Blomfield was dismayed by the appearance of 'horrible travesties' of his design, swords in relief 'freely pirated all over the country'.[55] The cross's popularity reflected the influence locally of war cemetery design, yet stylistic variations in local versions suggest that parish war memorial committees adapted Blomfield's original to match their limited budgets, site constraints and pride in their own designs.

Order of Ceremony

Sunday, 10th November, 1929,
At 3 p.m., at the

Unveiling

BY

Brig.-Gen. G. W. St. G. Grogan,
V.C., C.B., C.M.G., D.S.O.
(Member of the Egham Urban District Council),

THE

ACCEPTANCE OF THE CROSS

BY

Dr. J. W. BIRD, D.S.O., J.P.,
(Chairman of the Egham Urban District Council),

AND THE

Dedication

BY

THE VICAR OF EGHAM
(Rev. A. C. TRANTER).

The following representatives will assemble at the site of the Cross of Sacrifice at 2.50 p.m., and will take their places as shewn on the plan overleaf :—

A Detachment of the EAST SURREY REGIMENT.
Local Branch of BRITISH LEGION,
UNITED SERVICES CLUB.
A Detachment of POLICE and SPECIAL CONSTABLES,
EGHAM FIRE BRIGADE,
BOY SCOUTS, CHURCH LADS' BRIGADE and GIRL GUIDES,
EGHAM & DISTRICT BAND.

The following will proceed from St. Jude's Church to the site of the Cross of Sacrifice at 3 p.m. :—

THE VERGER.
CHOIR.
CHURCH WARDENS.
PARISH CLERK.
THE CLERGY.
Brig.-Gen. G. W. St. G. GROGAN, V.C., C.B., C.M.G., D.S.O.
Lt.-Col. W. RAE, D.S.O.
(Representing the Imperial War Graves Commission and the High Commissioner for Canada),
The CHAIRMAN and VICE-CHAIRMAN OF THE COUNCIL.
COUNCILLORS and OFFICIALS.

Order of ceremony for the unveiling of the Cross of Sacrifice at St Jude's Cemetery, Englefield Green, 10 November 1929 (SHC 2118/1/18)

The Muslim Burial Ground

In 1915, land on Horsell Common, requisitioned by the War Office to become a burial ground for Muslim soldiers who died in hospitals in southern England, comprised an unadorned fenced area and a hut. Maulana Sadr-Ud-Din of Woking's Shah Jahan Mosque campaigned for a permanent enclosure that would more fittingly honour the Indian Army's Muslim fallen.[56] The India Office Surveyor, T. Herbert Winney, designed arches, minarets and a domed (chattri) square entrance, influenced by the mosque's design and, possibly, by the 'Jaipur Portfolios' of Sir Samuel Jacob, who, in retirement in Weybridge after forty years in India, was the War Office's first choice as designer.

Following its completion in 1917, nineteen Muslim soldiers were interred with military honours under the supervision of the Shah Jahan. The IWGC assumed responsibility for the burial ground in 1921 and the graves were relocated to Brookwood Military Cemetery in 1969. Under the subsequent ownership of

Horsell Common Preservation Society some repairs were effected, but the structures were vulnerable in a space without formal use.[57] From 1999, the Shah Jahan, Woking Borough Council and the Horsell Common Preservation Society undertook the restoration of this Grade II–listed site and enabled the opening there in 2015 of the Muslim Burial Ground Peace Garden.[58] (See further Chapter 1.)

MOSLEM BURIAL GROUND, WOKING.   18

The Muslim Burial Ground, Horsell, 1937 (SHC PC/160/ALB1/84)

Recreation Grounds and Open Spaces

War memorials could be social amenities that might be 'useful for life's sake' by paying tribute to service as well as sacrifice.[59] The promotion of the health and happiness of returning ex-servicemen through providing free access to recreational space necessitated land purchase, if influential inhabitants were willing to fund such social betterment for the living. A donation of land to Capel Parish Council for a recreation ground initiated their work to widen access to the village's social amenities. The tablet erected at the recreation ground's entrance gates in April 1921 clarified that the gift was 'in memory of the men fallen in the war'.[60] New byelaws for managing the open space were followed by the construction of a pavilion and permanent cricket pitch, relocated allotments and facilities for the horticultural society.

At Horley, the purchase of a 5-acre site for a recreation ground was pursued in a well-documented nineteen-month search, but the offer of land at £1,400 was too expensive.[61] At Churt, Crossways Field was purchased by subscription appeal at the much reduced cost of £800 to express 'gratitude to the Dead and Living who fought and suffered for us'.[62] The field became a recreation ground and sixteen ¼-acre building plots for cottage construction. Applications for these cottages from Churt's seventy-five returned servicemen were preferred.

At Abinger Common, Abinger Hammer and Forest Green, open spaces were purchased, dedicated to the memory of parishioners who had fallen in the war and endowed and entrusted to the Parish Council in 1920. In 1919, an anonymous gift of £1,000 as a 'thank-offering for peace' enabled the acquisition of 70 acres of open country at Box Hill for the National Trust. Intent on commending the principle behind this gift, Lord Farrer, Chairman of the Box Hill Management Committee, hoped that dignified memorial expressions of 'irreparable loss' could preserve 'places of great natural beauty and their association with the names of those whom it is desired to commemorate'.[63] In 1923, funds for the acquisition of the 'remainder of Box Hill' included money that had been donated to the Country Life Fund; such donations were sometimes sent in remembrance of fallen relatives. In Surrey, the fallen were commemorated by preserving open spaces on high ground, whose slopes mattered so much to inhabitant and excursionist alike.

District and Cottage War Memorial Hospitals

Hospital extensions and cottage hospital construction provided another socially useful option. When a new memorial hospital fulfilled a pressing need in a district, it could be both useful and a tribute, and the impulse to fund additional beds related closely to the needs of resident wounded soldiers.

A surplus army hut was relocated to the grounds of Purley Cottage Hospital for the treatment of discharged servicemen by the British Red Cross VAD. An extension scheme rededicated the Purley and District War Memorial Hospital, which was opened in 1922.[64] The Carshalton, Beddington & Wallington District (War Memorial) Hospital originated from public subscription in three villages: 'to the memory of those in this district who gave their lives during the Great War 1914–1918.'

Early in 1919, the Mayor of Reigate's War Memorial Fund (Hospital Scheme) expected to finance a new wing for the Reigate and Redhill Hospital, but this was deemed 'impracticable' and abandoned in August.[65] Instead, despite rising costs, the donation of a 7-acre site in Redhill enabled the building of a new hospital for East Surrey. Much effort was made to clarify the purpose and commemorative function of its War Memorial ward, which was dedicated on 15 May 1924 in the presence of the Reigate War Memorial Committee.

Social Betterment in War Memorial Halls

During the war, Young Men's Christian Association (YMCA) Red Triangle and Young Women's Christian Association (YWCA) Blue Triangle clubs enshrined three elements: homely facilities, paid hut superintendents and informal religious observance. Behind front lines and at divisional base camps, British service personnel embraced fellowship over cocoa and buttered buns, wrote letters on headed stationery in reading rooms and attended concerts and the cinema.[66] This orderly, and often self-regulated, 'hut habit' impressed advocates of social reconstruction in towns and villages.[67]

At Westcott, the endowed reading room of 1872 enabled concert, lecture and library use, but the hut erected in 1919 had a billiards and smoking room. Moreover, men and women could attend dances and theatrical productions there.[68]

Above the decorative fireplace in East Clandon's village hall, built in 1920, a roll of honour lists men who served in the war. That year, the Forest Green Red Triangle Club was unveiled by YWCA patron Princess Helena Victoria (1870–1948). The hall in which the club was based, along with the village green, comprised the parish's memorial; a plaque outside lists the names of the fallen.[69]

East Clandon Parish parchment roll of honour (SHC 1773/1)

Horsell parish's scheme intended to maintain the Sociable Cottage in Russell Road, near St Andrew's Mission Church, as a 'place of comfort and enjoyment' for ever.

Gertrude Jekyll observed of useful memorials: 'As a heritage of war there are evidences of a considerable brightening of village life.'[70] Through self-help, peace might be rendered 'fruitful' at common meeting places for Comrades, the Women's Institute and other secular organisations.

Ashtead Potters and Memorial Homes

The short history of Ashtead Potters Ltd eloquently testifies to the ambition for social improvement for disabled soldiers, and the tireless command of practical detail, social contacts and entrepreneurial skills of its founders, Sir Lawrence (1876–1930) and Lady Kathleen Weaver (1886–1927). This 'modestly circumstanced pair' collected and administered funds for numerous public-spirited schemes.[71] On the village green, Lady Weaver's beneficent life is commemorated by a plaque on the memorial lamp standard.

In 1923, the Weavers leased the Victoria Works in Ashtead for art pottery work, where disabled servicemen produced beautiful objects in pleasant surroundings. Capital from the British Legion enabled the purchase of equipment and the Ministry of Labour Training Scheme was implemented.

At the 1924 Empire Exhibition, royal guests were 'firmly conducted straight to the Ashtead display' and news of their purchases was advertised.[72] In 1926, Ashtead had approximately thirty to forty employees, but without adequate housing. A total of £6,000 was raised and twenty-three cottages erected to form a small garden village on land purchased by the Housing Association for Officers' Families (HAOF), of which Sir Lawrence was treasurer.[73]

In 1930, financial crisis seized the enterprise and a final effort to sustain employment for ten skilled disabled soldier-potters, by raising £3,000 from 'the influential men of Ashtead', failed.[74] The cottages were transferred to the Douglas Haig Memorial Homes Trust, of which Sir Lawrence was a trustee. Ashtead Potters supplied Haig homes with black tiles for window sills, while the veteran potter Percy Metcalf produced ceramic plaques of Haig to embellish the homes.[75]

Elsie Knocker, later Baroness de T'Serclaes MM (1884–1978), found a haven at the Haig Memorial Homes at Park Lane, Ashtead. After 1926, her small cottage there was a 'real, secure home', following years without rest, security or comfort, having been gassed and invalided home in 1918.[76] This 'Heroine of Pervyse' had, with Mairi Chisholm, maintained a cellar nursing post for three and a half years, attached to the Belgian Army. In Surrey, her memories and lantern slides on 'Four Years in Flanders' were shared with ex forces audiences such as the 'Lest We Forget' Association in Epsom.

At Green Lane, Morden, Haig Memorial Homes were built on land gifted by London County Council near HAOF cottages. Unlike Ashtead's cottages, they were located in open space on London's metropolitan outskirts near more diverse occupational opportunities. Like the Ashtead Pottery, the Poppy Factory, which was relocated by the Disabled Society to Petersham Road, Richmond, in 1925, required worker accommodation nearby. Howson Terrace comprised flats on three floors with staircase access. In addition to its first hostel at Eden Manor, Beckenham (Kent), the Ex-Services Welfare Society acquired in the mid-1920s hostels and a workshop for shell-shocked veterans in Ashtead and Leatherhead, and in 1930 built twelve houses for veterans and their families in Leatherhead. The residences became known as the Sir Frederick Milner Homes after the Society's founder.[77]

Regimental War Memorials

In the shadow of All Saints' Church, the Market Place in Kingston upon Thames was the only appropriate location for the mayor to welcome home the cadre of the 2nd Battalion, the East Surrey Regiment, from France in November 1918.[78] Over three years before, on 27 July 1915, the Union flag had hung at half-mast for a memorial service for nearly fifty fallen officers of the regiment. A general memorial service for all ranks followed. The regimental symbolism of sacrifice was routinely brought to the Market Place, where commerce, royal borough and barracks entwined. Plans for the East Surrey Memorial Chapel were displayed inside All Saints' southern entrance. An appeal for £3,000 was launched in 1919 for the refurbishment and rededication of the Holy Trinity Chapel and the erection of memorial gates.[79] The six surviving battalions raised £1,800 by Armistice Day 1920. The regimental war memorial was dedicated incomplete on 4 May 1921, and a widow subsequently funded the screen.

The Queen's (Royal West Surrey) Regiment's war memorial was dedicated by the Bishop of Winchester at Holy Trinity Church, Guildford, where the colours of the 1st and 2nd Battalions had been laid up during wartime, on 4 June 1921. The Queen's Regiment's Mons Banner had been laid up at the regimental chapel on 6 January 1918. The war memorial cost over £2,000 and was designed by Captain E. Stanley Hall, who served in the regiment. A canopied niche held the 'Book of Life', which contained the names of 8,000 fallen men.[80] It was unveiled by General Sir Charles Monro (1860–1929).[81] Commander-in-Chief in India from 1916–20 and responsible for the successful Gallipoli evacuation, Monro was appointed colonel of the regiment in 1920, a role that 'he coveted more than any other'.[82] A sensitive understanding of the architectural power of remembrance is apparent in Monro's addresses at the unveiling of war memorials at Banstead (5 June 1921), Busbridge (23 July 1922) and Streatham (14 October 1922).

Conclusion

In 1926 *The Times* reported progress on erecting war memorials in Surrey. Eight years after the Armistice, there were sixty-two stone crosses or crucifixes, five village halls, three recreation grounds, a cottage hospital, figurative sculpture, cenotaphs, a sanctuary, a memorial garden and numerous wall tablets.[83] At much-loved corners, in spaces known to all, material expressions of thanksgiving and sacrifice, of gratitude and sorrow, strove to make sense of the great sacrifice and national deliverance. There was much beauty, dignity and simplicity of war memorial design and function in Surrey's towns and villages, in which social relations, economic conditions and political aspirations varied considerably, even in adjacent communities. Clarifying and maintaining the evolving rolls of honour in a long war brought the greatest responsibility to well-defined 'local worlds'. War memorial committees used traditional moral language for solace and ideas of social betterment to develop schemes whose monuments and amenities co-existed at intensely local sites of remembrance. The responsibility of commemorating in perpetuity the sacrifice of the fallen, and often the service of returned men and women, revealed home to be a highly differentiated place in a county that well understood the dictum 'Never Again'.

POSTSCRIPT

MICHAEL PAGE

When the guns fell silent on the Western Front, Frederick Moore, an infantry-man in 10th (Service) Battalion, Queen's (Royal West Surrey) Regiment, found his excitement easy to contain: 'So it as [*sic*] come 11th Nov 10.0 am and we are ordered to cease fire 11.0 am. Pouring with rain no sign of grub or drink so Armistice day passes dismally but it is Over.'[1]

Behind the lines in the French village of Rumegies, young Archie Forbes, a junior officer of 6th Battalion Queen's, and scarcely out of public school, felt both exhilaration and sorrow:

> It is useless to try and express my feelings of joy and relief … it's all too glorious for words. No doubt England is upside down with delight, and rejoicing from top to bottom, the same that we are doing out here. The men are absolutely off their heads with glee, and it's topping to think of the happy meetings and rejoicings that will take place when we all get back to England. But on the other hand it's terrible to think of the many sad homes and sorrowful hearts where this long looked for return will not be, and to them, I fear, peace will only bring their losses back more vividly.[2]

Eight months on, Viola Bawtree of Sutton looked on uneasily as the Peace of Versailles was celebrated. She hoped that the sense of purpose and patriotic con-sensus that the war had brought had not evaporated irretrievably:

> At dusk yesterday the fireworks started. I stood and watched them all round the horizon and first felt only like crying. But when I realized it was after all an historic night and that all over the world the same sort of thing was going on, I

became fascinated and could not tear myself away. There was no cause to rejoice but I liked to feel it was a great day in history and that all the world was taking part. And I knew there were all 'Those Others' too, looking on, those who had fought and died for it, and that they saw deeper than we did and knew really that they had not died in vain. All the frivolity and silliness is probably only reaction, but what a much nobler, finer England it seemed while the war was on. Do we already need another big trial to call out the good in us, or will it gradually assert itself as the world settles down a bit?[3]

Every November provided further opportunities for people to reflect on the war, its purpose and its cost. The Rector of Godstone observed that the parish war memorial, dedicated in 1921, looked both forward and backwards: 'It awakens many memories of the past years of service and sacrifice, it [is] also an inspiration for the future. The war was waged for ideals: men fought and died for ideals.'[4] It was hoped that those ideals, which had inspired so much sacrificial patriotism, would spur the creation of a better, more just world. In September 1914, James Chuter Ede had taken comfort from his conviction that, with the eventual return of peace, the recollection of comradeship and 'spontaneous rally to the nation's need' would mean that 'much now seemingly unattainable will be within reach'.[5] The Bishop of Winchester, while warning of the evils of class divisions, urged people to come together in 'general goodwill, disinterestedness, and unselfishness' to build a fairer post-war society.[6]

The reality was somewhat different as grand plans for reconstruction had to be curtailed because of Britain's economic prostration and old animosities and divisions reasserted themselves. Demobilisation of the armed services proceeded slowly (far too slowly for many disgruntled, impatient and bored soldiers). Returning men not only had to rebuild disrupted relationships with loved ones but were faced with an exhausted country, class tensions and industrial conflict, poor job prospects and a rundown and depleted housing stock.

Viola Bawtree (courtesy of Jeremy Gordon-Smith)

The job market was challenging enough for the able-bodied, but for those who were now disabled in body or mind the situation was far worse. Legislation of 1919–20 established the statutory right to receive a pension for all those 'suffering from a disability attributable to or aggravated by' military service and extended that right to widows and dependants, but awards were less than generous and many veterans, especially those suffering from mental trauma, had to undergo the humiliation of regular medical reassessments. Initiatives to provide training or employment for disabled ex-servicemen, such as Ashtead Potters Ltd (discussed in Chapter 8), the Thermega Electric Blanket Factory in Leatherhead, established in 1927 for shell-shocked men by the Ex-Services Welfare Society, and St Dunstan's, established by Sir Arthur Pearson (once of Frensham) for blinded veterans, went a little way to addressing the problem, but more was needed, which the country could not afford. Some of those most badly affected by their war experiences ended up in the specialist Ministry of Pensions Neurasthenia Hospital at St Ebba's, Epsom, until it closed in 1927, or as 'service' patients in the Surrey county pauper asylums at Brookwood and Netherne. Those of independent means might be committed to Holloway Sanatorium in Egham, a private asylum. Atop Richmond Hill, the massive Star & Garter Home for severely disabled ex-servicemen, first opened in 1916 and rebuilt between 1919 and 1924, provided a very visible symbol of the human cost of the war.

Other initiatives in social reconstruction went some way to addressing the needs of veterans. Christopher Addison's Housing and Town Planning Act, 1919, launched a programme of house building by urban and rural district councils, supported by Treasury subsidies, to erect the 'habitations fit for the heroes who have won the war' that Lloyd George had called for. However, the high cost of materials, a shortage of manpower and economic retrenchment meant that far less was achieved than had been hoped. Surrey, like other counties, also initiated, with government support, a programme to create smallholdings for ex-servicemen who wished to pursue a career in agriculture.[7] The county council bought up suitable estates, built cottage accommodation, controlled rents and provided loans to set up the ex-servicemen, but once again more ambitious plans had to be abandoned.

For women, too, many of the opportunities provided by the national emergency did not endure into post-war Surrey. Frederick Robinson had noted in his diary in 1916:

We are getting accustomed to seeing women in many occupations previously occupied by men. In banks half the clerks are now girls, we have women waitresses at the West End Clubs … we have women booking clerks and ticket collectors on the railways, and women conductors on the tramways, also little girl 'page-boys' at the hotels. And vast numbers are working at Red Cross Hospitals, not only as nurses but as cooks, kitchen-maids etc.

He had wondered then, 'How is all this going to be adjusted after the war? Will women be content to go back to their domestic duties, their sewing and cooking and what not?'[8] The answer was that they were given little choice, as munitions factories closed and returning men supplanted them. A 1918 directory of engineering firms undertaking munitions work records that over 12,000 women were then employed across Surrey (including Croydon) just in munitions; the 1921 census suggests that only 2,914 were then working in *all* sectors of manufacturing (excluding food and textiles). There were only three women employed as bus and tram conductors and six as railway ticket inspectors. Domestic service remained by far the biggest source of employment for women (77,689 in 1911, 69,734 in 1921).[9] Many of those who had laboured for the national cause in munitions factories still found themselves excluded from voting in parliamentary elections, as the 1918 Representation of the People Act only extended the franchise to women over 30.

As domestic problems and international tensions showed no sign of abating, so confidence diminished that winning the war had been worth the price paid. Writers and artists struggled to evaluate its meaning. Surrey playwright Robert Sherriff's response to what he had experienced while serving with the 9th Battalion East Surrey Regiment had a long gestation before emerging as the great play *Journey's End*, first performed in 1929. It is a compelling portrait of human endurance in the most appalling of circumstances, but the cause for which the men were fighting had slipped from sight. Sherriff's unpublished sequel depicted the peacetime struggles of the protagonists in a harsh, unsympathetic world.

Many of those who had served kept silent about their experiences except when they met with their former comrades in British Legion meetings or regimental reunions. Herbert

R.C. Sherriff in East Surrey Regiment uniform, *c.* 1917 (SHC 2332/6/4/2/2/1)

Boxer was a signaller in Sherriff's old unit. His family remembers him saying almost nothing about his wartime service. He confined his reminiscences to his unflinching memoir of his nineteenth year. Despite the horror of much of what he relates, it was the recollection of the intense comradeship that remained with him for the rest of his life: 'Do I regret those years in the Army, in particular my Nineteenth Year. No, the memory, those wonderful memories will live with me always.'[10]

A third member of the 9th Battalion of the East Surreys was Private Teddy Cutt, a gardening boy from Shalford. He rushed to enlist in 1914 and met Nellie Dabbs, a teacher, while billeted with her family in Broadwater for training. Despite few chances to spend time together, they quickly fell in love and got engaged. In August 1915, Teddy sailed for France and within weeks his raw and inexperienced unit was thrown into the suicidal attack of 72nd Brigade on the German line at Loos on 26 September. He was never seen alive again. Nellie made frantic efforts to discover what had happened to him, which are documented in the diary in which she had first started to record the progress of their relationship. A year later, she received official confirmation of Teddy's death. She suffered a breakdown and moved to Lincolnshire to be with her family. For the rest of her life she remained devoted to Teddy, never marrying. His *Pocket Gospel of St John* (issued to all troops), a lock of his hair and a photograph were all that she had to remember him by, a fate suffered by countless women of her generation.[11]

Just as the thunder of the far distant guns could be heard across miles of land and sea to trouble the tranquillity of the Surrey hills, so the aftershocks of the war to end wars reverberated down the years through politics, society and individual lives. They can be felt still.

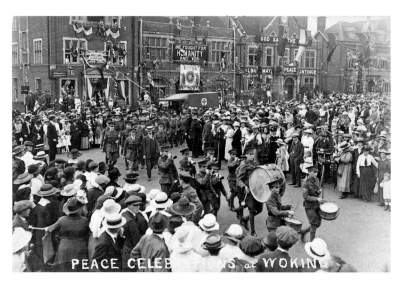

Woking Peace Day (SHC PC/160/ALB1)

NOTES

A note on references to newspapers: the figure following the date of the edition is the number of the page on which the relevant article is found. Within a page, columns are lettered from left to right, starting with 'a'. For example '4e' denotes 'page 4, column e' (the fifth from the left).

Chapter 1

1   *Dorking and Leatherhead Advertiser*, 1.8.1914, 4e.
2   *Ibid.*, 2e.
3   *Surrey Mirror*, 31.7.1914, 7h.
4   *Ibid.*, 4.8.1914, 2e and 2f.
5   *Ibid.*, 7.8.1914, 4f and 7.8.1914, 5c.
6   *Ibid.*, 7.8.1914, 5d and 5e; S. Badsey, 'Mass Politics and the Western Front', BBC History (http://www.bbc.co.uk/history/british/britain_wwone/war_media_01.shtml, p. 1; accessed 26.11.2018).
7   G. Corrigan, *Mud, Blood and Poppycock* (Cassell, 2003 [2004]), pp. 42, 207–12; R. Holmes, *'Tommy': The British Soldier on the Western Front 1914–1918* (Harper Perennial, 2005), p. 224.
8   H.W. Pearse DSO and H.S. Sloman CMG DSO, *History of the East Surrey Regiment II: 1914–1917* (Medici Society, 1923), pp. 3, 29; H.C. Wylly CB, *History of the Queen's Royal (West Surrey) Regiment in the Great War* (Gale and Polden, 1926), p. 3.
9   *Surrey Mirror*, 31.7.1914, 4.
10 C. Baker, 'Surrey Yeomanry (Queen Mary's Regiment)', The Long, Long Trail (http://www.longlongtrail.co.uk/army/regiments-and-corps/the-british-yeomanry-regiments-of-1914-1918/surrey-yeomanry-queen-marys-regiment/; accessed 1.12.2018).
11 C. Baker, 'British Army Reserves and Reservists', The Long, Long Trail (https://www.longlongtrail.co.uk/soldiers/a-soldiers-life-1914-1918/enlisting-into-the-army/british-army-reserves-and-reservists/; accessed 1.12.2018).
12 War Diary, 1st Battalion QRWS Regiment, 5–7 August 1914, Queen's Royal Surreys (http://www.queensroyalsurreys.org.uk/war_diaries/local/1Bn_Queens/1Bn_Queens_1914/1Bn_Queens_1914_08.shtml; accessed 1.12. 2018).
13 War Diary, 1st Battalion ESR, 5–8 August 1914, Queen's Royal Surreys (http://www.queensroyalsurreys.org.uk/war_diaries/local/1Bn_East_Surrey/1Bn_East_Surrey_1914/1Bn_East_Surrey_1914_08.shtml; accessed 1.12.2018).

14   *Surrey Mirror*, 7.8.1914, 5e; *Surrey Advertiser*, 8.8.1914, 4g & 4h.

15   *Dorking and Leatherhead Advertiser*, 8.8.1914, 5b; *Surrey Advertiser*, 5.8.1914, 1c; *Surrey and Hants News*, 14.8.1914, 3e.

16   *Surrey Advertiser*, 8.8.1914, 4g.

17   *Ibid.*, 8.8.1914, 4h.

18   *Ibid.*, 26.9.1914, 4h.

19   G. Winton, *Theirs Not to Reason Why: Horsing the British Army 1875–1925* (Helion and Company, 2013), pp. 262–63.

20   *Ibid.*, p. 266; Corrigan, *Mud, Blood …*, p. 45; *Surrey Advertiser*, 8.8.1914, 4a.

21   Winton, *Theirs Not to Reason Why*, p. 302.

22   *Surrey Advertiser*, 22.8.1914, 2f and 8.8.1914, 2d; Winton, *Theirs Not to Reason Why*, pp. 267–68.

23   *Surrey Advertiser*, 8.8.1914, 5b.

24   *Ibid.*, 1.8.1914, 3g.

25   C. Baker, 'The Territorial Force', The Long, Long Trail (https://www.longlongtrail.co.uk/army/the-territorial-force/; accessed 1.12.2018).

26   Surrey History Centre (SHC) QRWS/30/SLADEN/2/1 Diary of Lieutenant Colonel St Barbe Russell Sladen, 1914; M. Page, 'Lt-Col St Barbe Russell Sladen', Surrey in the Great War (https://www.surreyinthegreatwar.org.uk/story/lt-col-st-barbe-russell-sladen/).

27   C. Baker, '44th (Home Counties) Division', The Long, Long Trail (https://www.longlongtrail.co.uk/army/order-of-battle-of-divisions/44th-home-counties-division/; accessed 1.12.2018).

28   K. Atherton, *Dorking in the Great War* (Pen and Sword, 2014), pp. 34–42.

29   SHC CC7/4/4 Correspondence and Papers relating to Life Assurance Policies of Surrey County Council Staff 1914–23, Insurance Claims on behalf of Surrey County Council Education Department Employees Killed in Action, 1915–18.

30   SHC CC360/26 Surrey County Council Reports 1914, Finance Committee report 29.9.1914.

31   B. Gosling, 'Henry Robert Stanley', Surrey in the Great War (https://www.surreyinthegreatwar.org.uk/story/henry-robert-stanley/).

32   W.H. Oakley, *Guildford in the Great War* (Billings and Son, Ltd, 1934), pp. 35–36.

33   P. Simkins, *Kitchener's Army: The Raising of the New Armies, 1914–1916* (Manchester, 1988), pp. 238, 240.

34   Atherton, *Dorking in the Great War*, pp. 58, 66–80.

35   Oakley, *Guildford in the Great War*, pp. 126–27.

36   A. Riddoch and J. Kemp, *When the Whistle Blows: The Story of the Footballers' Battalion in the Great War* (Haynes Publishing, 2008).

37   J. Aston and L.M. Duggan, *The History of the 12th (Bermondsey) Battalion East Surrey Regiment* (Union Press, 1936), pp. 3–4; Pearse and Sloman, *History of the East Surrey Regiment II*, p. 28.

38   Simkins, *Kitchener's Army*, pp. 303–04, 314.

39   J. Schofield, 'Stage 1 Report: Army Camps History', in 'England's Army Camps', Archaeology Data Service, (http://archaeologydataservice.ac.uk/archives/view/armycamp_eh_2006/downloads.cfm; accessed 1.12.2018) p. 5.

40   G.H.F. Nichols, *The 18th Division in the Great War* (Blackwood, 1922), p. 2.

41   Schofield, 'Stage 1 Report: Army Camps History', p. 5.

42   'Woodcote Park Camp', Epsom and Ewell History Explorer (http://epsomandewellhistoryexplorer.org.uk/WoodcoteParkCamp.html; accessed 4.1.2019).

43   *The Times, The History of the Royal Fusiliers' U.P.S.: Universities and Public Schools Brigade* (The Times, 1917), p. 35.

44   *Ibid.*, pp. 64, 75–76.

45   H.C. O'Neill, *The Royal Fusiliers in the Great War* (Heinemann, 1922), pp. 14–16.

46   'Woodcote Park Camp'; *History of the Royal Fusiliers' U.P.S.*, pp. 44–45.

47 *Ibid.*, pp. 46–52.
48 'Woodcote Park Camp'.
49 *Surrey Advertiser*, 31.10.1914, 6e.
50 *The 60th CFA Battery Book* (Belgium, 1919), p. 19.
51 Information courtesy of Hannah Potter of Surrey County Archaeological Unit, which excavated the site in 2015.
52 *Surrey Advertiser*, 21.11.1914, 4e.
53 *Ibid.*, 13.2.1915, 11g.
54 Oakley, *Guildford in the Great War*, pp. 127–32.
55 SHC 6227/1/53–57 Annual Reports of the National Rifle Association 1914–18.
56 See further C. Baker, 'The Group Scheme (Derby Scheme)', The Long, Long Trail (https://www.longlongtrail.co.uk/soldiers/a-soldiers-life-1914-1918/enlisting-into-the-army/the-group-scheme-derby-scheme/; accessed 19.3.19).
57 The Military Service Act, 1916 (via https://www.legislation.gov.uk/ukpga/1916/104/pdfs/ukpga_19160104_en.pdf; accessed 18.2.2019).
58 The National Archives (TNA) MH 47/49/60, Ministry of Health Records, Middlesex Appeal Tribunal Minutes and Papers, Case Number M5361: Thomas Caley.
59 TNA MH 47/59/27 Case Number M5135: George Wheatley.
60 *Surrey and Hants News*, 17.8.1916, 3g.
61 SHC CC28/303B Clerk's Department Files, Surrey and Croydon Military Service Appeal Tribunal, Guildford Area Committee.
62 *Surrey Comet*, 18.7.1917, 2d.
63 SHC CC28/303B.
64 *Epsom Advertiser*, 27.10.1916, 6c.
65 *Ibid.*, 28.6.1918, 5d.
66 SHC CC418/1 Minutes of Surrey and Croydon Military Service Appeal Tribunal, 1916–19.
67 K. Atherton, *Dorking in the Great War* (Pen & Sword Books Ltd, 2015), pp. 108–09.
68 *Epsom Advertiser*, 2.8.1918, 8b.
69 Imperial War Museums, Docs. 11335 Diary of Frederick A. Robinson, 11.3.1916 and 8.7.1916.
70 D. Stiff, 'EM Forster (1879–1970)', Surrey in the Great War (https://www.surreyinthegreatwar.org.uk/story/em-forster-1879-1970).
71 Library of the Religious Society of Friends (http://fau.quaker.org.uk/; accessed 18.2.2019).
72 *Surrey Advertiser*, 29.12.1917, 5b.
73 B. Higham, 'Major Archer Hosking – Principal Medical Officer, Mount Felix Hospital', Surrey in the Great War (https://www.surreyinthegreatwar.org.uk/story/major-archer-hosking-principal-medical-officer-mount-felix-hospital/).
74 *Surrey Herald*, 8.3.1918, 7c (also 7.9.1917, 4b).
75 SHC 3434/9/6 United Racecourses (Holdings) Ltd Records, Epsom Grand Stand Association Minute Book 1907–19. N. Fryatt, 'Epsom Grandstand War Hospital', Surrey in the Great War (https://www.surreyinthegreatwar.org.uk/story/15223/).
76 C.W. Bird and J.B. Davies, *The Canadian Forestry Corps: Its Inception, Development and Achievements* (HMSO, 1919), pp. 5–6; 'Canadian Forestry Corps', Canadiansoldiers.com (https://www.canadiansoldiers.com/corpsbranches/forestrycorps.htm; accessed 6.11. 2018).
77 Bird and Davies, *The Canadian Forestry Corps*, pp. 5–6; 'Canadian Forestry Corps', www.canadiansoldiers.com/corpsbranches/forestrycorps.htm.
78 Bird and Davies, *The Canadian Forestry Corps*, p. 6.
79 *Surrey Advertiser*, 8.7.1916, 3f.
80 *Ibid.*, 24.6.1916, 3d.
81 Bird and Davies, *The Canadian Forestry Corps*, pp. 9–10; 'First World War Canadian Soldiers Buried at Englefield Green', Surrey in the Great War (https://www.surreyinthegreatwar.org.uk/story/first-world-war-canadian-soldiers-buried-at-englefield-green).

82 Bird and Davies, *The Canadian Forestry Corps*, p. 27.
83 *Ibid.*, pp. 22–23 (and map).
84 *Ibid.*, p. 33.
85 *Ibid.*, pp. 20, 31.
86 *Ibid.*, p. 30.
87 'Canadian Forestry Corps', canadiansoldiers.com (https://www.canadiansoldiers.com/corps-branches/forestrycorps.htm), accessed 1.12.2018.
88 Field Marshall Sir Douglas Haig, Despatch 17 December 1917, quoted in Bird and Davies, *Canadian Forestry Corps*, p. 38.
89 G.W.L. Nicholson, *Official History of the Canadian Army in the First World War: Canadian Expeditionary Force, 1914–1919* (Ottawa, Queen's Printer, 1962), p. 500.
90 'History of the Forestry Commission', Forestry Commission (https://www.forestry.gov.uk/forestry/cmon-4uum6r; accessed 1.12.2018); *Surrey Mirror*, 12.9.1919, p. 3.
91 George Morton-Jack, *The Indian Empire at War* (Little, Brown, 2018), p. 257.
92 'History of the Mosque – Part 2', Shah Jahan Mosque (http://www.shahjahanmosque.org.uk/history-mosque-part-2; accessed 1.12.2018); 'The First Muslim Soldier is Buried', Exploring Surrey's Past (https://www.exploringsurreyspast.org.uk/themes/subjects/military/india-woking/buried/; accessed 1.12.2018).
93 'Indian Soldier Buried at Woking', *Islamic Review* (December 1914), p. 534.
94 'Urdu Reports by Maulana Sdar-Ud-Din', The Woking Muslim Mission (http://www.woking-muslim.org/work/ww1/muslim-burials-report.htm; accessed 1.12.2018); *The Times*, 18.4.1916, 5.
95 S. Doherty and T. Donovan, *The Indian Corps on the Western Front* (Tom Donovan Editions, 2014), p. 167.
96 *Surrey Advertiser*, 27.5.1916, 5d.
97 'Second 'Id-ul-Fitr at Woking Muslim Mission, 13th August 1915', The Woking Muslim Mission (http://www.wokingmuslim.org/work/id-ul-fitr-1915.htm; accessed 1.12.2018).
98 *Surrey Advertiser*, 27.5.1916, 5d.
99 'Francis Pegahmagabow' in '100 Stories: Canadians in the First World War', Library and Archives Canada (https://www.bac-lac.gc.ca/eng/discover/military-heritage/first-world-war/100-stories/Pages/pegahmagabow.aspx; accessed 1.12.2018).
100 *Ibid.*
101 'John Baboo', in *ibid.* (https://www.bac-lac.gc.ca/eng/discover/military-heritage/first-world-war/100-stories/Pages/baboo.aspx; accessed 1.12.2018).
102 *Surrey Advertiser*, 1.6.1918, 7.
103 D. Morton, 'Kicking and Complaining: Demobilisation Riots in the Canadian Expeditionary Force, 1918–1919', *Canadian Historical Review*, 61, No. 3 (September 1980), pp. 334–60 (p. 342).
104 *Surrey Times and County Express*, 14.10.1916, 8c; *Surrey Advertiser*, 29.12.1917, 6h.
105 *Surrey Advertiser*, 16.06.1919, 1c and information courtesy of Hannah Potter. See also K. Gnap, 'Canadians at Witley Camp', Surrey in the Great War (https://www.surreyinthegreatwar.org.uk/story/surrey-and-the-great-war-canadians-and-witley-camp/).
106 *Surrey Advertiser*, 21.06.1919, 5f.

Chapter 2

1 Surrey History Centre (SHC) CC98/1/4-5 Surrey Constabulary Records, Reports of Chief Constable, 1909–23, report September 1914. See M. Edwards, '"A Policeman's Lot …": the Surrey Police in War Time', Part 1, Surrey in the Great War (https://www.surreyinthegreat-war.org.uk/story/a-policemans-lot-the-surrey-police-in-wartime-part-1-1914-1915/).
2 *Ibid.*
3 SHC CC98/1/4-5 Reports of Chief Constable, 1909–23, report November/December 1918.

4   SHC LA4/23/40-296 Dorking Rural District Council, Papers relating to London Defences, 1914–18.
5   The National Archives (TNA) WO 78/4420 War Office and Predecessors, Maps and Plans, Plan of London Defences, 1915; L. Spring, 'Surrey and the Defence of London', Surrey in the Great War (https://www.surreyinthegreatwar.org.uk/story/surrey-and-the-defence-of-london/).
6   A. Rawlinson, *The Defence of London* (Melrose, 1923), pp. 162–63.
7   SHC CC98/1/4-5 Reports of Chief Constable, report of May 1915.
8   See M. Edwards, 'Chilworth Gunpowder Factory in the Great War', Surrey in the Great War (https://www.surreyinthegreatwar.org.uk/story/chilworth-gunpowder-mills-in-the-great-war/).
9   *Dorking and Leatherhead Advertiser*, 9.3.1918, 5a.
10 B. Higham, 'Zeppelin Raid on Croydon, 1915', Surrey in the Great War (https://www.surreyinthegreatwar.org.uk/story/zeppelin-raid-on-croydon-1915/).
11 W.H. Oakley, *Guildford in the Great War* (Billings and Son, Ltd, 1934), pp. 149–48; *Surrey Advertiser*, 8.3.1919, 5c.
12 *Ibid.*, 16.2.1916, 1b.
13 K. Atherton, *Dorking in the Great War* (Pen and Sword, 2014), pp. 91–92; *Surrey Advertiser*, 27.10.1915; *Surrey Comet*, 25.8.1917, 7c; SHC 9841/1/4/1 Whyteleafe Grammar School Jubilee Book, 1957.
14 *Surrey Advertiser*, 4.10.1916, 1c; *Surrey Times and County Express*, 8.9.1916, 5d.
15 SHC 9117/Box 2 Papers relating to Hersham, Oatlands and Walton-on-Thames Special Constables, 1914–19, including memoir of Percy Webb.
16 SHC 6296/1/1/39-40 Horley Town Council Records, Records of Horley Committee for Defence of the Realm, 1914–19. See also L. Spring, 'Horley and the Defence of the Realm Act', Surrey in the Great War (https://www.surreyinthegreatwar.org.uk/story/horley-and-the-defence-of-the-realm-act/); SHC 2634/1 Dorking and District Emergency Committee, draft report on preparations in the event of a hostile landing, 1916. See also T. Brand, 'The Dorking and District Local Emergency Committee', Surrey in the Great War (https://www.surreyinthegreatwar.org.uk/story/the-dorking-and-district-area-local-emergency-committee/).
17 See M. Edwards, '"A Policeman's Lot …": the Surrey Police in War Time', parts 1–4, Surrey in the Great War (https://www.surreyinthegreatwar.org.uk/story/a-policemans-lot-the-surrey-police-in-wartime-part-1-1914-1915/; https://www.surreyinthegreatwar.org.uk/story/a-policemans-lot-the-surrey-police-in-wartime-part-2-1916/; https://www.surreyinthegreatwar.org.uk/story/a-policemans-lot-the-surrey-police-in-wartime-part-3-1917/; https://www.surreyinthegreatwar.org.uk/story/a-policemans-lot-the-surrey-police-in-wartime-part-4-1918/). Police numbers can be found in the Chief Constable's reports to the Standing Joint Committee, SHC CC360/26-30.
18 SHC CC98/22/1 Reigate Borough Force Annual Reports, 1899–1929; M. Edwards, 'Reigate Borough Police in the Great War', Surrey in the Great War (https://www.surreyinthegreatwar.org.uk/story/reigate-borough-police-in-the-great-war/).
19 Examples are SHC 898/4/1-74 Holmwood Local Committee records, 1914–16; SHC 7543/2/1 Ashtead Local Emergency Committee papers, 1914–18; SHC 8261/13/4 Memorandum for Special Constables for Albury Parish in the event of invasion, 1914. See also M. Edwards, 'Special Constables in Surrey', Surrey in the Great War (https://www.surreyinthegreatwar.org.uk/story/special-constables/).
20 *Surrey Times and County Express*, 15.5.1915, 5b; *Surrey Herald*, 17.1.1919, 4b.
21 *Surrey Times and County Express*, 26.2.1916, 5c.
22 SHC 9117/Box 2 Papers relating to Hersham, Oatlands and Walton-on-Thames Special Constables, 1914–19, including memoir of Percy Webb.
23 L. Spindler, *Leatherhead in the Great War* (Pen and Sword, 2016), pp. 75–82; Atherton, *Dorking in the Great War*, p. 53.

24   Oakley, *Guildford in the Great War*, p. 165.
25   L. Spring, 'Surrey Volunteer Regiment', Surrey in the Great War (https://www.surrey-inthegreatwar.org.uk/subjects/military/army/volunteer-regiment/).
26   *Surrey Advertiser*, 29.5.1915, 9c; Atherton, *Dorking in the Great War*, pp. 95–96.
27   Imperial War Museum, Docs. 11335, Diary of Frederick Robinson, 1914–18, entries for 19.8.1914 and 14.6.1916; A. Gregory, *The Last Great War* (Cambridge, 2008), p. 238.
28   *Surrey Advertiser,* 31.8.1914, 1e.
29   *Ibid.*, 2.10.1916, 1c.
30   SHC 9117/Box 2 Documents relating to Hersham, Oatlands and Walton-on-Thames Special Constables, 1914–19, including Percy Webb's memoir.
31   Oakley, *Guildford in the Great War*, p. 158.
32   SHC CC98/1/4-5 Reports of Chief Constable, report of May 1917.
33   L. Thomas, 'Frith Hill POW Camp at Frimley, Surrey', Frimley and Camberley Great War Memorial (https://sites.google.com/site/frimleyandcamberley/frith-hill-p-o-w-camp-at-frimley; accessed 18.12.2018); *Surrey Advertiser*, 15.8.1914, p. 2.
34   'Frith Hill POW Camp', Picture Postcards from the Great War 1914–1918 (https://www.world-war1postcards.com/pow-camp.php; accessed 29.12.2018); *Surrey Advertiser*, 3.10.1914, 3e.
35   *Surrey Advertiser*, 10.10.1914, 7d.
36   See Surrey Heath Museum, 'George Kenner (1888–1971), German Artist and Internee', Surrey in the Great War (https://www.surreyinthegreatwar.org.uk/story/george-kenner/).
37   Thomas, 'Frith Hill POW Camp'.
38   *Surrey Advertiser*, 27.9.1916, 1c; *Surrey and Hants News*, 28.9.1916, 3d.
39   R. Bartlett, 'The Working Life of the Surrey Constabulary 1851–1992', Part 2, International Centre for the History of Crime, Policing and Justice (http://www.open.ac.uk/Arts/history-from-police-archives/RB1/Pt2/pt2TL191221.html; accessed 30.12.2018).
40   *Surrey Advertiser*, 30.9.1916, 5c.
41   SHC CC98/1/4-5 Reports of Chief Constable, September and December 1917.
42   *Ibid.*, 1918.
43   *Woking News and Mail*, 6.9.1918, 2c.
44   *Epsom Advertiser*, 21.2.1919, 1g.
45   '*The Epsom Advertiser* incorporating the *Epsom Observer*, June 27 1919', Epsom and Ewell History Explorer (http://www.epsomandewellhistoryexplorer.org.uk/Sgt_Green_Riot_1.pdf; accessed 5.3.2019).
46   Crime statistics can be found in the appendices to the Chief Constable's reports to the Standing Joint Committee, SHC CC360/26-30.
47   *Surrey Herald*, 7.6.1918, 2c.

Chapter 3

1   Ministry of Munitions (henceforth MOM), *History of the Ministry of Munitions*, 12 volumes in 11 (HMSO, 1922), I: *Industrial Mobilisation, Part 1*, pp. 13–15.
2   *Ibid.*, p. 134.
3   *Ibid.*, I, *Part 4*, p. 5.
4   *Ibid.*, I, *Part 1*, p. 24.
5   D. Kenyon, *First World War National Aircraft Factories: Archaeological, Architectural and Historic Review* (Historic England, 2015).
6   Surrey History Centre (SHC) holds significant archival material about Dennis Brothers Ltd under the reference 1463. See also L. Spring, 'Dennis Brothers of Guildford and World War I', Surrey in the Great War (https://www.surreyinthegreatwar.org.uk/story/dennis-brothers-and-ww1/).

7   For records of Drummond Brothers Ltd, see SHC 1550 & 5179; L. Spring, 'Drummond Broth-
     ers, Lathe and Machine Tool Makers of Guildford', Surrey in the Great War (https://www.
     surreyinthegreatwar.org.uk/story/drummond-brothers-lathe-and-machine-tool-makers-of-
     guildford/).

8   The author would like to thank David Hassard of the Kingston Aviation Centenary Project (https://
     www.kingstonaviation.org/) for supplying information about the Sopwith Aviation Company.

9   The National Archives (TNA) AIR 1/754/204/4/77 Air Ministry and RAF Records, Air
     Historical Branch Papers, RFC Military Wing, 'Establishment of R.F.C. Wireless School at
     Brooklands, 1915'; R.W. Mint, 'Communications: An International History of the Formative
     Years', History of Technology, Series 32 (Institution of Engineering & Technology, 2004).

10 M. Page, 'Lang Propeller Ltd of Weybridge', Surrey in the Great War (https://www.surrey-
     inthegreatwar.org.uk/story/lang-propeller-ltd-of-weybridge/).

11 History of MOM, VIII: Control of Industrial Capacity and Equipment, Part 3, pp. 26–28.

12 D. Kenyon, National Aircraft Factories (Historic England, 2015).

13 History of MOM, IX: Review of Munitions Supply, p. 120.

14 History of MOM, VIII, Appendix IV.

15 Spring, 'Dennis Brothers of Guildford'.

16 The Times, 20 January 1916, p. 3.

17 J.H. Rowe, Air, Road, Sea, Addlestone: Bleriot, Weymann, Plessy Works 1916–88 (D.M. & J.L.
     Barker, 1992).

18 TNA AIR 1/727/152/6 Air Ministry and RAF Records, Air Historical Branch Papers, The
     'Blériot' Machines 1906–15.

19 See further M. Edwards, 'Inside Martinsyde: an Aeroplane Factory during World War I', Surrey
     in the Great War (https://www.surreyinthegreatwar.org.uk/story/inside-martinsyde-an-aero-
     plane-factory-during-world-war-i/); M. Edwards, 'Elephants and Buzzards: the Contribution
     of Martinsyde Aeroplanes to the War in the Air', Surrey in the Great War (https://www.
     surreyinthegreatwar.org.uk/story/elephants-and-buzzards-the-contribution-of-martinsyde-
     aeroplanes-to-the-war-in-the-air/); and J. Hyams, 'Sydney Camm and Martinsyde Limited',
     Surrey in the Great War (https://www.surreyinthegreatwar.org.uk/story/sydney-camm-
     1893-1966-and-martinsyde-limited/).

20 'Weyburn Engineering Co', Grace's Guide to British Industrial History (https://www.graces-
     guide.co.uk/Weyburn_Engineering_Co).

21 History of MOM, II: General Organization for Munitions Supply, Part 1, pp. 100–101.

22 Ibid.

23 TNA AIR 1/2302/215/11 Air Ministry and RAF Records, Air Historical Branch Papers, Air-
     craft Production, Instructions and Correspondence of Aircraft Supply Committee, 1918–19.

24 Many sources were used in the collation of the material in this paragraph, including TNA AIR
     10/516 Air Ministry and RAF Records, Air Publications and Reports, Preliminary Notes on
     the A.B.C. 'Dragonfly' Engine, 1918 and TNA AVIA 6/4754 Ministry of Aviation Records,
     Royal Aircraft Factory Reports, Examination of A.B.C. 'Dragonfly' Engine, 1921.

25 'Eyre Smelting Co', Grace's Guide to British Industrial History (https://www.gracesguide.
     co.uk/Eyre_Smelting_Co).

26 History of MOM, IV: Supply of Labour, Department of Engineering, MOM, 1918 Directory of
     Manufacturers in Engineering and Allied Trades (Wyman and Sons Ltd, 1918), no. 7656.

27 Woking News and Mail, 31.1.1919, 8d-e.

28 Alcock and Brown's Atlantic crossing of 1919 was made in a Brooklands-built Vickers Vimy.

29 'National Aircraft Factory No 1', Grace's Guide to British Industrial History (https://www.
     gracesguide.co.uk/National_Aircraft_Factory_No_1).

30 TNA AIR 1/2302/215/10 Air Ministry and RAF Records, Air Historical Branch Papers, Air-
     craft Production, Output figures for airframes and engines 1914–18.

31   TNA AIR 1/2302/215/12 Air Ministry and RAF Records, Air Historical Branch Papers, Department of Aircraft Production, Correspondence and data 1914–18.
32   David Hassard, Kingston Aviation Centenary Project (https://www.kingstonaviation.org/), personal communication, 2018.
33   *Ibid.*
34   TNA AIR 2/1040 and 2/1041 Air Ministry and RAF records, Air Ministry Registered Files, Lang Propeller Designs: Payment of Royalty.
35   *History of MOM, I, Part 1*, p. 102.
36   TNA AIR 2/13/AS31125/18 Air Ministry and RAF Records, Air Ministry Registered Files, Insurance Policies, Claim for damage by fire to Aero Engines Ministry Property on premises of Gordon Watney and Co. Ltd.
37   For example, *Epsom Advertiser*, 24.1.1919, 1c.
38   *The Times*, 11.9.1920, 8.
39   *The Times*, 7.10.1921, 7.
40   TNA MUN 5/116/670/13 MOM, Munitions, Munitions Council Records, Committee paper on application by Lang Propeller Company for permission to prepare for post-war furniture manufacture, 1918.
41   Surrey data analysed by Barry Oliver from *1918 Directory of Manufacturers in Engineering and Allied Trades*. See 'Making Munitions in Surrey: Private Contractors and National Factories', Surrey in the Great War (https://www.surreyinthegreatwar.org.uk/story/making-munitions-in-surrey-private-contractors-and-national-factories/).

Chapter 4

1   Surrey History Centre (SHC) 9497/1-2 'The Eaton Cottage Herald'. See further, M. Page, 'A Family at War: The Eaton Cottage Herald', Surrey in the Great War (https://www.surreyinthegreatwar.org.uk/story/a-family-at-war-the-eaton-cottage-herald/).
2   *Surrey and Hants News*, 31.5.1917, 2d; *Woking News and Mail*, 11.1.1918, 1e.
3   Imperial War Museums (IWM) Docs.11335 Diary of Frederick A. Robinson [hereafter Robinson diary], 1.1.1918.
4   V. Brittain, *Testament of Youth* (Victor Gollancz, 1933), Chapter 1.
5   E. Parker, *Memory Looks Forward* (Seeley, Service, 1937).
6   R. Macaulay, 'Picnic: July 1917'; C. Garrard, 'Listening to the Guns – "Picnic: July 1917" by Rose Macaulay', Surrey in the Great War (https://www.surreyinthegreatwar.org.uk/story/listening-to-the-guns-picnic-july-1917-by-rose-macaulay/).
7   Robinson diary, 29.9.1917.
8   *Ibid.*, 21.5.1916.
9   SHC 6094/2/1 *Surrey Teachers' Quarterly*, September 1914. See further, J. Hyams, 'James Chuter Ede, Politician, Educationist and Soldier (1882–1965)', Surrey in the Great War (https://www.surreyinthegreatwar.org.uk/story/james-chuter-ede-politician-educationist-and-soldier-1882-1965/).
10   SHC 9800/3/11 Godstone United Benefice Records, Godstone Parish Magazines 1908–16, September 1914 issue.
11   SHC 1786/6/1/4 West Byfleet Parish Records, Byfleet Parish Magazines 1914, September 1914 issue.
12   SHC GUHT/57/7/1 Letter of Bishop of Winchester, 5.8.1914, in Holy Trinity Church, Guildford, Scrapbook.
13   Robinson diary: 4.8.1917; 6.10.1917; 6.9.1914; 28.12.1915; 14.6.1916; 29.7.1917; 8.9.1916.
14   Sutton High School Magazine, autumn 1914, World War I School Archives (http://www.worldwar1schoolarchives.org/sutton-school/; accessed 1.2.2019); S. James and M. Page,

'Dora Black; A Volunteer with the Women's Emergency Corps', Surrey in the Great War (https://www.surreyinthegreatwar.org.uk/story/dora-black-a-volunteer-with-the-womens-emergency-corps/).

15 *Surrey Times and County Express*, 30.4.1915, 1e; *Surrey Mirror*, 4.12.1917, 3b and 9.7.1915, 3c.

16 *Surrey Times and County Express*, 3.3.1916, 5c.

17 C. Declercq and H. Baker, 'The Pelabon Munitions works and the Belgian village on the Thames: Community and Forgetfulness in Outer-metropolitan Suburbs', *Immigrants & Minorities*, 34 (2) (2016), pp. 151–170.

18 The National Archives (TNA) MUN 3/235 Ministry of Munitions Sunday Labour Return.

19 Robinson diary, 30.9.1917.

20 *Surrey Mirror*, 21.9.1917, 7e.

21 SHC 1786/6/1/4 Byfleet Parish Magazines, 1914, December 1914 issue.

22 SHC P2/7/1 St Peter's Chertsey Parish Records, Scrapbook of the Women's War Work Association, Chertsey, 1916–21.

23 W.H. Oakley, *Guildford in the Great War* (Billings and Son, Ltd, 1934), pp. 120–24.

24 SHC 9800/3/11 Godstone Parish Magazines 1908–16, February 1916 issue.

25 K. Atherton, *Dorking in the Great War* (Pen & Sword, 2014), pp. 84–85.

26 SHC 8909/8/1/4 Stoke D'Abernon Parish Records, Stoke D'Abernon and Oxshott Parish Magazines, 1911–19, March 1917 issue.

27 Robinson diary, 19.10.1916.

28 Oakley, *Guildford in the Great War*, p. 141.

29 Robinson diary, 18.11.1914, 3.6.1918, 5.4.1916, 14.8.1918.

30 *Ibid.*, 30.7.1918.

31 Oakley, *Guildford in the Great War*, pp. 135–39.

32 SHC 9800/3/12 Godstone Parish Magazines 1917–24, issues of July 1917, July 1918.

33 SHC CC1243/1/1/2 Whyteleafe School Records, Whyteleafe Council School (Infants) Logbook, 1906–40.

34 SHC CC360/30 Surrey County Council Reports 1918, Education Committee Report, 12.3.1918.

35 SHC CC42/1/3 Perry Hill Council School, Worplesdon, Records 1875–1977, Logbook 1904–33.

36 N. Watson, *The Royal Grammar School Guildford: An Illustrated History* (James & James Ltd, 2004), p. 53.

37 SHC CC360/30 Surrey County Council Reports 1918, Education Committee Report, 12.11.1918.

38 See S. James and M. Page, 'A Munitionette in the National Projectile Factory, Lancaster', Surrey in the Great War (https://www.surreyinthegreatwar.org.uk/story/a-munitionette-in-the-national-projectile-factory-lancaster/).

39 Sutton High School Magazines 1914–19 (http://www.worldwar1schoolarchives.org/sutton-school/; accessed 1.2.2019).

40 SHC CC360/29 Surrey County Council Reports 1917, Education Committee Report, 13.3.1917.

41 Reigate Grammar School Magazines, 1914–19, via World War I School Archives (http://www.worldwar1schoolarchives.org/reigate-grammar-school/; accessed 1.2.2019). See further, M. Edwards, 'Reigate Grammar School for Boys and its Officer Training Corps', Surrey in the Great War (https://www.surreyinthegreatwar.org.uk/story/reigate-grammar-school-for-boys-and-its-officer-training-corps/).

42 A. Seldon and D. Walsh, *Public Schools in the Great War: The Generation Lost* (Pen & Sword Military, 2013), Appendix.

43 *Surrey Times and County Express*, 25.2.1916, 4c; *Surrey Advertiser*, 1.11.1916, 1c.

44 With thanks to Martin Stilwell for contributing his research to this section on Surrey's food supply.

45   I. Beckett, *Home Front 1914–1918: How Britain Survived the Great War* (The National Archives, 2006), p. 111.

46   *Surrey Mirror*, 17.8.1917, 3e; *Surrey Herald*, 11.1.1918, 5a. The records of the Weybridge Urban District Food Control Committee, 1917–21, are held at SHC as Ac1229/2/31.

47   *Surrey Comet*, 22.12.1917, 7e.

48   S. Woodbridge, 'When Food was Scarce: Memories of a Female Control Officer in World War One', Surrey in the Great War (https://www.surreyinthegreatwar.org.uk/story/when-food-was-scarce-memories-of-a-female-control-officer-in-world-war-one/).

49   Oakley, *Guildford in the Great War*, p. 66.

50   *Dorking and Leatherhead Advertiser*, 5.1.1918, 5b.

51   Oakley, *Guildford in the Great War*, pp. 70–72.

52   SHC 9496/1 Rose Ponting Papers, Letters 1915–19, 6.10.1917.

53   Robinson diary: 3.1.1917; 7.4.1917; 30.12.1917; 26.7.1917.

54   SHC 9496/1 Rose Ponting Letters 1915–19, 1.6.1917.

55   *Surrey Herald*, 4.1.1918, 4e; *Surrey Mirror*, 8.2.1918, 2b.

56   Oakley, *Guildford in the Great War*, p. 74.

57   SHC 9496/1 Rose Ponting Letters 1915–19, 23.11.1917.

58   Oakley, *Guildford in the Great War*, pp. 74–77.

59   Robinson diary: 15.5.1918; 7.7.1918.

60   *Epsom Advertiser*, 6.4.1917, 1d.

61   SHC 8909/8/1/4 Stoke D'Abernon and Oxshott Parish Magazines 1911–19, issue of March 1918.

62   SHC Ac1321/7/3 Weybridge Urban District Council food advice pamphlet, from papers of Weybridge War Distress Fund, 1914–21. See J. Hawker, 'The Best Food for Nourishing Dishes', Surrey in the Great War (https://www.surreyinthegreatwar.org.uk/story/the-best-food-for-nourishing-dishes/).

63   SHC QS2/1/105 Surrey Quarter Sessions Order Book, pp. 172 and 198.

64   Robinson diary: 28.12.1917; 2.2.1916.

65   *Surrey Herald*, 15.2.1918, 6b; 11.10.1918, 3c; 6.12.1918, 6c.

66   *Surrey Times and County Express*, 16.8.1918, 3a.

67   *Surrey Mirror*, 7.2.1919, 5a.

68   SHC 6520/28 Hester Godfrey Papers, Printed notice from the Board of Trade, Coal Mines Department, concerning coal rationing, 1918. See also J. Hawker, 'Saving Coal at Home in WWI', Surrey in the Great War (https://www.surreyinthegreatwar.org.uk/story/saving-coal-at-home-in-ww1/).

69   Robinson diary, 13.10.1917.

70   *Ibid.*, 26.12.1916; 28.12.1917.

71   *Ibid.*, 23.7.1918.

72   *Ibid.*, 18.11.1916.

73   Reigate Grammar School Magazine, December 1918, World War I School Archives (http://www.worldwar1schoolarchives.org/reigate-grammar-school/; accessed 1.2.2019). See also M. Edwards, 'Forms, Forms and more Forms: Buying Margarine in 1918', Surrey in the Great War (https://www.surreyinthegreatwar.org.uk/story/forms-forms-and-more-forms-buying-margarine-in-1918/).

74   Robinson diary, 26.8.1918.

75   SHC 9496/1 Rose Ponting Letters 1915–19, 23.8.1918.

76   Oakley, *Guildford in the Great War*, p. 74. The 'YMCA' is the Young Men's Christian Association.

77   SHC 9800/3/12 Godstone Parish Magazines 1917–24, January 1918.

78   SHC GUHT/57/7/1 Letter of Bishop of Winchester, 5.8.1914, in Holy Trinity, Guildford, Scrapbook.

79   SHC 1786/6/1/4 Byfleet Parish Magazines 1914, December issue.

80 SHC 1925/2/19 Godalming Congregational Church Records, Magazines 1914, September issue.

81 *Surrey Herald*, 25.1.1918, 3d.

82 SHC 2151/5/1 Alwyne Road Wimbledon, Congregational Church Minutes, 1909–20.

83 *Surrey Advertiser*, 28.2.1916, 4a. See further J. Hyams, 'The Society of Dependents or Cokelers', Surrey in the Great War (https://www.surreyinthegreatwar.org.uk/story/the-society-of-dependents-or-cokelers-in-shamley-green/).

84 SHC 9800/3/11 Godstone Parish Magazines 1908–16, November 1916 issue.

85 Robinson diary, 15.10.1916.

86 *Farnham Herald*, 8.7.1916, 8c.

87 Atherton, *Dorking in the Great War*, p. 155.

88 Robinson diary, 13.10.1918.

89 SHC CC171/1/15-16 Surrey County Council Reports, Annual Reports of the County Medical Officer of Health, 1917–19.

90 SHC 9496/1 Rose Ponting Letters, 1915–19, 8.11.1918.

91 *Epsom Advertiser*, 25.10.1918, 1f.

92 *Surrey Comet*, 23.10.1918, 5c.

93 *Surrey and Hants News*, 9.5.1918, 2c and 19.4.1918, 3c.

94 SHC WIT/16/37 All Saints' Witley Parish Records, Witley Parish Magazines, 1918–21, December 1918 issue.

95 Robinson diary, 11.11.1918; 12.11.1918.

Chapter 5

1 1911 England & Wales Census, Online Historical Population Reports, Table 61: proportion per 10,000 of females aged 10 years and upwards engaged in certain groups of occupations, 1911, Histpop – The Online Historical Population Reports Website (http://www.histpop.org/; accessed 11.10.2018).

2 According to the 1911 England & Wales Census, just 0.2% of Surrey's working women then worked in agriculture.

3 G. Braybon and P. Summerfield, 'Women before 1914', *Out of the Cage: Women's Experiences in Two World Wars* (Pandora, 1987), pp. 11–29.

4 'Special Report as to the Establishment of a County War Agricultural Committee', 11.10.1915, *Surrey County Council Reports* (1915), 1361–73 (p. 1363).

5 *Dorking and Leatherhead Advertiser*, 10.4.1915, 4h.

6 Surrey History Centre (SHC) 3410/2/1/2 Surrey Federation of Women's Institutes Records, Surrey Women's Agricultural Committee minutes 1917–20, Report of training arranged by SWAC 1916–19, p. 1.

7 *Surrey and Hants News*, 11.2.1916, 3c.

8 SHC G173/212/16/11 Onslow Family Records, letter from J.M. Kelly, no date; SHC G173/212/16/6 Onslow Family Records, letter from George Ewing to Messrs Messenger & Morgan, 23.3.1916.

9 *Dorking and Leatherhead Advertiser*, 20.1.1917, 7c.

10 *Surrey Mirror*, 27.6.1916, 2b.

11 *Surrey Advertiser*, 23.4.1917, 2b.

12 *Ibid*. Film of the event is held by Screen Archive South East (title ID 1291; collection ID 198; http://screenarchive.brighton.ac.uk/detail/1291/).

13 SHC 8488/1 Florence Winifred Hooker Papers, *Women's Land Army Handbook*, 1918–19, p. 5.

14 'Fourth Report of the County War Agricultural Committee', 13.11.1917, Surrey County Council Reports, (1917), 937–60 (p. 941).

15   SHC G173/212/35 Onslow Family Records, letter from Miss C.L. Close to Lady Onslow, 16.4.1916.

16   SHC G173/212/61 Onslow Family Records, letter from Miss C.L. Close to Lady Onslow, 8.5.1916.

17   SHC 3410/2/1/2 Surrey Women's Agricultural Committee minutes 1917–20, minutes of 5 November, 10 November, 12 November and 20 November 1918.

18   'Sixth Report of the Surrey County War Agricultural Committee', 12.11.1918, *Surrey County Council Reports* (1918), pp. 893–917 (p. 911).

19   SHC 3410/2/1/2 Surrey Women's Agricultural Committee Minutes 1917–20, minutes of 22.6.1920.

20   Ministry of Munitions, *1918 Directory of Manufacturers in Engineering and Allied Trades* (Wyman and Sons Ltd) via Grace's Guide (https://www.gracesguide.co.uk/1918_Directory_of_Manu-facturers_in_Engineering_and_Allied_Trades; accessed 1.11.2018). See also M. Page, 'Making Munitions in Surrey: Private Contractors and National Factories', Surrey in the Great War (https://www.surreyinthegreatwar.org.uk/story/making-munitions-in-surrey-private-con-tractors-and-national-factories/).

21   David Hassard, personal communication, 17.8.2018. David Hassard is one of the founders of the Kingston Aviation Centenary Project: https://www.kingstonaviation.org/.

22   Historic England's collections include photographs of women undertaking such tasks in an aviation factory in Lancaster (https://historicengland.org.uk/whats-new/first-world-war-home-front/what-we-already-know/land/aircraft-factories/).

23   Ministry of Munitions, *1918 Directory of Manufacturers.*

24   Braybon and Summerfield, *Out of the Cage*, pp. 34–39.

25   *Ibid.*

26   *Surrey Mirror*, 26.10.1917, 4b.

27   *Surrey Advertiser,* 3.2.1917, 8a.

28   'How to Dress for Munition Making', Imperial War Museums MUN. v/1, LBY K. 5057 (1917).

29   *Surrey Comet*, 13.4.1918, 4d.

30   *Surrey Advertiser*, 2.10.1918, 1d.

31   *Ibid.*, 21.7.1917, 8d and 29.9.1917, 8d.

32   *Ibid.*, 3.2.1917, 5e.

33   *Ibid.*, 17.2.1917, 4d.

34   *Surrey Herald*, 24.1.1919, 4c. The article describes in detail the lady carpenters' work and living conditions in northern France.

35   *Ibid.*, 31.1.1919, 4b.

36   *Surrey Advertiser*, 5.12.1917, 4d.

37   *Dorking and Leatherhead Advertiser*, 13.10.1917, 4a, b. WAAC was formed in early 1917; it later became Queen Mary's Army Auxiliary Corps.

38   Elisabeth Shipton, *Female Tommies: The Frontline Women of the First World War* (The History Press, 2014), is a good source for women and the military.

39   SHC SGW/9 Rose Kate Overington Autograph Book, 1918–1945.

40   *Surrey Comet*, 8.3.1919, 7b; Casualty Database, Commonwealth War Graves Commission (https://www.cwgc.org/find-war-dead/casualty/401774/broad,-annetta-ellen-(netta)/).

41   *Surrey Advertiser*, 22.2.1919, 5e; Casualty Database, Commonwealth War Graves Commission (https://www.cwgc.org/find-war-dead/casualty/503380/luker,-doris-mary/).

42   SHC P2/7/1 St Peter's Chertsey Parish Records, Scrapbook of the Women's War Work Asso-ciation, Chertsey, 1916–21. Clipping from *Surrey Herald*, 27.12.1918, 2f.

43   SHC P2/7/1 Scrapbook of the Women's War Work Association, Chertsey, 25 February and 1 September 1916.

44   *Ibid.*, 8 December 1916.
45   *Ibid.*, 8 August 1919.
46   SHC 2572/123/1-14 Farrer Papers, Papers of Dorking War Hospital Supply Depot, 1916–17.
47   *Ibid.*
48   *Farnham Herald*, 12.5.1917, 4b and 19.5.1917, 4a.
49   *Surrey Comet*, 9.6.1915, 5e.
50   *Surrey Times and County Express*, 1.1.1916, 6g.
51   *Surrey and Hants News*, 19.11.1915, 2c.
52   *Surrey Comet*, 21.8.1918, 5c and 31.8.1918, 8c.
53   Susan Grayzel has discussed women's morality in WWI in *Women and the First World War* (Routledge, 2013), pp. 62–78.
54   Angela Woollacott, 'Khaki Fever and its Control: Gender, Class, Age and Sexual Morality on the British Home Front in the First World War', *Journal of Contemporary History*, 29, No. 2, 1994, pp. 325–47.
55   Clare Langley-Hawthorne, 'The Women's Police Service during the First World War' (http://www.clarelangleyhawthorne.com/pdf/WPS_Background.pdf; accessed 16.10.2018).
56   *Surrey Advertiser*, 4.12.1916, 3c.
57   *Surrey Comet*, 10.11.1915, 3b.
58   *Ibid.*
59   *Surrey Comet*, 3.3.1917, 8c.
60   SHC CC98/1/5 Surrey Constabulary Records 1851–1968, Reports of the Chief Constable 1916–1923, report of 5.12.1918.
61   *Ibid.*, 10.3.1919.
62   *Surrey Advertiser*, 9.5.1917, 1d.
63   SHC QRWS/30/ELIAA/2 Papers of A. Elias Morgan, Scrapbook, 'The Great War', p. 24; *Surrey Advertiser*, 5.7.1916, 1c.

Chapter 6

1   Thomas Middleton KBE, *Food Production in War* (Oxford University Press, 1923), p. 53.
2   *Ibid.*, p. 114.
3   *Ibid.*, p. 106.
4   *Ibid.*, p. 261.
5   'Fourth Report of the County War Agricultural Committee', 13.11.1917, *Surrey County Council Reports* (1917), pp. 937–60 (p. 956). See also S. Woodbridge, 'Land and Home: The Campaign to encourage more Land Cultivation in Surrey', Surrey in the Great War (https://www.surreyinthegreatwar.org.uk/story/land-and-home-the-campaign-to-encourage-more-land-cultivation-in-surrey/).
6   *Surrey Herald*, 11.1.1918, 5a.
7   'Third Report of the County War Agricultural Committee', 13.3.1917, Surrey County Council Reports (1917), pp. 287–301 (p. 293).
8   'Fourth Report of the County War Agricultural Committee', 13.11.1917, p. 951.
9   *Ibid.*, p. 943.
10   'Sixth Report of the County War Agricultural Committee', 12.11.1918, Surrey County Council Reports (1918), pp. 893–917 (p. 907).
11   The National Archives (TNA), Ministry of Agriculture, Fisheries and Food and predecessors: Statistics Divisions: Parish Summaries of Agricultural Returns, Surrey, 1914–19, MAF 68/-.
12   SHC 6200/ADD/Box 69 Records of Paine & Brettell Solicitors of Chertsey, Chertsey Rural District War Agricultural Committee Minutes 1917, meeting 3 March 1917.
13   For details see M. Stilwell, 'Food v Golf in WWI', Surrey in the Great War (https://www.surreyinthegreatwar.org.uk/story/food-v-golf-in-ww1-the-battle-of-the-golf-courses/).

14   *Illustrated Sporting and Dramatic News*, 21.4.1917, 209b.
15   'Fifth Report of the County War Agricultural Committee', 12.2.1918, *Surrey County Council Reports* (1918), pp. 441–60.
16   The data on these courses were collated by the author from various reports of the Surrey County WAC, 1917 onwards.
17   See further, M. Stilwell, 'Farming in World War I – Surrey's Contribution', Surrey in the Great War (https://www.surreyinthegreatwar.org.uk/story/farming-in-world-war-1-surreys-contribution/).

Chapter 7

1   'British Red Cross Society Surrey Branch, Second Annual Report, 1914' via Surrey in the Great War (https://www.surreyinthegreatwar.org.uk/story/british-red-cross-society-surrey-branch-annual-report-1914; accessed 11.12.2018); British Red Cross (BRC) Museum and Archives BRC/2/3/7/7 *Surrey Branch, British Red Cross Society. Historical Summary, April 1907 to 31 December 1953* (British Red Cross, 1954).
2   BRC Archives BRC/2/3/7/7, p. 19. By the end of the war there were sixty-six. See 'List of Auxiliary Hospitals during the First World War', Red Cross (https://vad.redcross.org.uk/Auxiliary-Hospitals, accessed 13.12.2018).
3   Surrey History Centre (SHC) 1688/1/1 Records of Thorncombe Military Hospital, Annual Reports 1914–19, report of 1914–15. See also M. Stilwell, 'Thorncombe Red Cross Military Hospital, Bramley', Surrey in the Great War (https://www.surreyinthegreatwar.org.uk/story/thorncombe-red-cross-military-hospital-bramley/).
4   SHC 1688/1/5 Records of Thorncombe Military Hospital, Annual Reports 1914–19, report of 1918–19.
5   SHC 5337/10/52/66 Onslow Family Records, letter from Lord Onslow to Lady Onslow, 6.7.1915.
6   SHC G173/1/6 Onslow Family Records, 'Clandon as a Military Hospital, 1914–1919', p. 1464. This document was clearly written by Violet herself, and then someone (presumably Onslow) edited it, changing personal pronouns from 'I' to 'she'.
7   *Ibid.*, p. 1468.
8   SHC 8792/2/18 Clandon Park Military Hospital Correspondence and Papers 1914–19, letter from Mary Pike to Lady Onslow, 1915.
9   SHC 5337/10/52/89 Onslow Family Records, letter from Lord Onslow to Lady Onslow, 5.8.1915.
10   SHC 8792/2/22–24 Clandon Park Military Hospital Correspondence and Papers 1914–19, letter from Mrs Locke King to Lady Onslow, 30.3.1915. The Cobham branch did eventually transfer to Lady Onslow.
11   SHC G173/1/6 'Clandon as a Military Hospital', p. 1482.
12   *Ibid.*, pp. 1557–58.
13   SHC 6857/File 11 Health Authorities' Publications, London County Council Asylums Committee, *Annual Report of the Council 1915–19, II: Asylums and Mental Deficiency*, p. 19.
14   Sir Marriott Cooke and C. Hubert Bond, *History of the Asylum War Hospitals in England and Wales* (HMSO, 1920), p. 7.
15   SHC 6857/File 10 *Annual Report of the London County Council 1914*, p. 36.
16   *Ibid.*
17   SHC 6857/File 11, p. 20; Cooke and Bond, *History of the Asylum War Hospitals*, pp. 14–15. See further, K. Arnould, '"Where possible, a change of clothes": Horton Asylum's forgotten war dead', Surrey in the Great War (https://www.surreyinthegreatwar.org.uk/story/where-possible-a-change-of-clothes-horton-asylums-forgotten-war-dead/).

18   SHC 6857/File 11, pp. 22–23.

19   Cooke and Bond, *History of the Asylum War Hospitals*, p. 45.

20   *Ibid.*

21   *Ibid.*, p. 39.

22   For more about the evacuation of soldiers from the battlefield, see Emily Mayhew, *Wounded: From Battlefield to Blighty 1914–1918* (Bodley Head, 2013).

23   *Woking News and Mail*, 16.4.1915, 7e.

24   *Ibid.*, 4.6.1915, 2f.

25   Cooke and Bond, *History of the Asylum War Hospitals*, p. 67.

26   *Surrey Advertiser*, 16.9.1918, 3e.

27   Cooke and Bond, *History of the Asylum War Hospitals*, pp. 64–65.

28   BRC Archives, T2 Van X/142 Memoir of Margaret E. van Straubenzee while a VAD at Clandon Park Hospital, p. 42. An extract of Margaret's memoir is also available at Surrey History Centre: SHC Zg/60/1.

29   Cooke and Bond, *History of the Asylum War Hospitals*, p. 45.

30   *Ibid.*, p. 45.

31   SHC 3043/7/9/1/35 Records of Brookwood Hospital 1867–1904, Brookwood Casebook 1913–15, p. 165.

32   *Ibid.*, p. 189.

Chapter 8

1   Surrey History Centre (SHC) 9667/1/1 Roll of voluntarily attested men prior to November 1915, Weybridge, undated.

2   SHC COH/9/3 Coldharbour Roll of Honour, undated.

3   SHC PC/64/ALB2/87 Hale Parish War Shrine, dedicated 30.12.1916, undated [*c.* 1917].

4   SHC 9800/3/11 St Nicholas Church, Godstone, parish magazines 1908–16, February 1916 issue.

5   *Ibid.*, November 1916 issue.

6   SHC 2337/13/8 List of ex-servicemen from Ham invited to the Welcome Home dinner, 1920.

7   SHC J/553/1 *The Journal of the East Surrey Regiment*, No. 22, November 1924, Armistice Sunday address.

8   E.D. Mackerness (ed.), *The Journals of George Sturt 1890–1927* (Cambridge University Press, 1967), Vol. 2, 11 November 1919 entry (p. 812).

9   *Surrey Advertiser*, 1.3.1919, 3d.

10   *Ibid.*, 3.5.1919, 7d.

11   SHC 3148/9/4 Invitation from All Saints' Church Kingston to a Welcome Home, 13 November 1919.

12   SHC 8591/1/1 Horsell Parish Magazine 1915–1925, January 1920 issue, p. 1; *Woking News and Mail,* 12.12.1919, 5f.

13   SHC 6520/64 Cranleigh Peace Celebrations Circular Letter, 12 July 1919.

14   SHC 1593/2/2 Henry R. Dunce Papers, Programme for Godalming concert to welcome home men who served in HM Forces, 26 July 1919.

15   H. Keatley Moore, *Croydon and the Great War* (Corporation of Croydon, 1920), p. 241.

16   SHC 1786/6/1/9 Byfleet Parish Magazines 1920, December 1920 issue.

17   SHC 5337/9/(31) Onslow Family Records, letter from Lord Onslow to Lord Midleton, 10.12.1917; SHC GU173/77/165 letter from Lord Midleton to Lord Onslow, 23.10.1920; *Surrey Herald*, 8.11.1918, 4d.

18   *Surrey Advertiser,* 8.2.1919, 4d and 15.2.1919, 5b; *Surrey Mirror*, 28.3.1919, 7b.

19   *Surrey Herald,* 15.2.1918, 6d.

20   *Surrey Advertiser*, 19.4.1919, 5e.

21   SHC 5337/9/(31) Onslow Family Records, letter from Lord Midleton to Lord Onslow, 8.8.1917; G. Wootton *The Politics of Influence. British Ex-servicemen, Cabinet Decisions and Cultural Change (1917–1957)* (Routledge, 1963), p. 87. See also S. Woodbridge, 'A "bond of mutual help": The Comrades of the Great War organisation in Kingston and Surbiton', Surrey in the Great War (https://www.surreyinthegreatwar.org.uk/story/a-bond-of-mutual-help-the-comrades-of-the-great-war-organisation-in-kingston-and-surbiton/).

22   SHC 2442/2 Mickleham Parish Council Minute Book, 1909–26, 15.3.1920, f. 164.

23   SHC 3148/9/4 Invitation from All Saints' Church, Kingston to a Welcome Home.

24   A. Howkins, *The Death of Rural England* (Routledge, 2003) p. 20; B. Bushaway 'Name upon Name: The Great War and Remembrance' in R. Porter (ed.), *Myths of the English* (Blackwell, 1992), pp. 136–67 (p. 142).

25   SHC HO/10/22 (1) Holmwood War Memorial Committee Minute Book, 1920–22, 27.1.1920.

26   SHC 8591/1/1 St Mary's Horsell Parish Magazines 1915–25, September 1919 issue, pp. 3–4.

27   SHC 3093/4/1 Churt Recreation Ground Records 1918–79, Minutes of Meeting of 'Returned Service Men', 18.2.1919.

28   SHC 6296/1/1/45 Horley War Memorial Committee Minute Book 1919–22, 3.5.1921.

29   *Surrey Herald,* 15.11.1918, 4d; *Surrey Advertiser*, 20.5.1922, 3e; T. Skelton and G. Gliddon, *Lutyens and the Great War* (Frances Lincoln Ltd, 2008), p. 148.

30   'Epsom – St Martin's Church', Returned from the Front (http://thereturned.co.uk/crosses/epsom; accessed 23.8.2018).

31   'Ranmore – St Barnabas', Returned from the Front (http://thereturned.co.uk/crosses/ranmore; accessed 23.8.2018); A. Mee, *Surrey* (Hodder and Stoughton, 1938), p. 252; Ranmore War Memorial, The Cubitt Chapel (http://ranmorewarmemorial.info/st.barnabas-church/the-cubitt-chapel; accessed 11.11.18).

32   K. Grieves, 'Commemorating the Fallen: The Lord Lieutenant's Soldier Sons in the First World War and the Making of the Memorial Chapel at St Barnabas Church, Ranmore', *Surrey History* 6 (2) (2000), pp. 107–24 (pp. 116–19).

33   L. Weaver, *Memorials and Monuments Old and New: Two Hundred Subjects chosen from Seven Centuries* (*Country Life*, 1915), p. 23.

34   *Ibid.*, pp. 38, 73, 161, 356; A.L. Baldry, 'Wall Tablets and Memorials by British Sculptors', *The Studio*, 66 (273) (1915), 186–96 (pp. 192–94).

35   SHC HO/10/22(6) and (1) The Holmwood, Photograph of War Memorial Tablet and Dedication Programme, 9.10.1921.

36   Royal Mail Group Memorial Database, Croydon and Epsom Post Offices Rolls of Honour (https://www.royalmailmemorials.com/memorial/croydon-post-office-war-memorial and https://www.royalmailmemorials.com/memorial/epsom-war-memorial; accessed 6.8.2018).

37   '9th Guildford Congregational Scout Troop WWI', Imperial War Museum War Memorials Register (http://www.iwm.org.uk/memorials/item/memorial/23305; accessed 19.11.2018). M. Nairn, 'Memorial to Guildford's 9th Congregational Scout Troop', Surrey in the Great War (https://www.surreyinthegreatwar.org.uk/story/memorial-to-guildfords-9th-congregational-scout-troop/).

38   *Surrey Advertiser*, 25.1.1919, 7d (a parishioner's letter quoted by the Vicar of Horsell).

39   J. Winter, *Sites of Memory, Sites of Mourning* (Cambridge University Press, 1995), p. 92; A. Borg, *War Memorials: From Antiquity to the Present* (Leo Cooper, 1991), p. 93

40   Christ Church Cross, Brockham, personal observation, 5.8.2018.

41   A. Mee, *Enchanted Land* (Hodder and Stoughton, 1936), p. 144.

42   St Peter and St Paul Church, West Clandon, personal observation, 29.8.2018.

43   SHC 8026/3/6 Plan of proposed memorial cross for St John's Church, Dormansland. On Celtic crosses see Borg, *War Memorials*, p. 8 and Weaver, *Memorials and Monuments*, p. 394.

44   On the medieval cross see A. Vallance, *Old Crosses and Lychgates* (Batsford, undated [1920]), p. 42; R. Blomfield, *Memoirs of an Architect* (Macmillan, 1932), p. 175; Weaver, *Memorials and Monuments*, p. 398.

45   SHC 7185/11/1 Bletchingley Parish, Unveiling and dedication of the Memorial Cross, 1921.

46   St John the Baptist Churchyard Cross, Kingston Vale, personal observation, 13.9.2018.

47   Mee, *Surrey*, p. 41; Skelton and Gliddon, *Lutyens and the Great War*, p. 166.

48   Historic England, 'National Collection of Lutyens War Memorials Listed', Historic England (http://historicengland.org/whats-new/news/lutyens-war-memorials; accessed 29.8.2018).

49   SHC SyAS 95/5 J.A. Gibbs, 'Inscriptions and Graves in Abinger Church and Churchyard', compiled 1934–39, with author's annotations June 1946; J.A. Gibbs, *Abinger Church* (Abinger, 3rd edition, 1946), p. 18; Historic England, 'Abinger Common War Memorial', list entry 1028839 (https://historicengland.org.uk/listing/the-list/list-entry/1028839; accessed 29.8.2018).

50   Skelton and Gliddon, *Lutyens and the Great War*, p. 148.

51   Blomfield, *Memoirs*, p. 179; P. Longworth, *The Unending Vigil* (Leo Cooper, 1967 [2003]), p. 36.

52   Blomfield, *Memoirs*, pp. 171–72.

53   SHC 2118/1/18 Order of Ceremony for unveiling of Cross of Sacrifice at St Jude's Cemetery, Englefield Green, 10.11.1929.

54   'Reigate War Memorial Cross', IWM War Memorials Register (http://www.iwm.org.uk/memorials/item/memorial/61186; accessed 19.11.2018).

55   Blomfield, *Memoirs*, p. 180.

56   'Design for Muslim Burial Ground, Woking', British Library Untold Lives Blog (British Library, 2016) (via https://blogs.bl.uk/untoldlives/2016/03/designs-for-the-muslim-burial-ground-woking.html; accessed 26.11.2018); 'Woking's Muslim Burial Ground', Exploring Surrey's Past (https://www.exploringsurreyspast.org.uk/themes/places/surrey/woking/woking/woking_muslim_burial_ground/; accessed 26.11.2018).

57   SHC Z/454/1/4 Correspondence of Councillor M.I. Raja, Woking Borough Council, and Shah Jahan Mosque regarding the history and repair of the Muslim Burial Ground; *Surrey Times and County Express*, 4.6.1915, 3g.

58   V. Ware, 'From War Grave to Peace Garden: Muslim Soldiers, Militarised Multiculture and Cultural Heritage', *Journal of War and Cultural Studies*, 10 (4) (2017), 287–304 (p. 297).

59   W.R. Lethaby, 'Memorials of the Fallen: Service or Sacrifice?', *The Hibbert Journal*, 17 (4) (1918–19), 621–25 (p. 625).

60   SHC P39/1/2 Capel Parish Council Minute Book 1913–36, meeting of 4.4.1921.

61   SHC 6296/1/1/45 Horley Town Council Records, War Memorial Committee Minute Book 1919–22, meetings 29.4.1919, 16.11.1920.

62   SHC 3093/4/1 Churt Recreation Ground Records 1918–79, Minutes of Public Meetings 21.11.1918 and 3.12.1918.

63   Letter, T.C. Farrer, 'A Permanent War Memorial', *The Times*, 15.7.1919, p. 8.

64   'Purley Hospital Extension', IWM War Memorials Register (http://www.iwm.org.uk/memorials/item/memorial/769; accessed 19.11.2018); Borg, *War Memorials*, pp. 139–40.

65   SHC 6818/3/8 Reigate and Redhill Hospital Correspondence 1919–20, letter from B.K. Field, Secretary, to A. Smith, Honorary Secretary, War Memorial, 23.8.1919.

66   A. Yapp, *Told in the Huts: The YMCA Gift Book* (Jarrold & Sons [*c.* 1916]), pp. 18–19; L. Weaver, *Village Clubs and Halls* (Country Life, 1920), p. 2; *Woking News and Mail*, 22.6.1917, 4c.

67   *Surrey Advertiser*, 14.6.1919, 5d.

68   Westcott Local History Group, *The History of Westcott and Milton* (Westcott Local History Group, 2000), p. 46.

69   SHC 2572/1/85 Farrer Letters and Papers. Programme, Forest Green Dedication of Seat of Remembrance, 19 September 1925.

70   G. Jekyll, *Old English Household Life* (Batsford, revised and enlarged by S.R. Jones, 1939), p. 5.

71   C. Williams-Ellis, *Lawrence Weaver* (Geoffrey Bles, 1933), p. 53; 'Notes', *The Architectural Journal*, 37 (7), 8 February 1930.

72   Williams-Ellis, *Lawrence Weaver*, p. 71.

73   Historic England, *Domestic Housing for Disabled Veterans 1900–2014* (Historic England, 2016) (https://content.historicengland.org.uk/images-books/publications/iha-domestic-housing-for-disabled-veterans-1900-2014/heag07; accessed 16.9.2018), p. 16.

74   SHC 2395/14/1 Cotton, Gumersall & Palmer Solicitors Records, Ashtead Potteries, 1935, letter from Edith Hillier, Hon. Secretary, Potters, to A.R. Cotton, 5.7.1935; SHC 8490/4 Letter from R. Stafford Cripps to Cecil Harmsworth, 24.3.1932.

75   See also M. Edwards, 'Helping the Disabled: the Ashtead Pottery', Surrey in the Great War (https://www.surreyinthegreatwar.org.uk/story/helping-the-disabled-the-ashtead-pottery/).

76   Baroness De T'Serclaes (formerly Elsie Knocker, née Elizabeth Shapter), *Flanders and Other Fields: The Memoirs of The Baroness de T'Serclaes* (George Harrap, 1964), pp. 131–32, 134.

77   F. Reid, *Broken Men: Shell Shock, Treatment and Recovery in Britain 1914–30* (Continuum, 2010 [2011]), p. 130.

78   SHC ESR/1/12/8 Scrapbook 'The East Surrey Regiment, 1914–1919', p. 9.

79   *Ibid.*, p. 6; *The Observer*, 28.12.1919, p. 8; SHC J/553/1 'The East Surrey Regimental War Memorial', *The Journal of the East Surrey Regiment*, 5 August 1920; *Surrey Advertiser*, 25.4.1921, 2e.

80   SHC QRWS/30/MERR L.W. Merrow-Smith Papers, p. 312: 'The Queen's Regimental War Memorial, Holy Trinity Church Guildford' (undated newspaper cutting).

81   *The Observer*, 5.6.1921, p. 15.

82   E.G. Barrow, *The Life of General Sir Charles Carmichael Monro* (Hutchinson, 1931), pp. 276, 249, 262; *Surrey Advertiser*, 21.5.1921, 4i; G.H. Cassar, 'Monro, Sir Charles Carmichael', *Oxford Dictionary of National Biography* (Oxford University Press, 2004).

83   *The Times*, 23.9.1926, p. 13.

Postscript

1   SHC QRWS/30/MOORF/1 Frederick Moore Papers, Diary 1915-19.

2   SHC QRWS/30/FORB/2 Archie Forbes Papers, Letters 1918-19.

3   Diary of Viola Bawtree, 29.6.1919, reproduced by permission of Jeremy Gordon-Smith.

4   SHC 9800/3/12 Godstone Parish Magazines 1917-21, February 1921 issue.

5   SHC 6094/2/1 *Surrey Teachers' Quarterly*, September 1914.

6   SHC WIT/16/37 All Saints' Witley Parish Records, Magazines 1918-21, January 1920 issue.

7   M. Stilwell, 'Homes Fit for Heroes', Surrey in the Great War (https://www.surreyinthegreatwar.org.uk/story/homes-fit-for-heroes/).

8   IWM Docs.11335 Diary of Frederick Robinson, 21.3.1916.

9   Ministry of Munitions, *1918 Directory of Manufacturers in Engineering and Allied Trades* (Wyman and Sons Ltd); HMSO, *Census of England and Wales, 1911 and 1921: County of Surrey* (1914 and 1923).

10   SHC Z/704/1 Herbert Boxer Papers, Diary 1917-18.

11   SHC ESR/25/CUTT/1-15 Papers of Edward Cutt 1914-2007.

CASE STUDY NOTES

A New Heaven

1   'Wilfred Owen – the New Officer', National Trust (https://www.nationaltrust.org.uk/witley-and-milford-commons/features/wilfred-owen-and-witley-common; accessed 4.1.2019); 'Witley Camps', Godalming Museum (http://www.godalmingmuseum.org.uk/index.php?page=witley-camps; accessed 4.1.2019).
2   Letter to Susan Owen, 18.6.1916 (C. Bent, 'Wilfred Owen's Letters Home from Witley Camp, Surrey in the Great War [https://www.surreyinthegreatwar.org.uk/story/wilfred-owens-letters-home-from-witley-camp/; accessed 21.3.19]).
3   *Ibid.*, 3.7.1916.
4   C. Bent, 'Wilfred Owen in Guildford and Godalming', Surrey in the Great War (https://www.surreyinthegreatwar.org.uk/story/wilfred-owen-in-guildford-and-godalming/; accessed 21.3.19).

The 'Willing Badge'

1   SHC Z/405/1 Walter Summerfield Papers, presentation letter October 1914.
2   Portable Antiquities Scheme, SUR-07E25F (https://finds.org.uk/database/search/results/q/strachey).

Roll Up!

1   *Surrey Advertiser*, 26.8.1916, 3a.
2   *Dorking and Leatherhead Advertiser*, 17.2.17, 4d.
3   *Surrey Mirror*, 10.9.15, 1h and 29.6.17, 3b.
4   'Elephants as War Workers', British Pathé Film no. 1864.25 (https://www.britishpathe.com/video/elephants-as-war-workers/query/elephant+war+workers).

Frank Lloyd Parton

1   *Surrey Advertiser*, 21.8.1918, 2c; L. Spring, 'Frank Lloyd Parton: a Conscientious Objector and the Military Tribunals', Surrey in the Great War (https://www.surreyinthegreatwar.org.uk/story/frank-lloyd-parton-a-conscientious-objector-and-the-military-tribunals/).

Edward Unmack

1   SHC CC98/14/8 Surrey Constabulary Records, enquiry regarding alleged German origin and sympathies of a clergyman, 1916–18.
2   *Surrey Advertiser*, 23.10.1916, 3e.

Noeline Baker MBE

1   L. Taylor, 'Noeline Baker: a Life in Two Worlds' (unpublished MA thesis: University of Otago, 1992), pp. 90–123 (http://hdl.handle.net/10523/353; accessed 31.10.2018).

Vickers' Virgins!

1   Sutton High School Magazine, Autumn 1915, p. 12, World War I School Archives (http://www.worldwar1schoolarchives.org; accessed 30.10.2018); see also Surrey in the Great War (https://www.surreyinthegreatwar.org.uk/person/105805).
2   Sutton High School Magazine, Summer 1916, p. 12, World War I School Archives (http://www.worldwar1schoolarchives.org; accessed 30.10.2018). See Surrey in the Great War (https://www.surreyinthegreatwar.org.uk/person/112556).

Flora Sandes

1   L. Miller, *A Fine Brother: The Life of Captain Flora Sandes* (Alma Books, 2012). Sandes wrote two autobiographies describing her life as a soldier: *An English Woman-Sergeant in the Serbian Army* (Hodder & Stoughton, 1916) and *The Autobiography of a Woman Soldier: A Brief Record of Adventure with the Serbian Army* (Frederick A. Stokes, c. 1927).

Rhoda Brodie MBE

1   H. Keatley Moore, *Croydon and the Great War* (Corporation of Croydon, 1920) (via http://archive.org; accessed 20.10.2018).
2   *Ibid.*
3   'GDST in the First World War', Girls' Day School Trust (https://www.gdst.net/article/gdst-first-world-war; accessed 25.11.2018). *Unknown Warriors* was republished by The History Press, 2014.

War Comes to Brooklands

1   *The Times*, 22.6.1914, 5b.
2   *The Red Cross Magazine*, July 1914, pp. 238–42. See also 'Red Cross Field Day at Brooklands', Surrey in the Great War (https://www.surreyinthegreatwar.org.uk/story/red-cross-field-day-at-brooklands); *Surrey Advertiser*, 24.6.1914, 4c.

A Family Affair

1   BRC Museum and Archives, VAD Records (accessed online at www.redcross.org.uk/ww1); TNA ADM 318/314 Admiralty, Women's Royal Naval Service, Personal Files of Officers, Service Record of MacDonald, Katharine Alleyne. See further P. Smee, 'John Doran MacDonald', Surrey in the Great War (https://www.surreyinthegreatwar.org.uk/story/john-doran-macdonald/).

Ethel Locke King DBE

1   E. Lovelock, *Reminiscences of Weybridge* (Walton & Weybridge Local History Society, 1969), p. 4.
2   *Ibid.*, p. 10.

Remembering VADs and Nurses

1   TNA WO 95/3988/3 War Diary, Headquarters Branches and Services: Matron in Chief, British Expeditionary Force, France and Flanders, January–April 1915; H. Keatley Moore, *Croydon and the Great War* (Croydon Public Library, 1920), p. 363.
2   Casualty Database, CWGC (https://www.cwgc.org/find-war-dead/casualty/4020716/pearse,-phyllis-ada/; accessed 21.12.2018).

FURTHER RESEARCH

Surrey History Centre

Surrey History Centre (SHC) is home to the county's archive; the oldest document in its care dates from the twelfth century. It holds substantial collections relating to many aspects of World War I, including records of the Queen's (Royal West Surrey) and East Surrey Regiments, private letters and diaries, school logbooks, parish magazines, records of military service tribunals, minutes of war agricultural committees and local emergency committees, and information about Belgian refugees to Surrey. Guidance on visiting SHC, how to search its catalogues, order documents and request research assistance can be found at www.surreycc.gov.uk/culture-and-leisure/history-centre, by phoning 01483 518737 or by emailing shs@surreycc.gov.uk.

Visit SHC to research individual soldiers who served in World War I, explore the personal papers of soldiers of the two Surrey regiments, and access online records such as medal index cards and service files via Ancestry.com and FindMyPast.com. Professional advice on family history research is also available.

For detailed information on Surrey's regiments, contact Surrey Infantry Museum, which is also the main repository for objects relating to Surrey's military history.

SHC's website, *Exploring Surrey's Past* (www.exploringsurreyspast.org.uk) is a superb, continually expanding resource on all aspects of Surrey's rich past and for information about the collections of SHC and several of the county's museums.

Surrey in the Great War: A County Remembers

The gateway to *Surrey in the Great War* is www.surreyinthegreatwar.org.uk. Our website holds a plethora of information about Surrey during the 1914–18 conflict, including biographical profiles of many thousands of World War I era Surrey people, articles covering all aspects of the county's wartime history, an index of over 80,000 references to the war in Surrey's contemporary newspapers, free learning resources for schools, research guides, information on Surrey's war memorials, photographs and contemporary film.

Newspaper Indices

Local newspapers are a valuable source of information about the Home Front during World War I. A major strand of the *Surrey in the Great War* project has seen volunteers indexing World War I related content in eleven Surrey newspapers of 1914–22. The resulting indices are searchable on the project's website and can be used to explore all sorts of fascinating and detailed information about the war's effect on the county. Our volunteers have tagged indexed articles thematically, so that entries relating to such subjects as women's war work, soldiers' obituaries, fundraising, economy and wartime advertising can be located readily.

   Our website holds only our newspaper indices. The following list shows where to view PDFs of the newspapers themselves:

Via the British Newspaper Archive website (www.britishnewspaperarchive.co.uk; accessible free of charge at SHC or at a branch of the county library network):
   Dorking and Leatherhead Advertiser
   Middlesex Chronicle, 1914–18 (Staines edition)
   Surrey Advertiser, 1914–18
   Surrey Mirror

Via DVD at SHC or at Caterham Valley and Redhill libraries (free of charge):
   Epsom Advertiser, 1913–22
   Farnham Herald, 1914–22 (including Haslemere and Alton editions)
   Middlesex Chronicle, 1919–22 (Staines edition)
   Surrey Advertiser, 1919–22 (including midweek editions)
   Surrey and Hants News, 1914–22
   Surrey Comet, 1914–22
   Surrey Herald, July 1913–December 1922 (Chertsey, Addlestone and Byfleet edition)
   Surrey Times and County Express, July 1914–1920
   Woking News and Mail, 1914–22

BIBLIOGRAPHY

Chapter 1: Surrey Goes to War

Archival Sources

Imperial War Museum, London

Docs.11335 – Diary of Frederick A. Robinson, 1914–18.

Surrey History Centre, Woking

3434/9/6 – Epsom Grand Stand Association minute book, 1907–19.
6227/1/53-57 – National Rifle Association annual reports, 1914–18.
CC7/4/4 – Correspondence and Papers relating to Life Assurance Policies for Surrey County Council Staff, 1914–23.
CC28/303B – Chairman's case notes, Surrey and Croydon Military Service Appeal Tribunal, Guildford Area Committee, 1916–18.
CC360 – Surrey County Council Reports, 1914.
CC418 – Surrey and Croydon Military Service Appeal Tribunal minutes, 1916–19.
QRWS/30/SLADEN – Papers of Lieutenant Colonel St Barbe Russell Sladen.
Z/405 – Papers of Walter Summerfield.

The National Archives, Kew

MH/47/49/60 – Ministry of Health records, Middlesex Appeal Tribunal minutes and papers, case number M5361: Thomas Caley.
MH/47/59/27 – Ministry of Health records, Middlesex Appeal Tribunal minutes and papers, case number M5135: George Wheatley.

Newspapers

The Times

Film

'Elephants as War Workers', British Pathé Film No. 1864.25 (https://www.britishpathe.com/video/elephants-as-war-workers/query/elephant+war+workers).

Books and Articles

Aston, J. and Duggan, L.M., *The History of the 12th (Bermondsey) Battalion East Surrey Regiment* (Union Press, 1936).

Atherton, K., *Dorking in the Great War* (Pen & Sword Books Ltd, 2015).

Basu, S., *For King and Another Country* (Bloomsbury, 2015).

Corrigan, G., *Mud, Blood and Poppycock* (Cassell, 2003 [2004]).

Doherty, S. and Donovan, T., *The Indian Corps on the Western Front* (Tom Donovan Editions, 2014).

Holmes, R., *'Tommy': The British Soldier on the Western Front 1914–1918* (Harper Perennial, 2005).

'Indian Soldier Buried at Woking', *Islamic Review* (December 1914).

Morton, D., 'Kicking and Complaining: Demobilisation Riots in the Canadian Expeditionary Force, 1918–1919', *Canadian Historical Review*, 61, No. 3 (September 1980), pp. 334–60.

Morton-Jack, G., *The Indian Empire at War* (Little Brown, 2018).

Nichols, G.H.F., *The 18th Division in the Great War* (Blackwood, 1922).

Nicholson, G.W.L., *Official History of the Canadian Army in the First World War: Canadian Expeditionary Force, 1914–1919* (Ottawa, Queen's Printer, 1962).

O'Neill, H.C., *The Royal Fusiliers in the Great War* (Heinemann, 1922).

Oakley, W.H., *Guildford in the Great War* (Billings and Son, Ltd, 1934).

Pearse, H.W. and Sloman, H.S., *History of the East Surrey Regiment II: 1914–1917* (Medici Society, 1923).

Riddoch, A. and Kemp, J., *When the Whistle Blows: The Story of the Footballers' Battalion in the Great War* (Haynes Publishing, 2008).

Simkins, P., *Kitchener's Army: The Raising of the New Armies, 1914–1916* (Manchester, 1988).

The 60th CFA Battery Book (Belgium, 1919).

Winton, G., *Theirs Not to Reason Why: Horsing the British Army 1875–1925* (Helion and Company, 2013).

Wylly, H.C., *History of the Queen's Royal (West Surrey) Regiment in the Great War* (Gale and Polden, 1926).

Website and Online Resources

Badsey, S., 'Mass Politics and the Western Front' *BBC History* (http://www.bbc.co.uk/history/british/british_wwone/war_media_01.shtml).

Baker, C., '44th (Home Counties) Division', The Long, Long Trail (https://www.longlongtrail.co.uk/army/order-of-battle-of-divisions/44th-home-counties-division/).

Baker, C., 'British Army Reserves and Reservists', The Long, Long Trail (https://www.longlongtrail.co.uk/soldiers/a-soldiers-life-1914–1918/enlisting-into-the-army/british-army-reserves-and-reservists/).

Baker, C., 'Surrey Yeomanry (Queen Mary's Regiment)', The Long, Long Trail (http://www.longlongtrail.co.uk/army/regiments-and-corps/the-british-yeomanry-regiments-of-1914–1918/surrey-yeomanry-queen-marys-regiment/).

Baker, C., 'The Group Scheme (Derby Scheme)', The Long, Long Trail (https://www.longlongtrail.co.uk/soldiers/a-soldiers-life-1914–1918/enlisting-into-the-army/the-group-scheme-derby-scheme/).

Bent, C., 'Wilfred Owen in Guildford and Godalming', Surrey in the Great War (https://www.surreyinthegreatwar.org.uk/story/wilfred-owen-in-guildford-and-godalming/).

Bent, C., 'Wilfred Owen's Letters Home from Witley Camp', Surrey in the Great War (https://www.surreyinthegreatwar.org.uk/story/wilfred-owens-letters-home-from-witley-camp/).

Bird, C.W. and Davies, J.B., *The Canadian Forestry Corps: Its Inception, Development and Achievements* (HMSO, 1919).

'Francis Pegahmagabow' in '100 Stories: Canadians in the First World War', *Library and Archives Canada. (*https://www.bac-lac.gc.ca/eng/discover/military-heritage/first-world-war/100-stories/Pages/pegahmagabow.aspx).

Friends' Ambulance Unit (http://fau.quaker.org.uk).

Fryatt, N., 'Epsom Grandstand War Hospital', Surrey in the Great War (https://www.surrey-inthegreatwar.org.uk/story/15223/).

Gnap, K., 'Canadians at Witley Camp', Surrey in the Great War (https://www.surrey-inthegreatwar.org.uk/story/surrey-and-the-great-war-canadians-and-witley-camp/).

Gosling, B., 'Henry Robert Stanley', Surrey in the Great War (https://www.surreyinthegreatwar.org.uk/story/henry-robert-stanley/).

Higham, B., 'Major Archer Hosking – Principal Medical Officer, Mount Felix Hospital', Surrey in the Great War (https://www.surreyinthegreatwar.org.uk/story/major-archer-hosking-principal-medical-officer-mount-felix-hospital/).

History of the Forestry Commission, Forestry Commission (https://www.forestry.gov.uk/forestry/cmon-4uum6r).

'History of the Mosque – Part 2', Shah Jahan Mosque (http://www.shahjahanmosque.org.uk/history-mosque-part-2).

'John Baboo', in '100 Stories: Canadians in the First World War', Library and Archives Canada (https://www.bac-lac.gc.ca/eng/discover/military-heritage/first-world-war/100-stories/Pages/baboo.aspx).

Page, M., 'Lt-Col St Barbe Russell Sladen', Surrey in the Great War (https://www.surrey-inthegreatwar.org.uk/story/lt-col-st-barbe-russell-sladen/).

Portable Antiquities Scheme, entry SUR-07E25F (https://finds.org.uk/database/search/results/q/strachey).

Schofield, J., 'Stage 1 Report: Army Camps History', in 'England's Army Camps', Archaeology Data Service (http://archaeologydataservice.ac.uk/archives/view/armycamp_eh_2006/downloads.cfm).

'Second 'Id-ul-Fitr at Woking Muslim Mission, 13th August 1915', The Woking Muslim Mission (http://www.wokingmuslim.org/work/id-ul-fitr-1915.htm).

Spring, L., 'Frank Lloyd Parton: a Conscientious Objector and the Military Tribunals', Surrey in the Great War (https://www.surreyinthegreatwar.org.uk/story/frank-lloyd-parton-a-conscientious-objector-and-the-military-tribunals/).

Stiff, D., 'EM Forster (1879–1970)', Surrey in the Great War (https://www.surreyinthegreatwar.org.uk/story/em-forster-1879–1970/).

'The Canadian Forestry Corps', Canadiansoldiers.com (https://www.canadiansoldiers.com/corpsbranches/forestrycorps.htm).

'The First Muslim Soldier is Buried', Exploring Surrey's Past (https://www.exploringsur-reyspast.org.uk/themes/subjects/military/india-woking/buried/).

The Military Service Act, 1916 (https://www.legislation.gov.uk/ukpga/1916/104/pdfs/ukpga_19160104_en.pdf).

'Urdu Reports by Maulana Sdar-Ud-Din', The Woking Muslim Mission (http://www.wokingmuslim.org/work/ww1/muslim-burials-report.htm).

War Diary, 1st Battalion QRWS Regiment, 5–7 August 1914, Queen's Royal Surreys (http://www.queensroyalsurreys.org.uk/war_diaries/local/1Bn_Queens/1Bn_Queens_1914/1Bn_Queens_1914_08.shtml).

'Wilfred Owen – the New Officer', National Trust (https://www.nationaltrust.org.uk/witley-and-milford-commons/features/wilfred-owen-and-witley-common).

'Witley Camps', Godalming Museum (http://www.godalmingmuseum.org.uk/index.php?page=witley-camps).

'Woodcote Park Camp', Epsom and Ewell History Explorer (http://epsomandewellhistory-explorer.org.uk/WoodcoteParkCamp.html).

Chapter 2: Keeping Surrey Safe

Archival Sources

Surrey History Centre, Woking

898/4/1-74 – Holmwood Local Committee, Dorking and District Area, Defence of the Realm Act, records, 1914–16.

6296/1/1/39-40 – Horley Committee for Defence of the Realm records, 1914–19.

7543/2/1 – Correspondence and papers of Ronald Peake of Howard House, Ashtead, Chairman of the Local Emergency Committee for Ashtead, under the Defence of the Realm Act, 1914–18.

8261/13/4 – Defence of the Realm memorandum for Special Constables for Albury parish in the event of invasion, 1914.

9117/Box 2 – Documents relating to Hersham, Oatlands and Walton-on-Thames Special Constables, including memoir of Percy Webb, 1914–19.

9841/1/4/1 – Whyteleafe Grammar School Jubilee Book, 1957.

CC98/1/4-5 – Surrey Constabulary, reports of Chief Constable to Standing Joint Committee, 1909–23.

CC360/26-32 – Surrey County Council annual reports, 1914–20.

ESR/25/MARSD – Papers of Quartermaster Walker Mason Marsden, 2nd Volunteer Battalion, East Surrey Regiment.

LA4/23/40-296 – Dorking Rural District Council papers relating to London defences, 1914–18.

The National Archives, Kew

WO 78/4420 – War Office and Predecessors. Maps and Plans: Plan of London Defences, 1915.

Books and Articles

Atherton, K., *Dorking in the Great War* (Pen and Sword, 2014).

Oakley, W.H., *Guildford in the Great War* (Billings and Son, Ltd, 1934).

Rawlinson, A., *The Defence of London* (Melrose, 1923).

Spindler, L., *Leatherhead in the Great War* (Pen and Sword, 2016).

Online Resources and Websites

Bartlett, R., 'The Working Life of the Surrey Constabulary 1851–1992', Part 2, International Centre for the History of Crime, Policing and Justice (http://www.open.ac.uk/Arts/history-from-police-archives/RB1/Pt2/pt2TL191221.html).

Brand, T., 'The Dorking and District Local Emergency Committee', Surrey in the Great War (https://www.surreyinthegreatwar.org.uk/story/the-dorking-and-district-area-local-emergency-committee/).

Edwards, M., '"A Policeman's Lot …": the Surrey Police in War Time', parts 1–4, Surrey in the Great War (https://www.surreyinthegreatwar.org.uk/story/a-policemans-lot-the-surrey-police-in-wartime-part-1-1914-1915/; https://www.surreyinthegreatwar.org.uk/story/a-policemans-lot-the-surrey-police-in-wartime-part-2-1916/; https://www.surreyinthegreatwar.org.uk/story/a-policemans-lot-the-surrey-police-in-wartime-part-3-1917/; https://www.surreyinthegreatwar.org.uk/story/a-policemans-lot-the-surrey-police-in-wartime-part-4-1918/).

Edwards, M., 'Reigate Borough Police in the Great War', Surrey in the Great War (https://www.surreyinthegreatwar.org.uk/story/reigate-borough-police-in-the-great-war/).

Edwards, M., 'Special Constables in Surrey', Surrey in the Great War (https://www.surreyinthegreatwar.org.uk/story/special-constables/).

Epsom and Ewell History Explorer (http://www.epsomandewellhistoryexplorer.org.uk/Sgt_Green_Riot_1.pdf).

'Frith Hill POW Camp', Picture Postcards from the Great War 1914–1918 (https://www.worldwar1postcards.com/pow-camp.php).

Higham, B., 'Zeppelin Raid on Croydon, 1915', Surrey in the Great War (https://www.surreyinthegreatwar.org.uk/story/zeppelin-raid-on-croydon-1915/).

Spring, L., 'Horley and the Defence of the Realm Act', Surrey in the Great War (https://www.surreyinthegreatwar.org.uk/story/horley-and-the-defence-of-the-realm-act/).

Spring, L., 'Surrey and the Defence of London', Surrey in the Great War (https://www.surreyinthegreatwar.org.uk/story/surrey-and-the-defence-of-london/).

Spring, L., 'Surrey Volunteer Regiment', Surrey in the Great War (https://www.surreyinthegreatwar.org.uk/subjects/military/army/volunteer-regiment/).

Surrey Heath Museum, 'George Kenner (1888–1971), German Artist and Internee', Surrey in the Great War (https://www.surreyinthegreatwar.org.uk/story/george-kenner/).

Thomas, L., 'Frith Hill POW Camp at Frimley, Surrey', Frimley and Camberley Great War Memorial (https://sites.google.com/site/frimleyandcamberley/frith-hill-p-o-w-camp-at-frimley).

Chapter 3: Forging the Weapons of War

Archival Sources

Surrey History Centre, Woking

1463 – Dennis Specialist Vehicles Ltd, vehicle manufacturers of Guildford and predecessor companies, records.

1550 and 5179 – Drummond Brothers Ltd, lathe and machine tool makers of Rydes Hill, Guildford, records.

The National Archives, Kew

AIR 1/727/152/6 – Air Ministry and RAF Records, Air Historical Branch Papers, The 'Blériot' Machines, 1906–15.

AIR 1/754/204/4/77 – Air Ministry and RAF Records, Air Historical Branch Papers, RFC Military Wing, Establishment of RFC Wireless School at Brooklands, 1915.

AIR 1/2302/215 – Air Ministry and RAF Records, Air Historical Branch Papers, 1914–19.

AIR 2/13/AS31125/18 – Air Ministry and RAF Records, Air Ministry Registered Files, Insurance Policies, Claim for damage by fire to Aero Engines Ministry Property on premises of Gordon Watney and Co. Ltd, 1918–21.

AIR 2/1040 and 2/1041 – Air Ministry and RAF records, Air Ministry Registered Files, Lang Propeller designs: payment of royalty, 1916–19.

AIR 10/516 – Air Ministry and RAF Records, Air Publications and Reports, Preliminary Notes on the ABC 'Dragonfly' Engine, 1918.

AVIA 6/4754 – Ministry of Aviation Records, Royal Aircraft Factory Reports, Examination of ABC 'Dragonfly' Engine, 1921.

MUN 5/116/670/13 – Ministry of Munitions, Munitions Council Records, Committee paper on application by Lang Propeller Company for permission to prepare for post-war furniture manufacture, 1918.

Newspapers

The Times

Books and Articles

Kenyon, D., *First World War National Aircraft Factories: Archaeological, Architectural and Historic Review* (Historic England, 2015).

Ministry of Munitions, *History of the Ministry of Munitions* (HMSO, 1922).

Mint, R.W., 'Communications: An International History of the Formative Years', *History of Technology*, Series 32 (Institution of Engineering & Technology, 2004).

Rowe, J.H., *Air, Road, Sea, Addlestone: Blériot, Weymann, Plessy Works 1916–88* (D.M. & J.L. Barker, 1992).

Website and Online Resources

1918 Directory of Manufacturers in Engineering and Allied Trades. See 'Making Munitions in Surrey: Private Contractors and National Factories', Surrey in the Great War (https://www.surreyinthegreatwar.org.uk/story/making-munitions-in-surrey-private-contractors-and-national-factories/).

Edwards, M., 'Elephants and Buzzards: the Contribution of Martinsyde Aeroplanes to the War in the Air', Surrey in the Great War (https://www.surreyinthegreatwar.org.uk/story/elephants-and-buzzards-the-contribution-of-martinsyde-aeroplanes-to-the-war-in-the-air/).

Edwards, M., 'Inside Martinsyde: an Aeroplane Factory during World War I', Surrey in the Great War (https://www.surreyinthegreatwar.org.uk/story/inside-martinsyde-an-aeroplane-factory-during-world-war-i/).

'Eyre Smelting Co', Grace's Guide to British Industrial History (https://www.gracesguide.co.uk/Eyre_Smelting_Co).

Hyams, J., 'Sydney Camm and Martinsyde Limited', Surrey in the Great War (https://www.surreyinthegreatwar.org.uk/story/sydney-camm-1893-1966-and-martinsyde-limited/).

'National Aircraft Factory No 1', Grace's Guide to British Industrial History (https://www.gracesguide.co.uk/National_Aircraft_Factory_No_1).

Page, M., 'Lang Propeller Ltd of Weybridge', Surrey in the Great War (https://www.surrey-inthegreatwar.org.uk/story/lang-propeller-ltd-of-weybridge/).

Spring, L., 'Dennis Brothers of Guildford and World War I', Surrey in the Great War (https://www.surreyinthegreatwar.org.uk/story/dennis-brothers-and-ww1/).

Spring, L., 'Drummond Brothers, Lathe and Machine Tool Makers of Guildford', Surrey in the Great War (https://www.surreyinthegreatwar.org.uk/story/drummond-brothers-lathe-and-machine-tool-makers-of-guildford).

'Weyburn Engineering Co', Grace's Guide to British Industrial History (https://www.gracesguide.co.uk/Weyburn_Engineering_Co).

Chapter 4: A County at War

Archival Sources

Imperial War Museum, London

Docs.11335 – Diary of Frederick A. Robinson, 1914–18.

Surrey History Centre, Woking

1786/6/1 – St John's, West Byfleet, parish records, Byfleet parish magazines, 1914.

1925/2/19 – Godalming Congregational Church records, magazines, 1914.

2151/5/1 – Alwyne Road Wimbledon Congregational Church minutes, 1909–20.

6094/2/1 – *Surrey Teachers' Quarterly*, September 1914.

6520/28 – Hester Godfrey papers, printed notice from the Board of Trade, Coal Mines Department, concerning coal rationing, 1918.

9496/1 – Rose Ponting letters, 1915–19.

8909/8/1/4 – St Mary's, Stoke D'Abernon, parish records, Stoke D'Abernon and Oxshott parish magazines, 1911–19.

9800/3 – St Nicholas, Godstone, parish records, Godstone parish magazines, 1908–16.

9497/1-2 – 'The Eaton Cottage Herald', 1915–16.

Ac1321/7/3 – Weybridge Urban District Council food advice pamphlet from papers of Weybridge War Distress Fund, 1914–21.

CC42/1/3 – Perry Hill Council School, Worplesdon, logbook 1904–33.

CC171/1/15-16 – Annual Reports of the County Medical Officer of Health, 1917–19.

CC360/26-32 – Surrey County Council annual reports, 1914–20.

CC1243/1/1/2 – Whyteleafe Council School (Infants) logbook, 1906–40.

GUHT/57/7/1 – Letter of Bishop of Winchester, in Holy Trinity, Guildford, church scrapbook, 5 August 1914.

P2/7/1-22 – St Peter's, Chertsey, parish records, scrapbook of the Chertsey Women's War Work Association, 1916–21.

QS2/1/105 – Surrey Quarter Sessions Order Book, 1914–19.

WIT/16/37 – All Saints', Witley, parish records, Witley parish magazines, 1918–21.

Reigate Grammar School magazines, 1914–19, World War I School Archives (http://www.worldwar1schoolarchives.org/reigate-grammar-school/).

Sutton High School for Girls magazines, 1914–19, World War I School Archives (http://www.worldwar1schoolarchives.org/sutton-school/).

The National Archives, Kew

MUN 3/235 – Ministry of Munitions, Dehon, Godar & Connell, shell manufacturers, Barnes, Sunday labour return, 1918.

Books and Articles

Atherton, K., *Dorking in the Great War* (Pen & Sword, 2014).

Beckett, I., *Home Front 1914–1918: How Britain Survived the Great War* (The National Archives, 2006).

Brittain, V., *Testament of Youth* (Victor Gollancz, 1933).

Declercq, C. and Baker, H., 'The Pelabon Munitions works and the Belgian village on the Thames: Community and Forgetfulness in Outer-metropolitan Suburbs', *Immigrants & Minorities*, 34 (2) (2016).

Oakley, W.H., *Guildford in the Great War* (Billings and Son, Ltd, 1934).

Parker, E., *Memory Looks Forwards* (Seeley, Service, 1937).

Seldon, A., and Walsh, D., *Public Schools in the Great War: The Generation Lost* (Pen & Sword Military, 2013).

Watson, N., *The Royal Grammar School Guildford: An Illustrated History* (James & James Ltd, 2004).

Websites and Online Resources

Edwards, M., 'Forms, Forms and more Forms: Buying Margarine in 1918', Surrey in the Great War (https://www.surreyinthegreatwar.org.uk/story/forms-forms-and-more-forms-buying-margarine-in-1918/).

Edwards, M., 'Reigate Grammar School for Boys and its Officer Training Corps', Surrey in the Great War (https://www.surreyinthegreatwar.org.uk/story/reigate-grammar-school-for-boys-and-its-officer-training-corps/).

Garrard, C., 'Listening to the Guns – 'Picnic: July 1917' by Rose Macaulay', Surrey in the Great War (https://www.surreyinthegreatwar.org.uk/story/listening-to-the-guns-picnic-july-1917-by-rose-macaulay/).

Hawker, J., 'Saving Coal at Home in WWI', Surrey in the Great War (https://www.surrey-inthegreatwar.org.uk/story/saving-coal-at-home-in-ww1/).

Hawker, J., 'The Best Food for Nourishing Dishes', Surrey in the Great War (https://www.surreyinthegreatwar.org.uk/story/the-best-food-for-nourishing-dishes/).

Hyams, J., 'James Chuter Ede, Politician, Educationist and Soldier (1882–1965)', Surrey in the Great War (https://www.surreyinthegreatwar.org.uk/story/james-chuter-ede-politician-educationist-and-soldier-1882-1965).

Hyams, J., 'The Society of Dependents or Cokelers', Surrey in the Great War (https://www.surreyinthegreatwar.org.uk/story/the-society-of-dependents-or-cokelers-in-shamley-green).

James, S. and Page, M., 'A Munitionette in the National Projectile Factory, Lancaster', Surrey in the Great War (https://www.surreyinthegreatwar.org.uk/story/a-munitionette-in-the-national-projectile-factory-lancaster/).

James, S. and Page, M., 'Dora Black: a Volunteer with the Women's Emergency Corps', Surrey in the Great War (https://www.surreyinthegreatwar.org.uk/story/dora-black-a-volunteer-with-the-womens-emergency-corps/).

Page, M., 'A Family at War: The Eaton Cottage Herald', Surrey in the Great War (https://www.surreyinthegreatwar.org.uk/story/a-family-at-war-the-eaton-cottage-herald/).

Woodbridge, S., 'When Food was Scarce: Memories of a Female Control Officer in World War One', Surrey in the Great War (https://www.surreyinthegreatwar.org.uk/story/when-food-was-scarce-memories-of-a-female-control-officer-in-world-war-one).

Chapter 5: Women in Wartime

Archival Sources

Imperial War Museum, London

LBY K. 5057 – Ministry of Munitions, 'How to dress for munitions making'.

Surrey History Centre, Woking

2572/123/1-14 – Farrer family papers, Dorking War Hospital Supply Depot papers, 1916–17.

3410/2/1/2 – Surrey Federation of Women's Institutes records, Surrey Women's Agricultural Committee minutes, 1917–20.

8488/1 – Florence Winifred Hooker papers, Women's Land Army Handbook, 1918–19.

CC98/1/5 – Surrey Constabulary, reports of Chief Constable to Standing Joint Committee, 1916–23.

G173/212/16 – Onslow family records, correspondence relating to Women's Farm and Garden Union and Women's National Land Service Corps, 1915–18.

QRWS/30/ELIAA/2 – Mrs M C Elias Morgan scrapbook, 'The Great War', 1915–21.

SGW/9 – Rose Kate Overington autograph book, 1918–45.

P2/7/1 – St Peter's, Chertsey, parish records, scrapbook of the Chertsey Women's War Work Association, 1916–21.

Surrey County Council Reports, 1915–18.

Sutton High School for Girls Magazine, World War I School Archives (http://www.worldwar-1schoolarchives.org).

1911 England & Wales Census (via Histpop – The Online Historical Population Reports Website: http://www.histpop.org/).

Books and Articles

Braybon, G. and Summerfield, P., 'Women before 1914', *Out of the Cage: Women's Experiences in Two World Wars* (Pandora, 1987).

Grayzel, S., *Women and the First World War* (Routledge, 2013).

Keatley Moore, H., *Croydon and the Great War* (Corporation of Croydon, 1920) (https://www.gdst.net/article/gdst-first-world-war).

Luard, K., *Unknown Warriors* (The History Press, 2014).

Miller, L., *A Fine Brother: the life of Captain Flora Sands* (Alma Books, 2012).

Roberts, J., 'A Biography of the Trousered Munitions Women's Uniform of World War 1', *Apparence(s)* (http://journals.openedition.org/apparences/1355).

Sandes, F., *An English Woman-Sergeant in the Serbian Army* (Hodder & Stoughton, 1916) (https://archive.org/details/englishwomanserg00sanduoft).

Sandes, F., *The Autobiography of a Woman Soldier: A Brief Record of Adventure with the Serbian Army* (Frederick A. Stokes, *c.* 1927) (https://archive.org/details/HeAutobiographyOfAWomanSoldierABriefRecordOfAdventureWithThe).

Scott, C., *Holding the Home Front: The Women's Land Army in the First World War* (Pen & Sword History, 2017).

Shipton, E., *Female Tommies: The Frontline Women of the First World War* (The History Press, 2014).

Stevens, J. and C., *Unknown Warriors: The Letters of Kate Luard* (The History Press, 2017).

Taylor, L., 'Noeline Baker: A Life in Two Worlds' (unpublished MA thesis: University of Otago, 1992) (accessed online at http://hdl.handle.net/10523/353).

Woollacott, A., 'Khaki Fever and its Control: Gender, Class, Age and Sexual Morality on the British Home Front in the First World War', *Journal of Contemporary History*, Vol. 29/2, (1994), pp. 325–47.

Websites and Online Resources

1918 Directory of Manufacturers in Engineering and Allied Trades, Grace's Guide (https://www.gracesguide.co.uk/1918); (directory_of_manufacturers_in_engineering_and_allied_trades).

Casualty Database, Commonwealth War Graves Commission (https://www.cwgc.org/); (https://www.cwgc.org/find-war-dead/casualty/503380/luker,-doris-mary/).

'GDST in the First World War', Girls' Day School Trust (https://www.gdst.net/article/gdst-first-world-war).

Historic England, photographs of women undertaking work in an aviation factory in Lancaster (https://historicengland.org.uk/whats-new/first-world-war-home-front/what-we-already-know/land/aircraft-factories/).

Kingston Aviation Centenary Project (https://www.kingstonaviation.org/).

Langley-Hawthorne, C., 'The Women's Police Service during the First World War' (http://www.clarelangleyhawthorne.com/pdf/WPS_Background.pdf).

Online Historical Population Reports (http://www.histpop.org/).

Page, M., 'Making Munitions in Surrey: Private Contractors and National Factories', Surrey in the Great War (https://www.surreyinthegreatwar.org.uk/story/making-munitions-in-surrey-private-contractors-and-national-factories/).

Women's Land Army (https://www.womenslandarmy.co.uk/world-war-one/).

Chapter 6: Working the Land

Archival Sources

Surrey History Centre, Woking

CC360/27-30 – Surrey County Council annual reports, Surrey War Agricultural Committee reports, 1917–18.

6200/ADD/Box 69 – Paine and Brettell, solicitors of Chertsey, records, Chertsey Rural District War Agricultural Committee minutes, 1917.

The National Archives, Kew

MAF 68 – Ministry of Agriculture, Fisheries and Food and predecessors, Statistics Divisions, Parish Summaries of Agricultural Returns, Surrey, 1914–19.

Newspapers

Illustrated Sporting and Dramatic News

Books and Articles

Bennett, M., *British Food Policy during the First World War* (Allen & Unwin, 1985).

Beveridge, W.H., *British Food Control* (Oxford University Press, 1928).

Middleton, T., *Food Production in War* (Oxford University Press, 1923).

Starling, J. and Lee, I., *No Labour, No Battle* (The History Press, 2009).

The Journal of the Board of Agriculture, 1914–1919; HMSO (full set held at Natural History Museum Library).

Websites and Online Resources

Stilwell, M., 'Farming in World War I – Surrey's Contribution', Surrey in the Great War (https://www.surreyinthegreatwar.org.uk/story/farming-in-world-war-1-surreys-contribution/).

Stilwell, M., 'Food v Golf in WWI', Surrey in the Great War (https://www.surreyinthegreatwar.org.uk/story/food-v-golf-in-ww1-the-battle-of-the-golf-courses/).

Woodbridge, S., 'Land and Home: The Campaign to encourage more Land Cultivation in Surrey', Surrey in the Great War (https://www.surreyinthegreatwar.org.uk/story/land-and-home-the-campaign-to-encourage-more-land-cultivation-in-surrey/).

Chapter 7: Treating the Wounded

Archival Sources

British Red Cross Archives and Museum, London

BRC/2/3/7/7 – Surrey Branch, British Red Cross Society. Historical Summary, April 1907–31 December 1953 (British Red Cross, 1954).

T2 Van X/142 – Memoir of Margaret E. van Straubenzee while a VAD at Clandon Park Hospital, 1953 (British Red Cross, 1954).

British Red Cross Society Surrey Branch, Second Annual Report, 1914. ('British Red Cross Society Surrey Branch Annual Report 1914', Surrey in the Great War (https://www.surrey-inthegreatwar.org.uk/story/british-red-cross-society-surrey-branch-annual-report-1914).

BRC: *The Red Cross Magazine*.

Surrey History Centre, Woking

1688/1/1 – Thorncombe Military Hospital records, annual reports 1914–19.

3043/7/9/1/35 – Brookwood Hospital, Woking, records, male case book, 1913–15.

5337/10/52 – Onslow family records, wartime correspondence between 5th Earl of Onslow and Violet Lady Onslow, 1914–19.

6857/Files 10 & 11 – London County Council Asylums Committee annual report, 1914 and 1915–19.

8792/2 – Clandon Park Military Hospital correspondence and papers, 1914–19.

G173/1/6 – Onslow family records, papers relating to Clandon Park as a Military Hospital, 1914–19.

The National Archives, Kew

ADM 318/314 – Admiralty, Women's Royal Naval Service, Personal Files of Officers, Service Record of MacDonald, Katharine Alleyne.

WO 95/3988/3 – War Diary, Headquarters Branches and Services, Matron in Chief, British Expeditionary Force, France and Flanders, January–April 1915.

Newspapers

The Times

Books and Articles

Cooke, M. and Hubert Bond, C., *History of the Asylum War Hospitals in England and Wales* (HMSO, 1920).

Keatley Moore, H., *Croydon and the Great War* (Croydon Public Library, 1920).

Lord, J.R., *The Story of the Horton (Co. of London) War Hospital: Epsom. Its Inception and Work and some Reflections* (Heinemann, 1920).

Lovelock, E., *Reminiscences of Weybridge* (Walton & Weybridge Local History Society, 1969).

Mayhew, E., *Wounded: From Battlefield to Blighty 1914–1918* (The Bodley Head, 2013).

Websites and Online Resources

British Red Cross, First World War Volunteers (VAD Records) (www.redcross.org.uk/ww1).

Commonwealth War Graves Commission Casualty Database (https://www.cwgc.org/find-war-dead/casualty/4020716/pearse,-phyllis-ada/).

Commonwealth War Graves Commission Debt of Honour (https://www.cwgc.org/find-war-dead/).

'List of Auxiliary Hospitals during the First World War' (https://vad.redcross.org.uk/Auxiliary-Hospitals).

Arnould, K., '"Where possible, a change of clothes": Horton Asylum's forgotten war dead', Surrey in the Great War (https://www.surreyinthegreatwar.org.uk/story/where-possible-a-change-of-clothes-horton-asylums-forgotten-war-dead/).

'Red Cross Field Day at Brooklands', Surrey in the Great War (https://www.surrey-inthegreatwar.org.uk/story/red-cross-field-day-at-brooklands).

Smee, P., 'John Doran MacDonald', Surrey in the Great War (https://www.surreyinthegreatwar.org.uk/story/john-doran-macdonald/).

Stilwell, M., 'Thorncombe Red Cross Military Hospital, Bramley', Surrey in the Great War (https://www.surreyinthegreatwar.org.uk/story/thorncombe-red-cross-military-hospital-bramley/).

Chapter 8: Peace, Veterans and Remembrance

Archival Sources

Surrey History Centre, Woking

1593/2/2 – Henry R. Dunce papers, programme for Godalming concert to welcome home men who served in HM Forces, 26 July 1919.

1786/6/1 – St John's, West Byfleet, parish records, Byfleet parish magazines, 1920.

2337/13/8 – St Andrew's, Ham, parish records, list of ex-servicemen invited to the Welcome Home dinner, 1920.

2395/14 – Cotton, Gumersall & Palmer, solicitors, Ashtead Potteries papers, 1935.

2442/2 – Mickleham Parish Council minute book, 1909–26.

2572/1/85 – Farrer family papers, programme, Forest Green dedication of seat of remembrance, 19 September 1925.

3093/4/1 – Churt Recreation Ground Trustees minutes, 1918–40.

3148/9/4 – All Saints', Kingston, parish records, invitation to a Welcome Home, 13 November 1919.

5337/9/(31) – Onslow family papers, correspondence between 5th Earl of Onslow and Lord Midleton, December 1917.

6296/1/1/45 – Horley Town Council records, Horley War Memorial Committee minute book, 1919–22.

6520/64 – Hester Godfrey, Quartermaster at Oaklands Red Cross Hospital, Cranleigh, papers, peace celebrations circular letter, 12 July 1919.

6818/3/8 – Reigate and Redhill Hospital correspondence, 1919–20.

8026/3/6 – St John's, Dormansland, parish records, plan of proposed memorial cross, undated.

8591/1/1 – St Mary's, Horsell, parish records, parish magazines, 1915–25.

9667/1/1 – Military Roll, Weybridge (undated).

9800/3/11 – St Nicholas', Godstone, parish records, parish magazines, 1908–16.

COH/9/3 – Christ Church, Coldharbour, parish records, Coldharbour roll of honour, undated.

ESR/1/12/8 – The East Surrey Regiment records, scrapbook, 1914–19.

GU173/77/165 – Onslow family papers, letter from Lord Midleton to Lord Onslow, 23 October 1920.

HO/10/22 – St Mary's, South Holmwood, parish records, Holmwood War Memorial Committee minute book, 1920–22.

J/553/1 – 'The East Surrey Regimental War Memorial', *The Journal of the East Surrey Regiment*, Vol. 5, August 1920.

P39/1/2 – Capel Parish Council minute book, 1913–36.

PC/64/ALB2/87 – Postcard collection, Hale Parish War Shrine.

QRWS/30/MERR – L.W. Merrow-Smith papers.

SyAS 95/5 – J.A. Gibbs, 'Inscriptions and Graves in Abinger Church and Churchyard', compiled 1934–1939, with author's annotations, June 1946.

Z/454/1/4 – Correspondence between Councillor Mohammed Ilyas Raja, Woking Borough Council, and Shah Jahan Mosque regarding the history and repair of the Muslim Burial Ground, 1996–2001.

Newspapers

The Observer
The Times

Books and Articles

Baldry, A.L., 'Wall Tablets and Memorials by British Sculptors', *The Studio*, 66 (273) (1915), 186–96.

Barrow, E.G., *The Life of General Sir Charles Carmichael Monro* (Hutchinson, 1931).

Borg, A., *War Memorials: From Antiquity to the Present* (Leo Cooper, 1991).

Bushaway, B., 'Name upon Name: The Great War and Remembrance' in R. Porter (ed.), *Myths of the English* (Blackwell, 1992), 136–67.

Cassar, G.H., 'Monro, Sir Charles Carmichael', *Oxford Dictionary of National Biography* (Oxford University Press, 2004).

De T'Serclaes, Baroness [Elsie Shapter Knocker], *Flanders and Other Fields. The Memoirs of the Baroness de T'Serclaes* (George Harrap, 1964).

Gibbs, J.A., *Abinger Church* (Abinger, 3rd edition, 1946).

Grieves, K., 'Commemorating the Fallen: The Lord Lieutenant's Soldier Sons in the First World War and the Making of the Memorial Chapel at St Barnabas Church, Ranmore', *Surrey History* 6 (2) (2000), 107–24.

Howkins, A., *The Death of Rural England* (Routledge, 2003).

Jekyll, G., *Old English Household Life* (Batsford, revised and enlarged by S.R. Jones, 1939).

Keatley Moore, H., *Croydon and the Great War* (Corporation of Croydon, 1920).

Lethaby, W.R., 'Memorials of the Fallen: Service or Sacrifice?', *The Hibbert Journal*, 17 (4) (1918–19), 621–25.

Longworth, P., *The Unending Vigil* (Leo Cooper, 1967 [2003]).

Mackerness, E.D. (ed.), *The Journals of George Sturt 1890–1927* (Cambridge University Press, 1967).

Mee, A., *Surrey* (Hodder and Stoughton, 1938).

Mee, A., *Enchanted Land* (Hodder and Stoughton, 1936).

'Notes', *The Architectural Journal*, 37 (7) (8 February 1930).

Reid, F., *Broken Men: Shell Shock, Treatment and Recovery in Britain 1914–30* (Continuum, 2010 [2011]).

Skelton, T., and Gliddon, G., *Lutyens and the Great War* (Frances Lincoln Ltd, 2008).

Ware, V., 'From War Grave to Peace Garden: Muslim Soldiers, Militarised Multiculture and Cultural Heritage', *Journal of War and Cultural Studies*, 10 (4) (2017), 287–304.

Weaver, L., *Memorials and Monuments Old and New: Two Hundred Subjects chosen from Seven Centuries* (Country Life, 1915).

Weaver, L., *Village Clubs and Halls* (Country Life, 1920).

Westcott Local History Group, *The History of Westcott and Milton* (Westcott Local History Group, 2000).

Williams-Ellis, C., *Lawrence Weaver* (Geoffrey Bles, 1933).

Winter, J., *Sites of Memory, Sites of Mourning* (Cambridge University Press, 1995).

Wootton, G., *The Politics of Influence. British Ex-servicemen, Cabinet Decisions and Cultural Change (1917–1957)* (Routledge, 1963).

Yapp, A., *Told in the Huts. The YMCA Gift Book* (Jarrold & Sons, no date [*c.* 1916]).

Website and Online Resources

'9th Guildford Congregational Scout Troop WWI', IWM War Memorials Register (http://www.iwm.org.uk/memorials/item/memorial/23305).

'Design for Muslim Burial Ground, Woking', British Library Untold Lives Blog (British Library, 2016) (https://blogs.bl.uk/untoldlives/2016/03/designs-for-the-muslim-burial-ground-woking.html).

Edwards, M., 'Helping the Disabled: the Ashtead Pottery', Surrey in the Great War (https://www.surreyinthegreatwar.org.uk/story/helping-the-disabled-the-ashtead-pottery/).

'Epsom – St Martin's Church', Returned from the Front (http://thereturned.co.uk/crosses/epsom).

Historic England, 'Abinger Common War Memorial', list entry no 1028839, Historic England (https://historicengland.org.uk/listing/the-list/list-entry/1028839).

Historic England, 'Domestic Housing for Disabled Veterans 1900–2014' (Historic England, 2016) (https://content.historicengland.org.uk/images-books/publications/iha-domestic-housing-for-disabled-veterans-1900-2014/heag07).

Historic England, 'National Collection of Lutyens War Memorials Listed', Historic England (http://historicengland.org/whats-new/news/lutyens-war-memorials).

Nairn, M., 'Memorial to Guildford's 9th Congregational Scout Troop', Surrey in the Great War (https://www.surreyinthegreatwar.org.uk/story/memorial-to-guildfords-9th-congregational-scout-troop/).

New Zealand High Commission, 'Remembering the New Zealanders in Walton-on-Thames' (New Zealand High Commission London, 2018) (https://nzhistory.govt.nz/files/documents/-walton-on-thames-hospital-booklet.pdf).

'Purley Hospital Extension', IWM War Memorials Register (http://www.iwm.org.uk/memorials/item/memorial/769).

'Ranmore – St Barnabas', Returned from the Front (http://thereturned.co.uk/crosses/ranmore).

'Reigate War Memorial Cross', IWM War Memorials Register (http://www.iwm.org.uk/memorials/item/memorial/61186).

Royal Mail Group Memorial Database, Croydon and Epsom Post Offices Rolls of Honour (https://www.royalmailmemorials.com/memorial/croydon-post-office-war-memorial and https://www.royalmailmemorials.com/memorial/epsom-war-memorial).

'Woking's Muslim Burial Ground', Exploring Surrey's Past (https://www.exploringsurreyspast.org.uk/themes/placess/surrey/woking/woking/woking_muslim_burial_ground/).

Woodbridge, S., 'A "bond of mutual help": The Comrades of the Great War organisation in Kingston and Surbiton', Surrey in the Great War (https://www.surreyinthegreatwar.org.uk/story/a-bond-of-mutual-help-the-comrades-of-the-great-war-organisation-in-kingston-and-surbiton/).

Postscript

Archival Sources

Private

Viola Bawtree diary, 29 June 1919, reproduced by permission of Jeremy Gordon-Smith.

Imperial War Museum, London

Docs.11335 – Diary of Frederick A. Robinson, 1914–18.

Surrey History Centre, Woking

6094/2/1 – Surrey Teachers' Quarterly, September 1914.
9800/3/12 – St Nicholas', Godstone, parish records, parish magazines, 1917–21.
ESR/25/CUTT – Edward Cutt papers, 1914–2007.
QRWS/30/MOORF – Frederick Moore papers, 1915–19.
QRWS/30/FORB – Archie Forbes papers, 1918–19.
WIT/16/37 – All Saints', Witley, parish records, Witley parish magazines, 1918–21
Z/704/1 – Herbert Boxer papers, 1917–18.
HMSO, Census of England and Wales, 1911 and 1921: County of Surrey, 1914 and 1923.
Ministry of Munitions, *Directory of Manufactures in the Engineering and Allied Trades*, 1918.

Websites and Online Resources

Stilwell, M., 'Homes fit for Heroes', Surrey in the Great War (https://www.surreyinthegreatwar.org.uk/story/homes-fit-for-heroes/).

Surrey Newspapers consulted by Authors

Dorking and Leatherhead Advertiser
Epsom Advertiser
Farnham Herald
Surrey Advertiser
Surrey and Hants News
Surrey Comet
Surrey Herald
Surrey Mirror
Surrey Times and County Express
Woking News and Mail

INDEX

INDEX